The Philosophical Actor

'...[some] actors...believe that any conscious factor in creativeness is only a nuisance. They find it easier to be an actor by the grace of God.'

Constantin Stanislavski

'There are almost no good books on acting'

Sydney Pollack

The Philosophical Actor
A Practical Meditation for Practicing Theatre Artists

Donna Soto-Morettini

intellect Bristol, UK / Chicago, USA

First published in the UK in 2010 by
Intellect, The Mill, Parnall Road, Fishponds, Bristol, BS16 3JG, UK

First published in the USA in 2010 by
Intellect, The University of Chicago Press, 1427 E. 60th Street,
Chicago, IL 60637, USA

A catalogue record for this book is available from the
British Library.

Cover designer: Holly Rose
Copy-editor: Rebecca Vaughan-Williams
Typesetting: Mac Style, Beverley, E. Yorkshire

ISBN 978-1-84150-326-4

Printed and bound by Gutenberg Press, Malta.

Contents

Acknowledgements

My heartfelt thanks go to Lise Olson for her careful reading of an early draft, to Theresa Larkin for reading and working through the ideas with graduate students at Cal State Los Angeles, and to David Grindrod, Suzy Lamb and Mel Balac for (somewhat unintentionally!) providing the funding for this book.

Thanks, also, to the staff at Intellect for their support and patience, and to the Bodleian and the Langson Libraries for all their help. This book is result of many years of working with wonderful students at Central, LIPA and the RSAMD – my thanks go to all of them for their patience and their perseverance.

This book is dedicated to the memory of my mother, Beverly Lee Soto.

ACKNOWLEDGEMENTS

Introduction

I t's hard to look out at the sea of books on acting – ranging from the ambitious and the inspiring to the more workaday guides on technique – without feeling, well… philosophical. What does the study of this particular art/craft mean? How, given its significant difference from all the other arts (a difference based on the fact that the actor has no external media or instruments to master and no fixed physical/technical criteria to meet) can one set about training without running immediately into the limitations of the subjective or the personal? Why – when we all know that there are successful actors who never trained formally – bother at all? What is the point of writing books about a subject so practical in its nature?

And, of course, philosophy (or indeed, for that matter, meditation!) would seem to be a pursuit that excludes practical action. It is this common conception of philosophy being inert and intellectual that made Karl Marx's dictum about philosophy so startling in its time (Marx, of course, famously wrote that 'philosophers have merely interpreted the world in various ways; the point, however, is to change it'). Certainly no acting teacher or director would deny that a great majority of their time is spent encouraging their actors to think in deeper, more rigorous ways and they encourage this intellectual activity not only in terms of something that the actor has to go away and do as part of preparation for rehearsal and performance. That thinking is also something the actor has to do while actively engaged in the process of rehearsal and performance.

No doubt we hope that the deeper, more rigorous thinking we encourage our actors to do outside of rehearsal will result in what looks like spontaneous brilliance in playing the role – because we're generally suspicious about any actor looking as if they're 'thinking too much' or 'over-intellectualizing' as they perform. As directors and teachers we know that there is a kind of dialogue that occurs between director/actor, teacher/student, actor/actor that continually broadens and deepens our understanding of the things that we're working on practically both in and out of rehearsal, and we recognize our own patterns in terms of preparation, analysis and articulation in a rehearsal process. And while we know that this thinking, analysing, verbalizing and sharing of ideas is a substantial part of any rehearsal, there is often little time spent on considering exactly how the language of all that intellectual activity translates into the practice of playing a role for the actor without being *too detectable in the playing.*

Of course, it could be said that the history of acting theory has been an attempt to see how these activities – the intellectual and the practical – come together to create the actor's art and practical applications like the 'magic if' or 'trigger objects' or 'psychological gesture' could all be said to be part of this process: 'translating' the labour of the mind into the practice of the actor, but it seems to me that far less time has been spent

> **It is true, of course, that some actors will say that they DON'T think about their process and don't WANT to think about it.**

considering just what the language of acting theory *means*. Phrases like 'affective memory' or 'emotional truth' or 'psychophysical technique' are common enough in these books, but clear definitions of just exactly what we're talking about when we use them are much harder to find.

It is true, of course, that there are any number of actors who will say that they *don't* think about their process and, more to the point, don't *want* to think about their process. Presumably they work from a kind of intuitive operation that allows them to 'feel' their way through a performance. I've met my share of these actors and while they are often perfectly capable of turning in an interesting performance, they usually seem to find sustaining that performance for a long run much more difficult than those actors who have identified some kind of consistent process or approach. I have to take a little gamble here. I have to bet that there are some 'Philosophical Actors' who *want* to think about their process and about the language used in rehearsal or classrooms. And I have to bet that s/he will find some pleasure in considering the possibilities present in a variety of approaches/ideas connected to the somewhat slippery notion of building a strong, sustainable performance process. But above all, I am betting that most of us pick up books on acting (if we do at all) in order to try and bring some fresh ideas into our own practice. We may do this because we're teaching and we want to be able to help others to become great actors. Or we may do this because we're trying to become better actors ourselves – but whatever point of view we start from, and whatever books we're reading, I think the fundamental question that underlies all is this: what makes a great actor? And this fundamental question is then accompanied by a few more, such as: why are some actors so much better than others? Can great acting be learned/taught? etc.

So what might a philosophical approach to the practice of acting look like? Well, amongst other things, we might want to start by questioning the relationship between 'intellectual labour' or analysis and practical expression and would no doubt come to agree that there is, of course, no simple distinction to be made between these things. We might want to examine the basis of memory, emotion and the actor's sense of self (in terms, perhaps, of how it is we have a sense of 'selfness', or what it is we can actually KNOW about ourselves, or how critical memory is to sense of self), or question how it is we read the often slippery language of great (and not so great) writers on the subject of acting and how we then go about applying what we understand – in other words how do we imagine the relationship between the acting theory text and the practice of the actor? We might want to consider how emotion works and how emotion is related to cognition, or we might want to question the kinds of psychological assumptions we bring into rehearsal. We could look more closely at what it is we're doing when we attempt to 'get inside' the head of a character. Perhaps we might look closely at the kinds of particular mental processes actors bring to what is arguably a highly complex intellectual function, in which imagination and fiction collide to create a world 'lived' within a world. We might also want to consider what we base our judgements on when we attempt to determine what 'good' acting is, and how we use terms like 'truth' in our response to performances or productions.

Because theatre is a manifestation of our desire to examine what it is to be human and of our curiosity about what it is that makes us human, I believe that it is never far from the fundamental project of philosophy. Terry Eagleton sees the three great questions of philosophy as 'what can we know? What ought we to do? and 'What do we find attractive?'[1] These areas roughly map out as epistemology, moral philosophy and aesthetics. It seems to me that we could profitably look at acting through all three of these areas, specifically asking some age-old philosophical questions like: what is the relationship between mind/body, and how does that affect what we know about the world? How do we determine meaning or find value in acting? What might be the aesthetic issues raised by representational acting and what is its place in the contemporary world? What are the moral issues involved in training actors? How can we know what others are thinking? Indeed these questions, while on the one hand 'intellectual', are precisely the stuff of great acting. And that, perhaps, is the unspoken argument of this book: that the process of acting could be said to be an activity that bridges the oppositional nature of these questions. I also think acting itself both solves and continually raises these issues within us.

There is no point in writing a book like this if it is simply another literary analysis or else poor philosophy or – worse yet! – another book on acting technique. There is only a point in writing this if the interdisciplinary approach in the thinking can stimulate more and better ways to approach the elusive quest to create great theatre – either as an actor or a director or both. It seems to me that there are some important and interesting books written specifically for the academic/theoretical market that look closely at critical theory and of course there are countless practical books. It is my humble hope that this book can bridge the gap between this more academic/theoretical and practical split. I hope that approaching some very old questions from some very different perspectives may bring inspiration to some. And perhaps in the writing I've hoped to clarify my own thinking which, after more than 30 years of acting, directing and teaching needed clarification. Thus the fundamental question of the book must be: is there something to be learned from a 'philosophical' examination of our conventions and our language – including our common sense ideas about 'mind', 'identity', 'meaning', 'emotion', 'truth', 'intention', 'behaviour' or 'body' – that can advance our practice as actors and directors?

> **'This book has no answers!'**

We need to remember from the outset that a philosophical approach often means examining things like language and ideas closely – but not necessarily to the point of resolution. There is a particularly wonderful moment in *The Simpsons Movie*, where Homer Simpson leafs frantically through the Bible at a moment of crisis, crying 'This book has no answers!' I suppose that is the state I wish to achieve with this book: not to provide answers but, perhaps, to lead experienced theatre practitioners through a series of questions that may help us to enrich, refresh and diversify our approach to acting, teaching and directing.

It seems evident from even this brief introduction that this book is not aimed at the general 'beginners' market. There are many books – some great and some not so – designed for this purpose. I hope instead that the book will appeal to and stimulate discussion amongst professional actors and directors as well as educators and more advanced students in Drama.

It is not in anyone's interest for this book to be too difficult for the practising actor or director to comprehend; therefore I will very determinedly attempt to avoid language that cannot be easily understood. This will no doubt be the greatest challenge of attempting this work, since so much of philosophical labour is about fine-tuning thought and language to a point that 'specializes' language beyond common usage. I hope that the clarity of language I have employed will not result in a 'reduction' of philosophical language or scientific ideas, but will perhaps be seen as an attempt to grapple with their larger rather than with their finer points. It is a commonplace in philosophy that often the questions under scrutiny seem simple enough at first: 'how do I know that this leaf is green?' But in the patient unraveling of all the possible answers to this question, we are slowly led into something much more complex and problematic. I have always thought that it is just here – in the 'patient unraveling' – where all the pleasure of philosophy lies.

Playing philosophy

Why does the word philosophy scare us so much?

In America it worried studio execs so much they changed the title *Harry Potter and the Philosopher's Stone* to *Harry Potter and the Sorcerer's Stone*. But why on earth should 'philosophy' be less attractive or scarier than 'sorcery'? Maybe it's because sorcery puts us in mind of Mickey Mouse and dancing mops whereas philosophy reminds us of those 'general ed' classes where we had to wade through things like Scholasticism. Or maybe we're permanently scarred from trying to read contemporary philosophy in the form of Derrida or Žižek (wouldn't be surprising!). But whatever it is that scares us about the word, I'm hoping we can remember for a moment that the word philosophy simply means a love of knowledge or wisdom. And in my experience we all love to think about the mysteries of our trade.

I want to concentrate in this book on the kind of acting theory based in the tradition of Stanislavski – that is to say, geared toward helping actors interpret a role as written. This means that I will be leaving aside some of the interesting and more radical practitioners of the twentieth century to look specifically at how actors interpret and play a role. Given the many 'how to act' books and training programmes available out there it would be logical to conclude that there are many competing schools of thought about what it is the actor does and how they do it. But while it is true that there are lots of different practical ideas about how best to approach acting, how to train actors and how to instil technique, there is surprisingly little on actually defining what acting IS. And in spite of variations in approach, there are really only two raging debates in the more theoretical area. The first is about the relationship of the actor's own feelings to the feelings that the actor portrays. The second is about the relationship of the actor's own personality to the personality of the character that the actor portrays.

The first debate is inspired by Diderot's classic work *The Paradox of Acting*, in which he suggests that the paradox of acting is that the actor who is consumed by his true emotion while playing is a 'middling actor', while the 'sublime actor' is most likely to be one that is in absolute control (and therefore distant from) his own emotion. This paradox has for years inspired debate about the relationship of the actor's emotion to the emotion of the character being portrayed. The second debate is really the result of the legacy of the American Method acting school, and its interpretation of Stanislavski, which inspired many generations of actors to 'play themselves' as the character.

> **Little wonder David Mamet was so tempted to lob his little hand-grenade of a book into the skirmish in 1997…**

If I look at two of the most interesting books to emerge in the 'sea' of acting books over the last two decades, *The Player's Passion* (2001) and *The End of Acting* (1992), it is clear that our theoretical ideas about acting remain locked in these two debates about Diderot (eighteenth century) and the teachings of Stanislavski (nineteenth century). It seems our philosophical 'whipping boy' is René Descartes (seventeenth century), whose idea of the body and mind as separate entities has bedevilled many, but is now more or less proven to be inaccurate. Little wonder, one supposes, that David Mamet was so tempted to lob his little hand-grenade of a book (*True and False: Heresy and Common Sense for the Actor*) into the skirmish in 1997.

I am bold enough to hope that by looking at the advances in other areas – philosophy, cognitive science, psychology, neuroscience – we can perhaps begin to bring our old debates up to speed. At the very least I think that these advances can shed some new light on the ways in which we think as practising theatre artists.

The discontents of the acting studio

My own experiences have no doubt shaped many of the thoughts in this work. In the early 1990s I found myself working at the Central School of Speech and Drama in London, where I became head of acting after a year. I spent a first year watching others and learning much as I went along, although mostly I learned that the British approach to actor training differed substantially from the way actors were taught in California, where I had trained. Up until this time I had either worked with other actors, been acting myself, or else directing actors, but with the exception of teaching a few 'acting fundamentals' classes (in which I largely repeated exercises and ideas I had been taught at that level) I had never really thought critically about any particular method for training actors. I had simply accepted that the things that had worked for me as a young actor (discovering intentions, 'playing to win' as Robert Cohen – the head of my department at UCI – might describe it, close analytical readings of plays, free improvisational exercises, etc.) would be helpful for my students. And the things that hadn't helped me (pretending to walk through a room full of jello, games called 'zip-zap-boing', etc.) simply didn't figure when I taught. I am aware now that this sounds marvellously naïve, but my focus up until this point had always been on directing – not on training actors.

Like most acting teachers I have spoken with, I started by cobbling together a number of ideas from various sources. I was, no doubt, strongly influenced by Robert Cohen's ideas, but also found that my adventures as an acting teacher were much like my adventures as a student: I didn't want to be taught. I wanted to find my own way through what seemed to me to be a pretty inexact 'science' of training actors. I read books but found most of them unhelpful. I simply didn't have the patience for many of them I think and I've come to recognize that my own 'learning style' is one of rugged experimentalism. Reading Stanislavski, Michael Chekhov, Richard Boleslavsky and Uta Hagen was compulsory in my undergraduate days. In all but Uta Hagen I found the language used in these books to be rather distant and definitely of another time. The things that were helpful in them were the things I took to be 'common sense' and the unhelpful things I simply didn't retain. But in that first year at Central I tried once again to go back to these books to see what I must have missed as an undergraduate. On the whole I found that there was a kind of resonance between these books (*An Actor Prepares*, *Respect for Acting*, *Acting: The First Six Lessons* and *To the Actor*) and what I was teaching, but for reasons I still didn't stop to analyse, I found that in re-reading them I was no closer to finding a way forward. Nor did I find that I had any more patience with the language employed in them. More often than not I felt frustrated in my attempts to translate language that seemed to me either strangely expressed: 'The whole mental and physical being of the actor must be directed to that which is derived from his facial expression'[2] or obscure:

> With this aim in view the actor must work out within himself not only the ordinary flexibility and mobility of action, but also the particular consciousness that directs all his groups of muscles, and the ability to feel the energy transfused within him, which, arising from his highest creative centres, form in a definite manner his mimicry and gestures and, radiating from him, brings into the circle of its influence his partners on stage and in the auditorium.[3]

Or else just too obvious to be of use: 'Find the energy you need for your work. God doesn't give you this energy. And without it your work is boring.'[4]

All too often I felt that the theory books I read were fairly consistent in their use of terms that went undefined and I grew weary with what appeared to me at times to be a combination of unwarranted certainty and unnecessary complexities. Of course my own arrogance, no doubt, played a part in these conclusions, but in the end I decided that rehearsal studio heuristics would be my best way forward.

The early years of my 'rugged experiments' produced a patchwork approach that was mostly adequate, and in some instances rather good. But as I watched the work of other acting teachers and directors around me (which in truth was fairly rare as conservatoire tutors work such intensive hours), it struck me that the greatest obstacle for me to overcome in training these young actors was in getting them to focus their concentration outside of themselves. The most consistently worrisome thing to me in that first year was the sense, in watching the students, that they had a strong tendency to 'isolate' themselves on stage. With rare exception I could see that even the first-year students were doing exactly what was asked of them and that they were 'making truthful emotional connections' (if not always at a very deep level), maintaining clear 'actions' or 'intentions' (if not always finding the most interesting ones) and exhibiting an understanding of the 'world' of the play, etc. But I was still aware of something about them that left the work I watched looking a bit careful and prescriptive rather than passionate and free. I was sure that the sense of isolation I kept seeing was at the bottom of this.

I noticed that more often than not young actors would always choose to look away, to occupy themselves with something on stage – a prop, a bit of furniture, staring into the middle distance – or to create a physical distance between themselves and the other actors. I could see good reason for this – we were continually encouraging them to hold their concentration and to maintain a relevant and concentrated thought process during a scene and this, along with keeping track of actions, lines, blocking, etc. is much to contend with if you are also expected to interact freely with others and to cope with the unexpected. But this latter ability is what makes acting teachers value and encourage students to be 'living in the moment' – the sense that everything is fresh and unplanned, everything is occurring for the first time and anything may happen. Yet throughout that first year, the classes I watched and the rehearsal techniques I witnessed seemed often to require that the actor spend a great proportion of their time on *self*-reflection.

I watched classes in which the actors were required to reproduce as accurately as they could ten full minutes of solitude in their bedrooms at home. I understood the point of the exercise and even agreed with the principle of attaining that 'public solitude'[5] that Stanislavski often alludes to, but noticed also that these exercises led more than ever to actors isolating themselves on stage. I watched exercises in which the actors were placed in a chair and asked to answer twenty minutes of questions 'in character'. Again, I understood entirely the principle behind the exercise, but noticed that while the exercise helped the actor gain a sense of 'mastery' over the

> **I watched silently as the panelists next to me would note 'OTT' on their audition forms and then proceed to redirect the student…**

15

character (if such a thing makes sense), the work often led to more isolation on stage, since the concentration in the exercise was all about sustaining 'character' choices consistently, and not about affecting the world around the 'character'. And of course, there were many more exercises that ultimately led me into wondering what it was about that 'isolated actor' that worried me so much and how I could disrupt and redirect the actor's energy toward more external action.

I was surprised often by the students' great reluctance EVER to be seen to be 'overacting' or hammy in any sense. Indeed I think their greatest anxiety about acting had to do with a fear that they would be overdoing it. I was keenly aware that this same anxiety used to run through our audition panel when a student came in to do a Shakespeare monologue with great energy. I watched silently as the panelists next to me would note 'OTT' on their audition remarks forms and then proceed to redirect the student by asking them to imagine that they were very, very tired. Leading the young hopeful through a series of exercises to induce a great sense of both physical and mental exhaustion, the auditionee would then be asked to begin their monologue once more. The kind of introspective but honest reading given by students in this state was often greeted by my fellow-panelists as a more tasteful and 'connected' performance. But I worried that the exercise would suggest to the student that Shakespeare is best played with this kind of low energy.

Throughout three years of training, students attended many hours of 'skills' classes – in voice, movement, dance, etc. They were attempting to achieve a kind of physical freedom while watching themselves constantly in the mirror. They were asked to attempt to keep their vocal energy 'flowing' while at times being continually interrupted with comment. They were advised in tutorials to allow themselves to fail and then, of course, faced some criticism in the next tutorials when they didn't 'fail' in quite the ways staff had wanted or expected. As they progressed, the questions increasingly became about overall self-awareness – particularly in the third year when actors began to think of themselves in terms of their 'casting' and marketability. They spoke as freely in tutorial as the staff did about when/whether they were cast 'to strength' in some productions or whether they were cast 'against type' in others. In fact, the more I watched, the more convinced I became that what we were doing was creating a kind of extraordinary self-consciousness that would always militate against 'ease', 'flow', 'play' and 'living in the moment' – indeed, it seemed to me that we were creating a method, a way of thinking that would always be contrary to creating the conditions for achieving the things we positively encouraged. And I began to wonder if the kind of actor training we were practising was a self-defeating exercise.

Of course, as a staff we never discussed this. There were many things we didn't discuss, and when I look back at this now I find it incredibly curious. We didn't, in that first year, discuss amongst ourselves what exactly we were talking about when we judged an acting performance. We didn't talk amongst ourselves about our own teaching methods, or our own approaches to directing. We didn't discuss in practical terms how we intended to help Actor A achieve the emotional depth that was consistently lacking in performances. We didn't discuss in practical terms how we were going to help Actor B find the intellectual curiosity that might lead to greater exploration. But we were happy to exchange terms that were (clearly!) ideological in the sense that they were put forth as if already defined and agreed upon. This was especially true during the critique sessions that followed every 'staff run' of a public show.

I can still so clearly remember the vocabulary of these sessions. We routinely described performances as:

- not fully connected
- understood but not felt
- accomplished (read: superficial)
- not fully inhabited
- general, unspecific
- not well-observed, not detailed
- not deeply/not fully explored
- a bit breathless/over the top (read: over-energized)
- not fully in the world/didn't bring the world on with them
- 'hand me down' (read: cliché)
- off the back foot (read: low energy/too casual)
- over-intellectualized
- external
- self-conscious
- emotive
- clotted/constipated/ponderous
- mannered/tricksy
- signalling emotion/intent
- anticipating the moment.

Some of these terms were new to me but I felt that I instinctively understood what they meant. It is remarkable that while I can easily reel off this list of traits of the unsuccessful performance, I don't remember quite as many descriptions for GOOD performances. It seems extraordinary to me now that we didn't, at any point in that first year, exchange views on what exactly we were looking for in a young actor's performance (although clearly we knew what we WEREN'T looking for!). We generally went through each actor by name and then waited – sort of staring fixedly at our shoes – until the Artistic Director made his first pronouncement. Once we knew the general direction of the wind (the Artistic Director was a man of strong opinion…), we would usually find the courage to bring up small additional comments about the performance. In an atmosphere like this, it isn't easy to suggest that we should all sit down and have a full and frank discussion about what it was, exactly, that made for a good performance – because to suggest such a thing was to suggest that you, personally, didn't know.

But what if I didn't know? If I look closely at the language employed above in describing some problems in performance, what would I conclude from this list? It is certainly true that these negative things do add up to a positive kind of 'desiderata' or list of what I might find desirable in the work of actors – but can it ever be anything more than that?

For example, let's see if we can build a list of positive traits in performance from the list of negative traits above. I think it would go something like this:

- connected
- felt
- profound
- inhabited
- specific
- well-observed, detailed
- deeply, fully explored
- fully in the imagined world
- unself-conscious
- ease of 'energy flow'
- straightforward
- spontaneous, 'in the moment'.

It certainly sounds good, and now that I have what I think might be the best positive list I can create on the basis of my negative list, what does it tell me about what, exactly, we were looking for?

There are many, many ways to approach actor training. I am sure that one of the most unique was practised by the late, great classical actor, Brewster Mason, whose work at the RSC was well known. Somehow Brewster found himself heading up a class in Advanced Shakespeare at UCI when I was a student there. We were instructed to bring in as many monologues as we wanted and Brewster would coach us through. At the beginning of classes, his response to every monologue was the phrase 'Yes, well, it's a difficult one, isn't it?' As a class, we slowly came to realize that Brewster had three ways of saying 'Yes, well, it's a difficult one, isn't it? The first carried a kind of subtext of respect, and we could feel that Brewster – while not altogether approving our reading – had some respect for the attempt that we had made. The second had a strong feeling of uncertainty about it – as if Brewster knew that we weren't quite getting it right but he needed time to think how he could possibly be of help. The third (and the most deadly) seemed to carry an unspoken rider that went something like 'Yes – it's a difficult one…but I never realized how difficult until I heard *your* version!'

By the time the end of term rolled around, Brewster would be waiting for us at the back of the darkened theatre. At this point Brewster didn't actually coach so much as simply shout things like 'No! You're murdering it!' or 'Dreadful! Try again!' If we asked for advice we were generally told simply to try again. No matter how you look at it, I suppose Brewster just wasn't cut out for this teaching lark, but he had endless patience for our fourth, fifth and even sixth attempt at Mistress Quickly or Hermoine. Once, by the very end of term, I delivered Cressida's 'By the same token, you are a bawd...' which – miraculously – went uninterrupted. At the end there was a very disconcerting silence, after which he simply said 'Ah! There you go!'

We would not, in these days of 'quality assurance' and 'learning outcomes' probably think much of Brewster's style. But in reflection I realized that I had learned quite a lot – even if I'd had to do that by examining my failures on my own and trying different approaches. I couldn't have said exactly, after the Cressida speech, what I'd done that had finally gained his approval but I certainly knew that I'd never put so much time into preparation. I'd never spent so much time on the language and the meaning of each and every word, and I'd never felt so keenly my imagined sense of desire for Troilus or my reasons for giving the advice to my younger, love-struck sister (which was the context I'd given the piece). I'd never felt quite that much energy in delivery and I liked that I wasn't quite sure where Brewster was seated, so my vocal energy had to reach the back of the house.

He wouldn't be everyone's teacher. But he was certainly one of mine. Being the kind of student who didn't want to be taught made me the kind of student who worked well with his singular – and unashamed – decision not to teach.

A common sense view of good acting might be similar to the challenge that I set for students when I teach acting fundamentals. I routinely say to these students that our only aim in this fundamentals class will be to be able, by the end of the sessions, to do a credible imitation of a human being. The phrase is glib, but worth exploring in this context. When we look at the 'positive' list above – what does it add up to for us? A credible imitation of a human being? Perhaps – but we would have to admit that the range of human beings is vast, so this is a very wide category indeed and the list above not only does NOT exhaust that category, it is missing many, many descriptions. Are we looking for something 'truthful'? Actors talk about being truthful and about being believed or being believable all the time. Directors routinely talk to actors about truth and believability. Every acting book you will ever pick up mentions the importance of 'truthful' performance. But what, really, are we talking about when we use the word truth in this way? It is true to me that my senses have perceived human beings going about their business, many of whom exhibit the following behaviours:

- *not fully connected*

  That is to say that I have met many people who, it seems to me, are not greatly in contact with their own deep feelings – indeed much of psychotherapy is based on trying to GET people to connect with and openly express feeling.

- *a bit breathless (read: over-energized)/off the back foot (read: low energy)*

  Of course, there are many people that we might routinely describe this way as being highly energized, even unnaturally so; equally we will have encountered many people whose snail-like pace is both a fact and often annoying.

- *self-conscious*

  Again, this is a regularly observable trait amongst people that I know – although the level of self-consciousness may be incredibly inconsistent. I have known some people though, who are almost never able to escape the confines of their self-consciousness in the company of others.

- *mannered/tricksy*

  One of my best friends at Oxford, Peter, used to manage five distinct gestures between picking up his cigarette from an ashtray and actually taking a puff. He was a marvellous and eccentric man, who was certainly full of mannerisms that made him incredibly memorable to me.

I won't go on. But I hope the point is clear. It isn't that these traits are not TRUTHFUL traits insofar as we might observe them and accept the evidence of our senses when observing the vast varieties of human behaviour. But perhaps it is the case that these truthful human traits are not ones that we like to see in an actor's performance during a sustained piece of 'realism' or 'naturalism' without very clear justification – such as playing very eccentric characters (Yepikhodov, or Lear's Fool perhaps). Might it be that in the context of 'psychological realism' or 'naturalism' some real people

> **Might it be that some people are perhaps 'too real' to be believed on stage?**

are perhaps too real to be believed on stage? Or perhaps we're looking not for truth but for, as Phillip Zarrilli puts it, 'an ideal-typical mode of aesthetic/experiential engagement'?[6] No doubt every actor, director or training tutor reading this will have their own list of good and bad acting criteria. They will agree with some of my terms and perhaps violently disagree with others. But I doubt that anyone will argue too strongly that the kind of TRUTH we value when watching an actor's performance is a splendidly elastic thing, and no doubt the product of history and culture.

It occurs to me that there were many paradoxes about my experiences at Central, and the ways in which we spoke about 'truth' was only one. These paradoxes were repeated wherever I worked. Another was that we trained actors in a manner almost guaranteed to make them self-conscious and yet continuously hoped to see them turn in 'fully inhabited' – unselfconscious – performances. Added to this, we spoke as if we were in agreement about the overall aesthetic criteria that make up good acting but had never once discussed it.

At a Central audition I recall a very talented young man, with a natural ease of voice and body and whose audition revealed him to be already at a stage in his artistry and development that would put most of our third-year actors to shame. We dithered about taking him, wondering whether in fact he shouldn't just be encouraged to get on with trying to find work. In the end we decided, given his age, that the training could only make a good thing better.

We were wrong. At the end of three years with us I was not the only staff member who believed that he was actually quite a bit worse than when he started. By his final performances, the wonderful freshness and ease that had allowed him to enter an imaginary world with playfulness, surprising depth and confidence had been slightly hampered by a subtle self-consciousness that had not been present in his first year. The range and depth of his expression had gone from seeming free and multi-chromatic to slightly overwrought and (yes!) mannered. Even he seemed aware of this in tutorial sessions when he spoke of suddenly feeling as if everything he had learned was making him overly analytical in approach and chipping away at what he had previously felt was his pretty limitless confidence on stage.

I saw him not long ago in a film, in which all the old passion and charisma seemed present once again. I can only hope that for him, the lack of confidence and the self-doubting, self-consciousness was a phase that has passed. But I would not be telling the truth if I said that over my nearly two decades of actor-training he was the only young person whose phenomenal natural abilities were not always well served by the sort of 'hot-house' environments produced by conservatoire training, and the rather rigid set of values that they engender in terms of what makes great acting.

And as I write this I am very aware now of how my descriptive language seems suddenly to invite a lot more analysis. My description of James as a young auditioning actor certainly tells you a lot about what it is that I value in actors. My description of how his work transformed over the next three years tells you much about the things I worry about when watching or training actors. In other words, it is important for us to note that while these descriptions feel, to me, like good criteria for judging actors, they cannot, without much deeper examination be thought to be universally accepted criteria.

As I moved on from Central to the Liverpool Institute and then the Royal Scottish Academy, my doubts about how we approached actor training and the kind of language we used in that endeavour did not diminish, but the daily demands of my work left little time to ponder what it was that was worrying me at a deeper level. I was aware that the students we were training were (mostly) getting better and responding to our various approaches, but they were also often becoming increasingly dependent upon us to make decisions for them. As head of department, I was always too busy to really confront my worries about the effect of constant scrutiny on the creative spirit. And as the years went by I found myself getting better at not really facing up to a whole range of intellectual issues about acting and training that were nagging away at me. Instead of tackling these issues, I found myself wanting to leave aside or rule out of court whole areas during rehearsal.

For example, I refused to discuss character in class or rehearsal. I insisted instead that if we must refer to the role they were playing we would use the role's proper name. This was not simple eccentricity or recalcitrance on my part – I was just all too painfully aware of the baggage that comes with talking about 'character': 'my character', 'building a character', 'what the character wants', etc. – all of it continuously reminded me of how unexamined our language was in this area, and how slender our conception of the profound questions raised by this particular aspect of the actor's craft – particularly when it came to areas like where, precisely, we locate our own conscious sense of ourselves in relation to a 'character's' sense of self, and what it is we mean when we refer to 'I', or 'selfness' or 'character' or 'acting as character' or 'acting from the self', etc. It was easier simply not to allow the word in the room.

> **I refused to allow the actors to discuss their emotions or feelings.**

Similarly, I refused to allow actors to learn lines prior to rehearsal. More often than not I encouraged actors to try and learn their lines *in* rehearsal if they could (and was always happy to have other actors on the sides of the rehearsal room reading their lines for them – particularly in very physical scenes. I would then simply ask the actors to join the 'read-in' lines on the parts they could remember as they worked through the scene physically). It seemed to me that I would rather have actors holding books than parroting lines that they had learned elsewhere, so I never set 'off-book' dates – which some actors found difficult as they wanted a 'date' to work from.

I also never allowed the actors to discuss their emotions or feelings (either their own or their character's). They were encouraged instead to focus on changing or influencing the feelings of the actors around them. Again, this was not a question of being difficult or tyrannical – I think I just innately sensed that to get into this area would entail a much greater consideration of some very challenging questions about how we conceive the relationship between our various mental states and our sense perception of the world; how our intellectual faculty works in terms of reason and emotion, where, precisely, emotion resides in the body, etc. I also felt as if, apart from talking with the actor about what kinds of thoughts and emotions a particular scene might invoke, I wasn't sure that I wanted to get into areas like asking the actor to produce any specific emotion. It seemed better to me to ask them to focus on what they were trying to make other actors feel and trusted that the sheer frustration or desperation in the face of that difficulty would usually generate enough emotion to fuel a scene in a pretty compelling way. Where this wasn't adequate (in scenes like, for example, the company gathering at the death of King John, etc.), I found that once the actors truly understood a play and truly understood what a particular scene represented within that moment of the play and in the likely future immediately beyond that scene, the only way to help was not through language, but through music.

For example, in our production of the *Henry IV Part II*, when Morton comes to tell Northumberland of the death of his son, we simply worked the scene through in terms of its action. Of course it's difficult to predict how a father will react in the immediate aftermath of hearing of the death of his son, and although Northumberland's response is described as 'strained passion', I wasn't sure myself what that might mean in specific emotional terms. I also never felt comfortable saying to an actor 'Well, I think you should cry here' or 'I think he has a breakdown here' – I'm sure I'm not alone in this. But once we'd worked the scene through many times in terms of its action, I simply played Samuel Barber's *Adagio for Strings* quietly during the scene in the last few rehearsals. At this point the actors quite simply seemed to know instinctively what was right then. For the actor playing Northumberland this varied – but the depth of his feeling was always apparent. Still – actually talking about emotion – how to produce it, when to produce it, was something I never wanted to engage in. Again – easier just to keep it out of the room and work on my ongoing obsessions, such as redirecting self-consciousness in the hope of keeping actors from becoming isolated on stage, and trying to gently eradicate the repeatedly voiced fears of 'overacting'. I grew similarly wary of talking to actors about their use of 'trigger memories' or 'inner monologues' – ideas that they often brought with them from other directors/tutors, and simply asked that they leave all of this out of the rehearsal room.

In short, I seemed to be becoming an acting teacher/director who was working against the grain of much of what I was taught when I was training, and although it appeared I was growing more eccentric in terms of what I wanted to allow in the rehearsal room, I was rarely disappointed in what we came up with. But I never really took the time to analyse exactly why I was doing these things and simply remained content with their efficacy. The very point, for me, in writing this book is to have the courage to do what I haven't managed in acting classes or in the rehearsal room over the last two decades: to face some of these difficult questions but to do so with a kind of clarity that I hope gives the examination some immediate value for practitioners.

What follows is not a book of acting technique, but it is a book *about* acting technique; one that I hope prepares you for (and perhaps in some cases I mean defends you from) the things you encounter in acting books and in the rehearsal studio. It is an attempt to look very closely at how the philosophical questions we outlined earlier are or addressed (or NOT addressed) in acting theory and practice. And it is also an attempt to see if we can, through the lens of some remarkable contemporary research in areas like cognitive science and psychology, bring our thoughts about acting theory up to date and perhaps leave behind some ideas that have lost their currency.

As far as I know this book is the first sustained attempt to consider acting theory and practice in light of the 'cognitive revolution'. Over the last 30 years or so, this revolution has completely redrawn the disciplinary map in the areas of psychology, philosophy and neuroscience. The ability to understand the workings of the brain at the neural level has the potential to redraw the relationship between other disciplines as well, as V.S. Ramachandran points out:

> [W]e are poised for the greatest revolution of all – understanding the human brain. This will surely be a turning point in the history of the human species for, unlike those earlier revolutions in science, this one is not about the outside world, not about cosmology or biology or physics, but about ourselves, about the very organ that made those earlier revolutions possible. And I want to emphasise that these insights into the human brain will have a profound impact not just on scientists but also on the humanities, and indeed they may even help us bridge what C.P. Snow called the two cultures – science on the one hand and arts, philosophy and humanities on the other.[7]

I will begin in Part One with a fairly traditional philosophical approach, but in the following sections (particularly Parts Three, Four and Five) I'll be turning to recent research to see if we can uncover some of the mysteries of cognitive processes, emotion and the ways in which we theorize the minds of others – and the minds of dramatic characters. Above all, this book is an attempt to wrestle with the question of what acting IS.

It has been a terrific learning journey for me and throughout my writing I've been inspired by seeing the many ways in which the work of scholars like Ramachandran, Antonio Damasio, Joseph LeDoux and Daniel C. Dennett 'map' onto the whole area of acting and acting theory. It is my fondest hope that you will also find their work stimulating, thought-provoking and useful.

Notes

1. Terry Eagleton, *The Ideology of the Aesthetic* (Oxford: Blackwell, 1990), p. 366.
2. C. Stanislavski in *Acting: A Handbook of the Stanislavski Method* (New York: Three Rivers Press, 1983), p. 32.
3. *Ibid.*, p. 36.
4. Stella Adler, *The Technique of Acting* (New York: Bantam, 1988), p. 10.
5. *Acting: A Handbook of the Stanislavski Method*, compiled by Toby Cole (New York: Three Rivers Press, 1975), p. 31.
6. Phillip Zarrilli, 'Action, Sturcture, Task, and Emotion' in *Teaching Performance Studies* (Carbondale: Southern Illinois University, 2002), p. 149.
7. V.S. Ramachandran, *A Brief Tour of Human Consciousness* (New York: Pi Press, 2004), p. 2.

Chapter 1

Am I ACTING?

There is a fascinating love/hate thing going on with actors and the people who train actors about the whole notion of 'acting'. Indeed, there are books with titles like *No Acting Please* or *How to Stop Acting*. Of course it isn't that actors don't want to act. Nor is it that acting teachers are fed up and don't want to teach acting anymore. Of course authors of books with titles like *No Acting Please* don't really think that there is no such activity as acting in plays, nor are they issuing a general proclamation like 'No unsolicited manuscripts' or 'No smoking', by which the author means that there is to be no theatrical activity is his/her immediate area.

Instead these titles are taken to mean that the author proposes a method of training and working whereby the actor's activity is so seamlessly parallel to what our senses perceive as human behaviour that we will not be able to distinguish seeing an actor at work from greeting the woman at the dry cleaners or encountering our friends on a night out. It must also mean that the authors of such books value actors who do not attempt to alter their own perceived 'natural' behaviour when they are 'pretending' to be a person in a play. The questions that might concern us here is whether we should ALL value this kind of acting, or if there are only specific contexts in which we should ALL value this kind of acting. When we're teaching or taking an acting class, perhaps the first question should probably be this: what kind of acting do we value, and what kind of acting are we aiming to teach or learn in this class? Of course every time we watch a performance and then share our opinion we are answering this question in that context. In this section I'd like to consider what acting is, how we determine what it is we value in acting, and to look at the issues that bedevil us when we attempt to articulate a view about these seemingly straightforward questions.

A quick survey of acting books reveals their tendency to anchor critical judgement on 'truth'. Some of these kinds of foundational statements are short, and some are more complex, but all of them require that in order to judge acting (either our own or others) we can simply refer to our own innate ability to know the 'truth' when we see it. Now of course, it may be a commonplace to observe that truth is a relative concept that always needs careful thought about context and point of view. However, it seems that even this pretty mundane observation needs to be kept in mind if we want to make any progress amongst our pile of acting books. In most of these books, this foundational basis – the TRUTH – is sometimes bound up with character, and sometimes critically bound up with attempts to define what acting IS.

It's fairly easy to find some pithy observations on what acting is or should be, and these generally invoke being or doing as foundational activities, and the implication is that 'being' and 'doing' are immediately connected to something truthful in a way that 'acting' is not:

'I am' is living. 'I am Being' is acting.[1]

The foundation of acting is the reality of doing.[2]

The well-made play, scene, design, the good performance, must be true.[3]

Stella Adler appeals directly to truth as the bedrock of good acting:

> You must be truthful in what you do or say. Feel the truth within yourself.[4]

Some are longer but still involve 'truth' directly:

> My students spend the entire first year of their training developing themselves into truthful acting instruments.[5]

> the difference between BEING and acting was glaringly obvious to all of us. Once the actors had tasted these moments of BEING, their appetites were whetted for more. Both actors and audience became dissatisfied with less than the truth…[6]

> Stanislavski's 'big thing' was 'truthful' acting…There's an inherent paradox in good acting, particularly when it comes to psychological realism. You create the illusion of absolute 'truth' and naturalness, as if you're really 'living in the moment' and conjuring up those particular words in that particular moment of performance…Yet, in most cases, you can only seem that spontaneous if your *technique* is finely honed.[7]

Some involve truth but do so in some rather convoluted formulations:

> Since love is the highest emotional choice in life and bliss the deepest desire, so it is when working on stage. I have seen the acceptance of this truth to be the very thing that finally seats the character into place for an actor when he was having difficulty finding the character, because that deep desire is the truest one in every person and, there, in every character.[8]

Some are strangely circular:

> Integrating with the character, mastering it in depth, means that what you do in a situation will always correspond truthfully to the needs and intentions of the play. You'll know how to behave within given circumstance, how to function within your environment, how to listen to your partner, and what action to take.

When you interpret a role, you look for the character's 'truth'. Here, I use the word 'truth' to mean the endowment of the character with particular traits and behavioural patterns belonging specifically to that character. You make choices of interpretation by clear insight into the character's nature without imposing inconsistent traits on it.[9]

All of these statements are based on some unproblematic assumptions about the way in which acting involves a relationship between being, doing and truth, and seem to suggest that we will arrive at the truth as actors if we just relax and get on with doing and that we can judge the 'truthfulness' or otherwise of our performance for ourselves. Michael Chekhov provides some welcome relief by outlining a more complex understanding of different kinds of truths that the actor must be aware of:

There are several facets of truth. (1) Individual or psychological truth…(2) Being true to the given circumstances of the script. (3) Historical truth…(4) Stylistic truth…(5) Being true to the character…(6) The truth of relationship…[10]

But still, rather like the others he seems to assume that we will get better at judging these 'truths' as we go along. For Sandy Meisner acting 'is the ability to live truthfully under imaginary circumstances'. Stanislavski, of course, has a view that is typically full of tensions:

I am not interested in a truth that is without myself; I am interested in the truth that is within myself, the truth of my reaction to this or that event on the stage, to the properties, the scenery, the other actors…to their thoughts and emotions…Scenic truth is not like truth in life; it is peculiar to itself…on the stage truth is that which the actor sincerely believes.[11]

It's difficult to intuit much from this, apart from the overall sense that truth is something that we, as actors, must judge for ourselves – and yet we know that Stanislavski, as a teacher, had much to say about whether his pupils could judge truth for themselves. Stella Adler's version of truth seemed to be distilled from her time studying directly under Stanislavki's tutelage: 'You will hear me say very often what Stanislavski said: truth in art is truth in circumstances.'[12] This, of course, leaves the whole category of truth pretty wide open.

And related to the problem of figuring out just how it is that we make this judgement about whether our acting is truthful, is the issue of whether our acting is *detectable*, or whether acting is something that *should* be detectable. That is to say, that along with debates about method acting approaches, there has been a growing concern over the last decades about whether acting should be about personality, self-revelation, introspection and absolute verisimilitude OR about transformation, technique, character, etc., and a clear worry that actors whose acting is *detectable* may be compromising truth when they perform.

True for who(m)?

When Richard Hornby considers what it was that Stanislavski valued as truth in an actor's performance, he concludes that Stanislavski wasn't asking the actor to consider his/her own emotional life or circumstances:

> ...Stanislavski could not have been more plain about what kind of truth he was talking about: 'To play truly means to be right, logical, coherent, to think, strive, feel and act in unison *with your role*' [Hornby's emphasis]. The actor does not 'reality test,' checking everything he does against real life; nor does he churn himself up into a 'truthful' emotional frenzy. Reality testing not only makes all nonrealistic drama impossible, even with realistic material it takes the actor's imagination away from where it ought to be, on the role itself.[13]

The basic thesis of Hornby's book, *The End of Acting*, seems to me a sound one: that too much emphasis on self, emotion, personality and 'real life' have taken the pleasure out of acting. While we may be sympathetic with the basic thesis of his book, this particular assertion about truth is puzzling. Surely it all depends on what it is that we look for when we're checking ourselves against reality? And how can an actor rely solely on the role for guidance? Of course we have many, many clues about character and action from the text, but these clues are bound to change whenever we change the historical and cultural context and the personal circumstances of the actor involved. An actor's imagination does not reside in the text. Such a thing would be impossible. Surely the actor brings his or her imagination with them into the world and the character they seek to understand and portray. And while we know that most actors are hoping to create a 'truthful' performance, how else can we judge 'truth' unless we refer to the world beyond the text?

Truth is an incredibly tricky thing to write about, to attempt to 'create' in the theatre or to judge. I think instinctively actors know that, if only because – despite what Chekhov's or Stanislavski's words might imply – most of us have a hard time judging 'the truth' of our own performances while we're acting. This difficulty is surely the only reason we take acting classes or listen to directors' comments and notes in the first place. There are certainly some things we can judge for ourselves. For instance, we know when we think a scene is working. Most actors have a sense of feeling when a scene is going well, just as we know when it's going badly. I've never encountered an actor of some experience who didn't have the ability to sense when something is working or not. I would venture to say that when we get this sensation that a scene is working, it is because we achieve a kind of 'oneness' with the scene and with ourselves. That sounds very zen and mysterious, but I don't think working actors will be confused by this idea. When we sense a 'oneness' with the work we've usually achieved a strong level of self-belief. We're not 'outside' of ourselves criticizing our performance; we're not struggling to remember things, we're not worrying about believing, we simply are. When it's all 'clicking' we have the kind of sensation we had as kids when our imaginations felt so strong we just *knew* we were soldiers or cowboys or detectives. Of course, it often requires that we have scene partners for whom it's also 'clicking'. But having an inner sense of 'truth' for ourselves *does not necessarily guarantee that this sense is transferable*. The difficulty for an actor is that even when it's 'clicking' for us, it may not be for a director or an audience. Indeed, it may not feel 'truthful' for anyone *but* the actors. Or it may only seem 'truthful' for some. I've been on all sides of this difficulty as both actor and director.

But let's go back for a moment to Richard Hornby's idea that the actor is not 'checking everything he does against real life' – what can he really mean here? Can we ever say that anything is true without reference to something else? In other words, are there some brute facts that exist without reference to anything else? In a sense, this was something the French philosopher René Descartes set out to discover when he decided to reduce the whole world around him to simply things he KNEW he could KNOW. But of course, for many other philosophers, this is precisely where Descartes comes a cropper – because any knowledge that exists solely in our heads is pretty useless. In other words, we can't simply sit in a cave and discover by ourselves that our eyes are blue, unless we never intend to discuss this discovery with another human being. If we DO discuss this with another human being we may find out that our eyes are brown. Or at least, we'll find out that what we call 'blue' everyone else is calling brown, and we might as well go along with that or else we'll never be able to communicate. And if I DON'T intend to discuss my blue eyes with another human being, then it is all very well for me to sit in my cave and assert that my eyes are blue, but calling my eyes blue because I think they are blue remains pretty meaningless.

One of the fascinating things about theatrical creativity is that, although it raises so many philosophical issues, it does at least pretty neatly sidestep some of them, simply because it is a collaborative art. In other words, we are – in this collaborative arena – always testing out our theories of 'truth' and what is 'coherent' and what makes sense in the context of the play we're working on. We also test our sense of values and our moral judgements. And we are forced to acknowledge that when we present our personal conclusion that Hamlet is gay to the rest of the company, this observation is likely to be pretty controversial, and we are likely to encounter some other – possibly more persuasive – interpretations. It is true that all our work in theatre is public and dialogical. There are always many points of view in the room bearing on a single issue, and we regularly come up against other beings and strange points of view.

This doesn't, however, guarantee that what we all find truthful, wonderfully observant or riotously funny in our collaborative rehearsal process will strike others the same way once we've left the rehearsal room. Most actors and directors will have a story about a terrific and creative rehearsal period that met with stony silence or dreadful reviews.

Still, I've sometimes wondered if the history of philosophical thought might not have changed quite radically if ALL philosophers were pretty much forced (like most theatre artists) to work in the same room with other philosophers all the time…

When we start to think about acting as an activity that 'seamlessly parallels' what our senses perceive as 'true' human behaviour in varying contexts, we are already making the jump from our own heads out into the world. As we know, there are any number of ways in which we can accept certain behaviours in a theatrical contexts, and ways in which we seem less able to 'believe' or buy certain human behaviours (no matter how well founded they may be in the world we observe around us). But in the case of 'true' human behaviour, we're looking at the way in which what an actor does might correspond with truthful human behaviour as we observe it in the world, and then taking that simple connection to be the keystone of our judgement about the performance. In philosophical terms we're talking about 'correspondence theory'. The main idea behind correspondence theory is summarized by George Lakoff and Mark Johnson this way: 'A statement is true when it fits the way things are in the world. It is false when it fails to fit the way things are in the world.'[14] In other words, we work out what is true by testing it against something we consider to be 'reality'. Now at first glance, this may seem all too obvious to merit further consideration, and no doubt this is why so many acting books begin by talking about the 'truth' without any preamble that might explain how the particular acting theorist defines that word or concept. But let's consider this little philosophical 'correspondence' formula:

X is true if, and only if, X corresponds with the fact Y

This is one version of 'correspondence theory', which appears to work out well if the X is 'rain is wet' or 'rocks are hard'. It is more difficult of course if the X is 'Hamlet wants to die.'[15] This idea may be true, or it may not, but in this case we can't necessarily say that it is FALSE. We can only say that there seems to be an absence of truth in terms of our 'correspondence theory' formula, because there is no identifiable 'fact Y' out in the world against which we can test this idea. Of course, some philosophers feel that the whole way in which the question of correspondence theory is framed makes it too trivial to consider. There are too many ambiguities to allow us to formulate anything simple between 'truth' and its relationship to facts or observed states of affairs. Perhaps more interesting is to question the *relationship* itself. If our first statement X (rain is wet) is related to fact Y (wet rain) in the world, HOW is it related? Indeed, it is only a collection of words that refer to a condition in the real world, but how do we relate that collection of words to what-is-out-there? Or we might want to question the whole idea that there is a 'true' way that things 'are-in-the-world' – in other words, could we ever ascertain that there is some kind of brute, mind-independent state of things in the world? These questions are more important than they might seem on first reading. Acting books refer to the truth with regularity. Many acting books proceed on the assumption that the truth is relatively unproblematic (except insofar as young actors may have difficulty creating 'truthful' acting), and their general advice about the relationship between acting and observing human behaviour suggests a kind of tacit subscription to the correspondence theory of truth. But the theory is not without its critics.

Describing objections to correspondence theory, *The Stanford Encyclopedia of Philosophy* offers this:

> In a nutshell, the objection is that a correspondence theory of truth must inevitably lead into skepticism about the external world because the required correspondence between our thoughts and reality is not ascertainable…It is typically pointed out that we cannot step outside our own minds to compare our thoughts with mind-independent reality. Yet – so the objection continues – on the correspondence theory of truth, this is precisely what we would have to do to gain knowledge.[16]

There are many more objections to correspondence theory that can be made, not the least of which is that it puts its claims forth as if all truths can be 'stated at once from a neutral perspective'.[17] And if as actors or directors or acting teachers, we can never have the 'mind-independent reality' or the implied neutrality that would help us determine that the relationship between our ideas/words and reality is solid, we must admit that our access to 'truth' is kind of shaky – or at least, *relative*. No doubt this explains the lack of precision when theorists refer to the truth in relation to acting and judgements about acting. But does the acknowledgement of its inherent difficulty excuse the ways in which we use/encounter TRUTH when reading about, practising, teaching or studying acting? Would it help if we modified the word truth with the adjective 'relative'?

Beyond boring relativism

In his consideration of what he calls 'The Lair of Relativism', Stephen Law suggests that there are two kinds of relativism: Boring and Interesting.[18] Interesting relativism comes about when the same claim is made by two people, but is true for one person and false for another. I've been party to many post-performance discussions that we might see as 'interesting relativism' in which it is clearly true for me that Actor X's performance was inspired and extremely well executed, and yet for a colleague it is 'true' that Actor X's performance was utterly unbelievable. In order to determine who is right in this case we would have to assume that there is some objective form of 'Actor X's' performance that exists outside of either my or my coleague's perception of the performance. But even if such an objective form did exist, we would have to find ways to test the performance against something like an objective reality (although these ways seem hard to imagine), and determine who is 'right'.

> **Do we have to talk about 'truth' all the time? Can't we bypass the idea somehow when we're talking about acting?**

But of course, there is no such objective form of Actor X's performance that exists outside of our individual perceptions of it, nor any objective reality against which to test it, so talking about who is right and who is wrong will get us nowhere. And herein lies the whole problem of attempting to apply correspondence theory unproblematically when judging an actor's performance. But it is also, critically, the problem we encounter when we continually use truth as a kind of foundation stone in our theories about acting and actor training.

Stanislavski himself exacerbates these problems when he distinguishes between a 'stage truth' and a 'life truth': 'On stage truth is whatever you believe and in life truth is what actually is.'[19] Stanislavski's stage truth is therefore NOT related to simple correspondence theory is quite the way that his 'life truth' might be. While this is not surprising in itself, what is surprising to me is that – despite all the writing and debating and consideration that his acting theories have had – the way in which he (and Chekhov and Adler and so many others) builds his theoretical edifice on the foundation of 'truth' has had so little consideration. Perhaps Sharon Carnicke comes closest to considering why the language of acting theory is often so woolly:

> Actors, like writers, are practitioners, not theorists. As Peter Brook so aptly notes, theatrical 'aesthetics are practical, based upon an assumed, and often unexamined 'working system' which constantly prompts 'value-judgements'…The words 'better', 'worse', 'not so good', 'bad' are [used] day after day, but these words which rule decisions carry no moral sense whatever…[A]s a pragmatic system, theatre knowledge can contain mutually contradictory ideas as theory can not; it can evolve and shift dynamically from day to day as need demands, with each practitioner tinkering and adjusting it to suit the moment.[20]

It's difficult for me to swallow this sort of 'get-out-jail-free' card because the stubborn fact is that Stanislavski, Adler, Chekhov and others – despite their very practical experiences – *were* theorists. And as such, the 'assumed' and the 'unexamined' in their writing cannot be tucked away under the guise of some sort of contradictory pragmatism – whatever that might mean.

For too many of us, the experience of hearing a critical response about whether or not a performance is 'truthful' remains highly problematic, and it is the point at which we, as writers, directors or actors, stop talking. If I cannot convince you that my performance is truthful by performing, I certainly won't convince you by *talking about* my performance. In that sense wielding the weapon of TRUTH is the way in which theatrical battles are won. And this is not because the weapon is clean, shiny and rational – but only because, rather like the 'death star', there is no defence against it unless we can manage to infiltrate and 'blow it up from the inside'.

But do we need to worry or to talk about 'truth' in this way? Can't we bypass the idea somehow when we're talking about acting? **Surely we could if we didn't continue to base so many textbooks and so much of our response to an acting performance on the issue of whether or not an actor's performance is 'truthful'**. We can talk in other ways – we can talk about whether the performance was interesting or surprising or whether it made us see things in a new light, or whether the performance made us listen to a voice or a point of view we'd never heard before – indeed, there are any number of ways we can talk about how we judge acting. Still, when it comes to teaching, reading or writing about acting, we seem much tied to 'truth' as the bedrock of our judgements – this language has been entrenched in every place I've worked or studied.

What is acting?

Is acting just 'true being' as some theorists would seem to have it? Perhaps any attempt to answer this question needs to begin by asking what it is that we want to *encounter* in the theatrical experience. This might help us determine what it is we want actors to achieve, and allow us to avoid always relying on 'truth' as the basis of our judgements. We know, for example, Antonin Artaud wanted an encounter that was dangerous and spontaneous and wholly independent of the theatre traditions of set texts and 'masterpieces'. This certainty about what he wanted to encounter meant that Artaud knew what he might value in the performer who could create such works.

Stanislavki described clearly his idea of a great experience in the theatre:

You come in and take a seat as one of the audience. Without being aware of it, the director transports you from the world of the audience to that of the stage where you become a participant in the life being depicted in the play. Something has happened to you. You no longer feel like one of the audience. When the curtain goes up you immediately say: 'I know that room. Here comes Ivan Ivanovich, and now Marie Petrovna. That man is a friend of mine…Yes, I know all this. But what will happen next?' You are all attention. You look at the stage and say: 'I believe everything, everything, everything…'[21]

This little passage of Stanislavski's description of the ways in which the well-trained company can 'penetrat[e] deep into the heart of the audience'[22] presupposes a number of things, many of which would rankle Artaud or Bertolt Brecht. But supposing it is Stanislavski's experience that we want to have when we go to the theatre? By the description above, this means that whatever it is we see on stage, we want first and foremost to RECOGNIZE what we see. We want, in 'common sense' language, to be able to gather up our sense impressions of the theatrical experience and to be able to 'file' these in our minds somehow under the category of THINGS I HAVE ENCOUNTERED BEFORE or THINGS I RECOGNIZE. Perhaps, then, this is what I mean when I talk of 'truth' in the theatre. It means that I want to see things that I recognize – either from my direct lived experiences, or perhaps indirectly through films or television or other media – and that therefore have an immediate correspondence in my mind with past experience. Is it this correspondence, then, that makes my experience of watching *Uncle Vanya* or *Hedda Gabler* truthful? Let us suppose for a moment that the answer is yes. In this case, it would seem that I am suggesting a kind of formula about truth based on Stanislavski's observation that goes something like this:

RECOGNIZING = BELIEVING = TRUTH

We know that Stanislavki's description seems in many ways to equate these three terms. But of course, they are not necessarily synonymous. I might believe in a God of Trees. I might decide that the God of Trees is the entity with whom I must commune in order to bring about all my earthly wishes and desires. I wouldn't, however, necessarily claim to recognize this God of Trees if I were to see her. And I might also not necessarily see my belief in the God of Trees as being the same sort of thing as the statement 2 + 2 = 4. In fact, it is almost certainly the case that most of us have things we divide between the category of beliefs that seem true to us (believing that spiders are scary, that our horoscope is worth following or that Sunderland will one day win the Premiership) and the category of truth (all mortals will die, children have biological parents, the square root of 81 is 9).

With this in mind let us see if we might improve our formula in this way:

RECOGNIZING = BELIEVING = 'TRUTH'

How might this help? Well, the inverted commas remind us that truth is always a construct of some sort – and that what we might routinely recognize as 'theatrical truth' is constructed out of a sense of what we have come to value in watching theatre, or perhaps what we want to believe when going to the theatre. When we say that we value 'truthful' performances (which is a phrase I've heard often – and used! – in my years of training actors) we're using a kind of shorthand that ignores all the difficulties of explaining what truth means in a theatrical context.

We know that for Stanislavski at one point, the ideal encounter involved recognition, the sense that he was seeing the world as he knew it, with people he recognized and who therefore inspired in him a sense of belief. This was not only the result of the representation of a physical world that held true to him, but also a world that was psychologically 'real'; a 'psychological realism'. And on a common sense level many of us would have sympathy with this view – although we would no doubt want to remember that what seemed so easily 'recognizable' in Stanislavski's world probably is not recognizable to us, today in London or Los Angeles. Indeed, for many in London and Los Angeles in the twenty-first century, nineteenth-century Russian characters are very mysterious. Still, we might agree that when we watch a realistic play we want the whole theatrical experience to represent this kind of recognizable world. And if so, then we need actors who can convince us that we are seeing complex and recognizable human beings in conflict. But this still doesn't answer the question: what is acting?

Given all the obvious difficulties of invoking truth as part of our definition of acting, let us try a challenge. Let us set out to try creating a proposition about what acting is but do so in a way that DOES NOT INVOLVE THE WORD TRUTH. And based on our statements above, let us imagine that our first proposition about acting is this:

> ## ACTING IS THE ABILITY TO PORTRAY RECOGNIZABLE HUMAN BEHAVIOUR IN A PERFORMANCE CONTEXT

We need to test this a bit, and from the outset we would want to acknowledge that we need to consider whether our proposition holds true in all cases. As we are talking about 'realist' plays, let's concentrate on what we might call 'realistic' acting in the commonly accepted sense of that term – even though we understand that there are 'realist' plays which may have expressionistic or 'heightened' realist tendencies in them. Our definition proposes that there is human behaviour we 'recognize' in varying ways, and in our minds we are willing to make adjustments over what we see. We 'recognize' a young man who climbs buildings in a spider costume because, amongst other reasons, we have come to 'recognize' this particular fantasy. Indeed, if we watch a Spider-Man film closely enough we can routinely see all the laws of physics and the natural world violated, but we don't tend to storm out of the cinema crying 'Oh come on, the velocity and displacement here are utterly out of sync with the principles of classical mechanics – I don't recognize this world!' We KNOW that Spider-Man and his world aren't real, but in these films we are still presented with acting that seems to adhere to the principles of psychological realism and we seem, by and large, able to accept that. We know that we are watching an insecure young man trying to find his place in a rather fantastic world. And no matter how strange the laws of physics in this world, we are not surprised (and in fact, I think we expect) to find ourselves talking about his acting as 'realistic' and believable.

But let's go back and look closely at the language in our proposition. We quickly get into some interesting issues here if we ask ourselves what 'recognizing' means in Stanislavski's sense. If we take Stanislavski at his word in the quotation earlier, he seems to be referring to worlds that *he has experienced*. He seemed to recall what he was seeing as if he had experienced it before. Now of course with this kind of experiential recognition we would not be expecting anything TOO exact. When he says 'I know that room' he does not literally mean that he takes the set to be a room that he has actually, physically been in before. And of course when we watch Spider-Man, we do recognize much of his behaviour, despite his habit of defying the laws of physics, because there are enough things operating in the film that bear a resemblance to our everyday experience. In the same sense we also recognize Hamlet's world, although it is indeed more remote from us, or the worlds of Lady Bracknell or Nora Helmer despite their similar remoteness in terms of society and historical time. Perhaps, though, it isn't the 'world' that I am recognizing here – but something else, something which I might consider to be essential qualities that relate to being human, or perhaps even essential qualities that I recognize to be part of storytelling.

Consider two productions: I set the first production on one of the icy, sulphurous moons of Jupiter. In the play, two married people, after years away from Earth, have fallen in love with each other but are tormented by their vows of faithfulness to their partners back on earth.

I set a second production in a council flat in Croydon. In the play, a happily married couple awake, sit down to their morning coffee and then proceed to saw off their own toes with kitchen knife.

Now it may be that we would be equally interested in seeing both of these productions, but we might not immediately say that either was wholly recognizable in terms of our own experience – although still both would be recognizable in parts. Rather like Spider-Man. Could we say that the human behaviour in these plays is recognizable? We would have to admit that when we say we recognize things in the theatre, and that we value that recognition, we don't mean that we must – like Stanislavski certainly seemed to in his description – recognize *all* of the elements of what we see in a homely, everyday sense. But we still have a problem with the word 'recognize'. Because while we've never been to one of the sulphurous moons of Jupiter (let us say Io), we will still recognize it (which is to say 'recognize' in the sense of word's actual definition: to 'know again' or to identify as if already known or seen.

We will not recognize Io by experience, but we could of course recognize it either by pictures we may have seen or more likely we would recognize Io as a place very like another place we may have been or seen on Earth – the desert perhaps, or films set in Antarctica. And we would certainly recognize the psychology of the thwarted lovers. Much more provocative and no doubt disturbing to us will be the sight of the happily married couple sawing off their toes.

> **The more we think about it, the more difficult it is to say just what ISN'T recognizable in the theatre...**

This is extraordinary behaviour. It is difficult for us to watch. But let us think about it further. Would we say (if the scene was portrayed realistically) that even this extraordinary behaviour could be put into a context where we might conclude that we recognized this behaviour? The more we think about this, the more difficult it grows to determine just what ISN'T recognizable in the theatre. And it raises all the questions about how the conventions operating when we watch theatre seem to defy attempts to use a word like 'recognize' without carefully considering its context.

But when we are watching extraordinary human behaviour portrayed by an actor, is it the case that we want to see activity that seamlessly parallels human behaviour exactly as our senses perceive it (as, perhaps, a 'method' actor might do)? Or is it that we simply want the behaviour displayed by the actors to be recognizable in SOME way? If the actors laughed heartily as they cut off their toes would this be unrecognizable behaviour? Well, probably not, in a performance context. We would simply decide that we were watching a comedy. If the actors screamed and cried in agony this would of course be recognizable – because although I have to hope that most of us have not hacked off our toes after the morning coffee we would certainly expect that such activity would result in agony. If the actors simply had a quick chat about the neighbours as they were cutting off their toes would we not quickly adjust our viewing frame again and assume that we were watching some 'theatre of the absurd'?

We can imagine any number of things the actors could do while sawing away and all of them seem pretty recognizable – if not psychologically 'real' – but of course this does not mean that we 'recognize' any of that behaviour in Stanislavski's more homely everyday way of theatre demonstrating synchronicity with our lived experience.

One of my closest friends at university, Shaun, worked as a professional stand up comic. He used to say that there was a kind of audience 'forgiveness' about the way that a comedian sets up a joke. It was his contention that an audience would forgive ANY premise as the set up for a joke. He used to test this in his nightly routine by changing the set up to various jokes from 'There were these three eggplants hang gliding...' to 'A corkscrew, an onion and a ghost walk into a bar...', etc. The audience's attention is wholly on the joke and its outcome – and they don't care how the teller sets up the premise. The set up is in fact just part of a convention of the stand up performance. Of course, the theatre is a similar convention. The focus of our attention is on the story and where it will take us, and we're willing to overlook the sulphur on Io or the blood on the kitchen floor if the experience adds up to something satisfying to us in some way in terms of the overall experience. So it seems on the whole that 'recognizable' isn't a very helpful description for us in terms of trying to pin down what it is we want to see when we go to the theatre. But can we throw it out as a description when it comes to acting?

If we go back and look closely at Stanislavski's words it seems that the recognizability of the overall production – from scenery to acting – had the effect of making Stanislavski 'believe everything, everything, everything'. But if we know that we can believe without necessarily recognizing, can we leave 'recognizing' out and just say that it is actually the ability to inspire a sense of belief that we should value in acting? On a common sense level, surely this makes sense and is less troublesome than trying to identify the unrecognizable in a theatrical context. It seems that 'recognizible' – rather like 'truth' – is a tricky thing to define or depend upon, so let us amend our proposition then:

ACTING IS THE ABILITY TO PORTRAY HUMAN BEHAVIOUR IN A BELIEVABLE WAY WITHIN A PERFORMANCE CONTEXT

Of course, Stanislavski has set us the challenge of facing two kinds of belief – the actor's belief in him/herself and the audience's belief in what the actor is doing. As we know, belief and truth are not necessarily the same thing. But at least by substituting belief for truth we get around the problems of trying to 'square the circle' of correspondence theory. But, of course, we are still up against a couple of stubborn difficulties. Not only do we have to admit (given our productions above) that while we may not believe it is possible to brutally hack off our own toes while casually discussing the neighbours, we could *accept* this activity in a performance context and would probably assume that the director was saying something meaningful about the ways in which human beings are capable of inflicting tremendous damage upon themselves without noticing; or perhaps we will see this strange experimental production as a statement on the way that contemporary life in council flats has the propensity to numb our senses. The actors might be demonstrating psychological consistency and may then be 'believable' within the director's concept, but their behaviour is not consistent with how we *usually perceive the world*. How then do we apply some kind of judgement in terms of the actors' performances, or our demand that they be believable? Well surely when we are talking about such 'high-concept' productions as this one, we aren't going to apply the same criteria in judging the acting as we would if we were watching *The Lower Depths*. Are we? Well, again that might depend on exactly how the director has framed the production.

It may be that he/she has decided that the best way for us to take in the point about the ways in which council flat living numbs us is by juxtaposing some rather outrageous behaviour within a psychologically 'real' frame. In other words, the director wants us to have the same kind of experience in watching these actors as Stanislavski had: he/she wants us to believe everything about them. But what happens at the moment when they start the do-it-yourself surgery? If they don't scream (because they are numb) – could we possibly see this behaviour as believable? If we don't, is it because the actions don't strike us a psychologically real? Perhaps we have to be in agreement about what 'psychological realism' is. But let us agree for the moment that it is a literary/theatrical convention which is detected in the theatre as the ability to portray a kind of fully rounded human being with complex desires and motivations. But aren't we still left with a problem? If psychological realism is an acting style in which the actor's efforts are aimed at revealing the deep inner psychological workings of their characters, then that revelation depends critically on the expression. And of course it can be said that one person's excellent performance in the style of psychological realism might be another person's inarticulate, 'off-the-back-foot' actor. (Indeed – it is often a charge levelled at 'method' actors: 'For many, Brando was the quintessential method actor: mumbling, introspective, intense.')[23]

Of course what all this means is that there are varieties of 'real', and varieties of 'truth' that will no doubt affect the varieties of 'believable'. It might also mean that in an undeniable way actors – when they are not inarticulate and 'off-the-back-foot' – might often be manipulating the 'real' part of psychological realism, and 'cleaning up' their representation of the world. In other words, they are portraying 'real' people but very often they are doing so in relaxed bodies with well-modulated voices and clarity of intent (which is not, of course, our universal experience with real-people-in-the-world). And doesn't this further problematize the issue of what we, individually, find believable on stage? If, as an actor, I base my character squarely on the true mannerisms of my friend Peter (who consistently executes five distinct gestures between ashtray and inhalation), wouldn't your sense of believing me have something to do not only with whether the play's text somehow accommodates this behaviour as psychologically consistent, but also to do with whether or not you've ever encountered someone like my friend Peter?

But, of course, we all know that it is a commonplace to accept that there is an element of subjectivity in our reception to art and that the question of belief is indeed still ineluctably tied to the question of recognition (I recognize Peter's behaviour as real, therefore believable, even if you don't). So, if we accept this then surely we only have to make a minor modification in our proposition:

> **ACTING IS THE ABILITY TO PORTRAY HUMAN BEHAVIOUR IN A WAY THAT SEEMS BELIEVABLE IN THE EYES OF THE INDIVIDUAL OBSERVER WITHIN A PERFORMANCE CONTEXT**

We have to admit that this leaves out Stanislavski's description of the actor believing themselves. And it is not precisely the same as defining acting as the ability of the actor to portray a character in a manner so seamlessly parallel to what our senses perceive as everyday human behaviour that we will not be able to distinguish seeing the actor from greeting the woman at the dry cleaners. Because now we have introduced the element of subjectivity and what constitutes believability for a given individual. And for some individuals (I would include myself), this 'seamless' representation stuff is not the bedrock of our critical judgement anyway – even when viewing those stalwarts of psychological realism – Chekhov or Ibsen. So does this perhaps mean that I should be writing books with titles like *Let's Have a Bit More Acting Please*? Well, yes, if the idea is that I actually enjoy sensing the actor at work sometimes.

But this is the point at which – like it or not – we're once again facing an issue of what constitutes believability. Can we really get into that argument without talking about truth? I would say that we can if we acknowledge that for some people believability is not compromised by 'sensing the actor at work'.

The 'working' actor

We know that many actors and many acting teachers worry about overacting. Acting theorists and teachers have lots of ways of talking about this – notably by invoking the notion that 'overacting' is not truthful. And while this worry is not universally held, it seems to be common:

> When I ask actors why they have made such dull, mundane choices and why they won't take risks with extravagances and extremities, they tell me they are afraid of overacting... Almost all American actors are terrified of overacting. Yet almost all I ever see is underacting. Where did this ridiculous and widespread fear of overacting come from?[24]

It's clear that there is a sense that overacting (whatever, exactly, that might mean...) will distort TRUTH. Of course this needs much more consideration – not the least part of which is in determining what makes a performance 'overacted'. It seems to me (and to others, like Richard Hornby) that we've grown afraid of acting that is too much like, well…acting. I happen to like seeing the acting part of acting, and when I say this I mean that I really enjoy the full-blooded 'over-the-topness' of Kenneth Branagh's *Henry V* or Derek Jacobi's BBC *Hamlet*, or the 'mannered' repression of Anthony Hopkins in *The Remains of the Day*, or the studied ponderousness of Alan Rickman as Severus Snape. I don't want to encounter an everyday reality in these experiences – I want to see the actor's bold choices and eccentricities. And now that I've laid my cards on the table, could I be said to be enjoying these performances because they are *believable*? Well, yes and no. To me these particular performances are notable for their very theatricality – for the ways in which the actors made big, bold choices and sustained them. The very dimension of their choices reminded me at all times when I was watching them that I was watching an actor at work. Surely that means that I didn't actually find them believable, but that I was admiring their artistry as actors? Hmm…this gets tricker. Because the paradox is this: for me it is possible both to admire them as actors (in other words to be consciously aware that I am perceiving an actor pretending to be Severus Snape) and also to find something about the performance both psychologically consistent and believable. It isn't that I genuinely BELIEVE that Severus Snape exists, that he has greasy black hair and an incredibly low metabolic response rate and that I might at some point encounter him on the Central Line.

But within the context of watching a Harry Potter film I not only find pleasure in the suspense of disbelief generally, but also find pleasure in apprehending the craft detectable on all levels – from the screenwriting to the computer-generated images to the highly premeditated, somewhat constipated and 'mannered' acting of Alan Rickman. Does the fact that I perceive him as an actor make him unbelievable? I would argue that it doesn't. I find what he has created *believably* eccentric, a character's whose psychological depth is more gradually exposed in every ensuing episode. Somehow, it all adds up in a believable way to me in the context of this imagined world.

Richard Hornby also loves the 'acting' part of acting:

> …*character acting* (which Stanislavski himself considered good acting) needs to be valued much more highly than it is in the United States. This kind of acting, in which the actor plays a role significantly *different* from his everyday self, is neither taught nor much appreciated in this country, with the result that our acting so often seems timid and narrow.[25]

I can imagine some objection here – you may argue that what Hornby has alluded to above and what Alan Rickman is doing when playing Severus Snape is 'character' acting, and not only do we routinely recognize the difference between 'real' acting and 'character' acting, but we bring a different set of criteria to judging it. But why should we? At what point do we make this distinction, and can we say that it is in any way helpful? I begin to believe that it ISN'T. Surely Hamlet or Henry V are not 'character' roles, and yet I still detect that over-the-top, larger dimension in the works cited above, which can only mean that when

I am watching acting in these examples, I am aware of the process and I still find the work satisfyingly believable. When we talk of character acting in the normal course of things we're usually thinking about acting in which the expressive dimension of the work is exaggerated. But how is the actual process of this work any different from the process that we employ – apart from adjusting dimension – when playing *any* character in a play? I would argue that *process* isn't different – but that the expression is enhanced.

But of course, this is the much debated territory we considered earlier – the 'acting as character' and 'acting as self'. There is often an unspoken corollary of this distinction, which is the idea that we judge 'character' acting differently than we do 'straight' acting. But if it is true that we bring a different set of judging criteria to 'character' acting than those we bring to 'straight' acting, surely we would need a clear distinction between a 'straight' role and a 'character' role. And that distinction is very hard for me to imagine.

There are a lot of ways of talking about this and I can remember a discussion with a wonderful director, George Roman, who, in my first year of working at Central, explained to me that the British had two great and somewhat conflicting models of acting. The first was 'the school of Laurence Olivier', which held that great acting was about transformation and brilliant match of inner/outer transformation in the creation of a sustained 'character'. The second was the 'school of John Gielgud' which held that acting was not about transformation but about the deep revelation of the actor's soul through the work. Being Hungarian, George found the distinction a curious one and wholly unhelpful.

I have come across this idea since, posed as the difference between the British and the American schools of acting. Robert Brustein had considered the problem in his 1973 article 'Are British Actors Better than Ours?' Indeed, Hornby's book *The End of Acting* is an impressive polemic against the 'playing out of self' sort of method approach, and, like Brustein, he identifies strong cultural distinctions between the US and the UK in their approach to acting:

> It is not surprising, therefore, that the American approach to acting should be so ruthlessly individualistic, stressing self at the expense of text, fellow actors, artistic value, or social benefit. Unlike actors in foreign countries, who typically belong to long-established repertory companies, the American actor is an individual entrepreneur, who sells himself, and looks only to himself in preparing a role.[26]

We may have every sympathy with Hornby's distaste for the rather minimalist effect of introspective 'personality' acting (which, like many, he sees emanating from the influence of American Method guru Lee Strasberg), but he is taking a slightly rosy view of non-American (or at least British) approaches. As my director friend from Central so aptly pointed out, the Gielgud/Olivier distinction is still a strong one in many British actor's minds, and while I think there remains more sympathy in Britain and other countries for performances in which the actor 'transforms' into a character or else makes huge expressive choices, the prevalence of the 'personality actor' remains. Still, the Americans seem to be having a good time arguing the toss amongst themselves, alternately praising and blaming their theatrical heritage.

David Krasner mounts a spirited defence of the Method in his contribution to *Twentieth Century Actor Training*, beginning with a critique of the Brustein critique:

> For Brustein, this 'subjective, autobiographical approach to performance is reflected in the most prominent American acting method, where the current jargon includes phrases like "personalisation" and "private moment", signifying techniques with which to investigate one's own psychic history' (1973:1). What Brustein fails to realise is that the self is neither static nor fixed, but evolving – in other words, human beings reinvent themselves continuously. The self changes by entering into new relationships, and the actor must bring new ideas to each successive characterisation…Brustein's view of the Method is a common albeit misleading opinion present in such academic writing on the subject.[27]

In reading this passage all I can say is that Krasner never met my grandfather. There are people who may demonstrate a chameleon-like transformational self (and indeed, actors may be more prone to this than others) but I think the best we can say of this is that it seems to be another rosy view – this time in terms of the ways in which most human behaviour evolves. We certainly evolve and we respond to context – but to claim that all of us continually reinvent ourselves is somewhat overstating things. If this were true, surely there would be far less criticism of method acting and much less debate about the 'playing out of self' idea.

Of course it may be true that the American Method techniques must take the blame for a kind of 'mumbling, introspective' style. But in all the writing about this that I've encountered, there's been little recognition of the fact that historically both the widespread awareness and practice of American Method techniques (which we might date to the Actor's Studio, founded in 1947) and the widespread access to television (and television drama) were occurring simultaneously. Many of the actors who came through both the Group Theatre and the Actor's Studio in these early days (with teachers such as Harold Clurman, Stella Adler, Lee Strasberg, Sandy Meiser) were better known for their film and television roles than their stage work (Marlon Brando, Eli Wallach, Maureen Stapleton, Marilyn Monroe, Ben Gazzara, Martin Landau, Sally Fields, et al). I would strongly suggest that there is something significant to be considered here – even in a review of the great American Method teachers as recent as David Krasner's there is no consideration of the historical context and technological revolution that surrounded the rise of their work. And just as Stanislavski and Copeau were reformulating acting for new kind of theatre and new writers like Chekhov (and reacting against a context of empty academic convention in the theatre), the American Method teachers were working at a powerful historical juncture: the rise of new explorations particularly in small screen, television realism, as well as the rise of serious American dramatists like O'Neill, Odets and Miller – whose work demanded new approaches.

But enough! The Philosophical Actor may be curious but is also busy. We will leave these issues aside for the further contemplation of the Historical Actor, and content ourselves with acknowledging that for the last decades we have come, commonly, to think of acting as happening in two ways. We play 'out of ourselves' or we play 'character', and these two 'traditions' have inspired much debate amongst theorists. If we sustain these distinctions, does it not necessarily follow that we would need two different definitions of what acting *is*? I think it does – but I'm willing to bet that most actors would agree with me that two distinct definitions would be hard to frame.

Often actors and directors use the term 'character acting' as a kind of shorthand – to mean taking on a role that you can't simply play 'as yourself' – either because the role as written (let us say the Fairy Queen, Titania) simply requires traits, either physical or expressive, that don't marry up easily with the actor cast (let us say a 20-year old from Sutton Coldfield). In these cases we might expect that the young actor will be spending some time thinking about how to transform some of her own natural behaviour in such a way that she can convince an audience that she is the Queen of the Fairies. And of course she will attempt to do this in a way that she herself finds believable. Presumably, she will also hope that you, as an audience member, also find it believable. But what exactly does believable mean when we are talking about a fairy queen? Yes, of course, playing a fairy queen is precisely the moment when most of us think about calling upon our 'character' acting skills (although we know this idea still needs unpacking).

But what about *Henry V*? Must he be played with 'character' acting skills? He's a Shakespearean creation, of course, so speaks in heightened language. That in itself may seem to call for something more than a 'soap opera' approach to realism. But does heightened language in itself mean that Shakespearean texts are not realist texts? For *Henry V* to work, surely we must believe in Henry. We must hope and even expect that the young king will, by sheer effort of will and physical prowess, be capable of galvanizing his troops to realize victory. Our sense of belief is surely strengthened when we see the young Kenneth Branagh, an actor of seemingly effortless physical presence, urge us once more into breech, since this is a strong match of actor to part. It takes tremendous energy to carry off the role and terrific skill with language, both of which Branagh has. Do these things somehow mean this his performance spills over into the category of 'character' acting? Is Branagh not 'playing-out-of-self'?

Perhaps my appreciation of Branagh's performance simply betrays my own prejudice. There are some more inclined to believe in a Shakespeare of more prosaic delivery. Some people greatly prefer the performances in Baz Luhrmann's *Romeo and Juliet*. There may be those, of course, who hold the view that all Shakespearean acting is 'character' acting by virtue of its heightened language. In this case we need another example, so let us take an example of 'transformational' acting in film – perhaps Dustin Hoffman in *Midnight Cowboy*. The role he played in the film was a young man, about his own age at the time of playing. Rizzo's language was anything but heightened. Yet most people would consider Hoffman's work in *Midnight Cowboy* to have been 'character' acting. Was there something innate to the role of Rizzo that made this particular part a 'character' part? Or is it simply the boldness of Hoffman's choices that made Rizzo a 'character'? If the difference between Hoffman and Rizzo is simply one of bold expressive choices, then, why isn't Hoffman *simply acting*? On considering these differences Stanislavski put his views quite simply:

> To my way of thinking there can be only one type of actor – the character actor. Perhaps this is beyond the powers of those who are not gifted…Then they will be divided into only two categories: good actors and bad actors…[28]

For Michael Chekhov, the issue was similarly simple. In writing about the actor who is a 'real artist', working from the higher ego, there is no thought of 'playing-out-of-self':

> …he would never need to repeat his personal life experience on the stage. He would never try to be on the stage 'as he is in life', because this would seem tasteless to him.[29]

You may not agree with any of the views expressed above concerning actors' eccentricities, the helpfulness or otherwise of terms like 'character' acting, or what it is that appeals to my own sense of belief, but none of this matters, because our latest proposition about acting can accommodate whatever you, as the individual observer, find believable and whatever you, the individual observer, consider good acting. But if this is so, does our proposition about what acting is now mean ANYTHING? Can it have any force anywhere outside our own minds? If not, how can we write books about acting unless we continuously acknowledge that everything we put into them is really just a question of trying to get *YOU* to become an actor whose work *I* find believable? If so, what are we to make of Stanislavski's assertion that 'stage truth' is all a matter of 'that which the actor sincerely believes'? If we follow Stanislavski's idea here, we'll need to shift our proposition once again.

What if we try this:

**ACTING IS THE PROCESS WHEREBY IN A PERFORMANCE CONTEXT
WE PORTRAY A WORLD/CHARACTER IN WHICH WE OURSELVES
BELIEVE SINCERELY**

If we take this proposition to be a working definition, we get around some of our former difficulties – certainly in terms of truth and recognizability – but more importantly we also get around worrying about whether anyone finds our performance believable or truthful. There is no longer any need to talk about truth and the proposition allows ANY kind of acting – method, 'character', overacting, etc. – to stand, as long as the actor sincerely believes in themselves and their imagined world.

Of course it leaves us, the audience, out of the equation, except insofar as we can respond by saying 'that actor did/did not believe in their own portrayal/world'. And the disturbing conclusion of this kind of proposition is that it ultimately isolates the actor – under this proposition the actor's performance is either working or not working solely in terms of whether the actor can believe it. But as we know, this is not how theatrical experiences work.

The more we look at these difficulties, the more it seems that our best way forward is not to try and construct some universal proposition about acting, but only to agree that acting always includes certain things. We might come to agree that it always includes the actor's imagination and expressive ability working together in a theatrical context. If we leave our proposition this loose, we can manage to get around most of the philosophical/ definitional problems we have encountered so far. But is this sufficient? Can we ever answer the question: what is acting?

Art and craft

It is almost certainly the case that most of the descriptive language we employ in acting classes and 'how to act' books (post Stanislavski and Chekhov) are not usually about the ART of acting, but only about TECHNIQUE. Surely, like books on how to paint in oils, or how to write fiction, the great majority of acting books have been largely concerned with imparting that knowledge about which we can speak in a language that is fairly unambiguous: tips and advice on how to relax, how to get the most from your voice, various theories about how to use your memories and your ability to empathize with others; helpful observations on how to analyse a play script, etc. In other words, they are concerned with teaching us techniques to help us imitate a human being in a dramatic context, and they are not in the business of describing or implying that they describe the ART of acting any more than a book on how to paint in oils is going to lead its reader to become the next Caravaggio, or a book on how to write fiction is pretending to impart the kind of knowledge that will endow its reader with Tolstoy's insight. But even as we acknowledge this, we also know that we need to find some way of talking about the art of acting – sublime, wonderful, inspirational acting – both in terms of what it is and how to achieve it. And we're not likely to be able to do that simply in terms of technique. Nor are we likely to get to the heart of talking about acting by limiting our consideration to questions about 'character acting' or simply taking refuge in claiming 'truth' as the (unexamined) bedrock of our judging criteria. And this 'other thing', this slippery practice that involves the human mind, body, personality, expression in the process of creating something artful, has confounded most theatre theorists and lured even some lucid thinkers into the realms of disquieting convolution:

> The actor is a primordial sensing-sensible, the actor can be touched and he can touch himself. In this respect, there is an aspect of the actor that is open only to himself. No one can touch the actor as he can touch himself. And yet the actor is open to others… The actor is a performer, both for others and for himself. But beyond this, the actor is

also an other for himself. As an other for himself, the actor is a character situated in a different world from the performer, a realm of imagination. Finally, the actor falls short of completely taking over an other. This is to say that despite the actor's ability, the actor cannot touch the other as the other can touch himself.[30]

While I find this description puzzling, there is something to respect in the attempt to talk about what acting is without the usual recourse to 'acting is doing' or 'acting is truth' reductions. There are some who have attempted to circumvent the difficulties in talking about acting by looking at non-traditional, non-Western approaches to performing. Phillip Zarrilli has written much about performance and his project is both to broaden the ways in which we define 'performance' and to think much more philosophically both about language and about the ways in which performers cast the mind/body relationship. This desire leads him into some pretty obscure articulation when trying to write about acting 'as process and practice in the performative moment':

> One of the most important modes of theorizing theatre is through the more comprehensive notion of 'performance'. Performance can be defined as one mode of social, cultural, aesthetic, and/or personal praxis through which experience, knowledges, discourses, and meanings have been and are constantly (re)negotiated and (re)positioned through daily and/or extra-daily performance practices.
>
> In all performative events per se, performers and spectators alike could be described as materalizing (sub)culture, context specific ways of experiencing the performative moment...But many of our current critical theories and methodologies have not taken sufficient account of the body/experience/emotion at this site of materialization of experience and meaning in the theatrical performative event, either from the perspective of the performer or the audience.[31]

While it is refreshing to see the audience included as part of the big picture in terms of constructing meaning, Zarrilli's style is pretty challenging, and it's hard not to conclude that in trying to craft a careful and inclusive view of the possible ways in which performance and its significance might be described, he loses what is specific to acting amongst all the modifiers:

> Training in voice, acting, movement, and the like are specific psychophysiological techniques practiced to shape and potentially 'transform' the practitioner to attain a certain normative and/or idealized relationship between the 'self' and one's 'agency' or 'power' (often in the form of virtuosity), and/or behaviour. In this sense, actor training, acting, as well as spectating are 'incorporating practices' through which the bodymind (as I refer to it), and therefore experience and meaning, are 'culturally shaped in its actual practices and behaviours' (Connerton 104).

Embodied practices are those modes of doing through which everyday as well as extra-daily experiences, realities, and meanings are shaped and negotiated.[32]

What I take some of this to mean is that when we are expressing something or when we are interpreting, listening or watching something, we are creating meaning as we go. That meaning is not simply something like intuiting that Hamlet's indecision is the basis of his tragedy, but has critically to do with the ways in which there are values and ideas being shared about performance and its place in our cultural lives that come under consideration as well and therefore form part of a larger meaning. But it's hard to see that this idea is not equally applicable to any number of other modes of expression.[33]

Still, there are some specifics to be found and one centres on an idea of performance and 'virtuosity'. All the other wider considerations about phenomenology, Cartesian dualism, interculturalism and historically specific contexts aside, Zarrilli does lay a little 'foundational' stone in the ground when discussing Eugenio Barba's approach to what it is the actor does:

> Barba's research has called attention to the dynamic psychophysiological nature of such important 'principles' as 'balance', 'dilation', 'energy', and 'equivalence', which can become *points of departure* for practical performance work. Implicit is an understanding of the importance of the performer's virtuosic actualization of a particular psychophysiological state or condition.[34]

That last sentence feels to me like a very straightforward little marker in an otherwise heavily hedged consideration. Zarrilli is too philosophically savvy to weigh in with simple references to acting and its relationship to truth, but what are we to make of the thing he considers to be 'implicitly understood': the performer's virtuosic actualization of a particular state or condition? Is he just finding another way of saying that the actor must find a bloody good way to pretend that a given state or condition is actually occurring? What else could this mean? This reference to virtuosity is interesting because it provokes some thought about whether what we commonly take to be virtuosity (great technical skill) is really what all of us would consider 'implicit' when describing what is important in acting. I'm not sure that it is. I may revel in the joys of a performance by Jack Nicholson but I'm not sure that what I'm watching is virtuosic technical skill. Somehow the term feels loaded in a way that won't comfortably accommodate the pleasures of watching Severus Snape, but no doubt this all depends on what you mean by virtuosic when it comes to acting.

It's very clear what Zarrilli means. His own extensive training and interest in Kathakali dance drama means that he values the kind of technical skill resulting from years of dedicated practice:

> I gradually began to sense a shift in the quality of my relationship to my bodymind in exercise or on stage – I was discovering an internal energy which I was gradually able to control and modulate physically and vocally whether in performance or when extending my breath

or energy through a weapon when deliver a blow. I was moving from a concern with the physical, external form to awareness of the subtler internal (psycho-) dimension of how to fully embody an action. My mind and body were beginning to become one *in practice*.[35]

The virtuosic skill he strives for is aimed at achieving something like an active, integrative, meditative state: calm and 'in readiness'. While there's much to be said for this approach for any kind of performance – from sport or music to acting – there remains the stubborn question of just how we articulate a judgement about whether actors who employ such techniques are somehow better than, say, actors trained in Meisner technique. It's obvious that Zarrilli has great enthusiasm for this kind of training, based on what he sees as its ability to overcome the inevitable mind/body opposition. But it's hard not to wonder why this old 'Cartesian dualism' issue remains so prominent in books about acting when most cognitive scientists or philosophers have (as Zarrilli himself notes) long left this issue behind.

Zarrilli's bigger challenge, though, is how to write about the superiority of this Kathakali-based psychophysical approach without making claims about how it is or is not related to 'truth' in performance. And much as I admire Zarrilli's intellectual sharpness, that difficulty is not sufficiently met through some of his description:

> Working within the 'sense of appropriateness' (*aucitya bodham*) to the dramatic context, the actor assumes a physical attitude of thoughtful reflection. Nala's state is subtly conveyed to the audience through the actor's use of his eyes and facial expressions, both of which are infused with the 'emotional' resonance of the moment through subtle and skilful manipulation of his breath (*prana vayu*)…The actor playing Nala lingers thoughtfully on his beloved, taking sufficient time to allow this performative elaboration of Nala's inner mental state to be relished by those connoisseurs in the audience who know the story and Nala's state of mind well enough to 'taste' both his act of reflection and the resultant pain in an aesthetic experience of *rasa*.[36]

This passage raises some fascinating questions. Is a 'sense of appropriateness' just another way of describing a 'truthful' representation? How do we judge what is appropriate without making such judgements? Should 'connoisseurship' be a requirement for fully appreciating an acting performance? Does the performance he describes differ, materially, from any good acting performance? Zarrilli describes a set of emotional transitions which 'involve psychophysiologically moving through this temporal progression from reflection, to sorrow, to pain'.[37] His conclusion is that the psychophysiological embodiment of such states as being/consciousness/emotion requires years of intense training. He makes clear that his admiration is centred specifically on the performer's ability to convey with powerful stillness and lucid transparency the character's evolving inner state of mind. It may be that part of what is difficult for me in Zarrilli's descriptions is that he is very admirably reaching toward a kind of nearly ineffable experience of performance but having to describe this experience in a language that doesn't always accommodate its depth or complexity.

But it's also hard for me not to wonder if this ability of the actor to 'engage his bodymind fully in each specific action' is quite so unique to the Kathakali-trained performer as Zarrilli might contend. I could describe a similar scene from *The Godfather, Part II*, where Robert DeNiro – in a scene set entirely without dialogue – opens a mysterious package that he is asked by his unknown neighbour to conceal. DeNiro's 'full engagement' both with the object he has uncovered (which turns out to be a gun) and his own surprise conveys 'a detailed series of psychophysiological elaborations' which seem to move from intense curiosity to surprise, to the moment where he looks over his left shoulder at the imagined presence of the unknown neighbour, to weighing his options carefully and then deciding to conceal the weapon, as asked. It's a performance of powerful stillness and lucid transparency. I could argue that there is much, much more to be gleaned in watching this brief silent scene, but my point is clear enough here I hope: DeNiro trained with Stella Adler.

Quite apart from whether one actor's technique is somehow superior to another's or, indeed, whether they are equally skilled, what is found in both of our descriptions above is the problem that arises when discussing representational art – which is to say that we are describing these performances in *synthetic* terms. It may help at this point to consider A.J. Ayer's explanation of the Kantian distinction between synthetic and analytic ways of thinking:

> A proposition is analytic when its validity depends solely on the definitions of the symbols it contains *[2 + 2 = 4 or 'this work of art is a work of art']*, and synthetic when its validity is determined by the facts of experience.[38] [Italicized text is mine.]

Of course, to say that 'this work of art is a work of art' is tautological, but that is precisely Ayer's point – he asserts that only tautologies can be certain propositions. As soon as we frame our propositions about acting as an empirical or synthetic proposition, then we are always 'tempted to "verify" the proposition empirically'[39] which not only brings us back to problems of correspondence theory but condemns us to endless discussions about 'truth' or 'falseness' in performance.

So the question remains – can we build our language (when discussing acting or trying to define it) in a way that does not involve verification or reference to the world beyond the performance? Could we speak in ways that centre on things like the sincerity of the performance itself, which we might judge in terms of the actor's ease? This is still a synthetic proposition, but does at least contain the field of verification to the sphere of the actor and the immediate performance and does not require that we are 'flung out of art's orbit into the "infinite space" of the human condition'?[40] We would recognize, of course, that any sincerity experienced by the actor may still not be to our liking or within our power to judge absolutely. But perhaps we could grant that the actor is sincere when we can see little or no trace of self-consciousness. This could be considered the point at which the actor's ability to pretend is at its strongest. It could be considered that what the actor is sincerely pretending is REAL does not necessarily refer to a world beyond the actor's imagination. In which case we do not need to test the actor's imagined world against the real world – the actor is simply, sincerely, pretending.

Of course we still need to look more closely at whether the issue of self-consciousness is really the best or only test of the actor's sincerity, but perhaps we could at least agree that when an ability to pretend or imagine is strong enough, it could seem tangible enough to overtake all else and therefore 'crowd out' the kind of stiffness or unease engendered by self-consciousness. Now we might at least be at a position where we can consider the acting performance without being tempted to 'verify' it empirically against the world as either true or false.

But we still need more. Because even assuming that we leave 'insincere' performances aside, we still need to be able to talk about a sincere performance aesthetically.

That abstract thing beyond technique

What would happen if we were to forget about technique for a moment? Suppose we forgot utterly about emotional memory exercises, repetition exercises, perfecting the psychological gesture or getting in touch with the breath and the body in lengthy meditative/yogic physicalizations? What would be left in our acting books, apart from general statements about truth? It isn't the case, of course, that all acting books are quite so technique-based in their conception. It probably just seems that way these days when books published on acting over the last five years include: *Acting Characters: 20 Steps From Rehearsal to Performance*, and *Actions: An Actor's Thesaurus* (an entire book based on transitive verbs) – as if all we need to bring Lear to life is a twenty-step programme or an understanding of the finer shades of the transitive verbs 'to intimidate' or 'to dominate', etc. Of course, the really fascinating, complex, deep-thinking theorists of acting (Stanislavski, Michael Chekhov, Adler and Zarrilli for example) continually keep the much larger questions of the actor's spirit/soul, sense of consciousness and historical/political contexts in the picture. Indeed, once he gets past all the technique (tips on how to relax, how to analyse a text, a character's desires, how to exercise sense memory and how to apply his 'magic if' idea, his method of physical action, etc., all of which takes up much time in description), Stanislavski always invokes the subconscious: 'It is fair to say that this technique bears the same relation to subconscious creative nature as grammar does to poetry...We see, hear, understand, and think differently before and after we cross the threshold of the subconscious.'[41] While it may be difficult to pin down just what he means when he uses this word, there are many references to subconscious activity throughout Stanislavski's work.

Sharon Carnicke is keen to point out that Stanislavski did not see the subconscious in Freudian terms but that he saw it as the fount of creativity. His entire system was about activating the subconscious so that it would induce a sense of 'oneness' with a role.

Similarly, Michael Chekhov describes a 'Fourth Stage' which comes after all the advice about technique, which he calls the 'divided consciousness' – a mental state which allows the actor's 'higher ego' to take the actor beyond the realm of technique.

For Chekhov, as well as for Stanislavski, there is clearly a part of acting to consider that lies beyond technique or method, but it isn't an area that lends itself easily to description. There are many areas in their writings where you can sense them wrestling with the larger concepts of artistic practice and aesthetic effects. If pressed, we might say that what they were wrestling with is the 'spiritual' element in the work. Indeed, toward the end of his great meditation, *My Life in Art*, Stanislavski concludes that: 'The only king and ruler of the stage is the talented actor. But alas, I cannot find for him a true scenic background which would not interfere with, but would help with his complex spiritual work.'[42] There have indeed been theorist/practitioners (Jerzy Growtowski comes most immediately to mind) who do want to contemplate the spiritual aspect of acting, but such considerations seem almost 'quaint' in contemporary books.

Our consideration so far has been on how we judge an acting performance, and what acting actually IS, but we haven't explicitly specified whether we are considering acting to be divisible in terms of art/craft or – more difficult – whether there is a difference between these two things: art, craft. We know, however, that the great acting theorists whose works we've been contemplating so far centre their attention on how to achieve the 'real' in Realism. So under consideration here is an interpretative practice in realist art (which explains why we leave out theorists like Artaud or Brecht[43]). This means that – following the lead of Chekhov and Stanislavski – we are bound to see the practice both as art (and in order to avoid the massive philosophical considerations involved in trying to define art, let us say here that we mean art as an act of expression that transcends its constituent parts – in this case perhaps relaxed body, well-modulated voice, sound emotional 'recall', etc. – to become something that engages us on a more 'spiritual' or more profound level) and a a craft (in which we are judging technique or those things that might lend themselves more easily to 'objective' observation and discussion: the actors' voice, movement, analysis, etc.). On a common sense level surely most people would agree that it is one thing to teach someone how to mix colour or to draw with accuracy when painting, but another thing entirely to teach aesthetics of painting. Should we be clearer about this when we're talking about technique on the one hand and aesthetics on the other? Can we leave transitive verbs aside and bring ourselves to talk about aesthetics? How else are we to read these rather mysterious statements from Chekhov and Stanislavski about the importance of the subconscious and the higher ego? And perhaps more to the point – how are we to understand them?

> **When it comes to acting, can we leave transitive verbs aside and bring ourselves to talk about aesthetics?**

In 1929, Michael Chekhov had a strange kind of 'vision' while on stage during the premiere of a piece called *Artists*. The vision resulted in a 'revelation' of Chekhov's about feeling on stage as if he were watching himself: 'My consciousness divided – I was in the audience, near myself, and in each of my partners'. Chekhov called this visionary sighting Divided Consciousness.[44]

From this point, Chekhov considered that the finest, final stage in great acting resulted from the actor having acquired this 'divided consciousness', which he claimed was 'the aim of the whole creative process, the true desire of the higher ego of the actor'.[45] It is reported that following Chekhov's 'revelation' he met with Stanislavski a few months later in Berlin, where he attempted to explain his experience to his former teacher – a conversation which apparently was the beginning of the great disagreement between the two theorists about the use of 'affective memory' or emotional recall exercises (which Chekhov claimed led to 'uncontrollable hysteria'[46] in actors). Whatever their disagreements, it seems clear that they agreed on one thing: technique alone isn't enough.

When addressing his company for *The Blue Bird*, written by Maeterlinck, the great symbolist poet, Stanislavski considered that he had three main difficulties to overcome. The first was that his company 'must express on the stage the inexpressible', the second was the public's difficulty in 'comprehend[ing] abstract thoughts and feelings' and the third was that they would have to find a way to 'personify sleep, a dream, a presentiment, a fairy tale'.[47] He sums up what he sees to be Maeterlinck's theme:

> Man is surrounded by the mysterious, the awful, the beautiful, the unintelligible. These mysterious intangible things fall upon something young and vital and frail and quivering, or cover with snow the hopelessly blind, or astonish and dazzle us with their beauty. We are drawn toward the mysterious, we have forebodings, but we do not comprehend. At times, in exalted moments, our eyes perceive barely visible contours beyond the clouds of reality.[48]

Stanislavski's point, it seems to me, is that art is in the business of engaging with the 'mysterious intangibles'. Acting – while both collaborative and interpretative – is an art, and it must surprise as well as frustrate us to acknowledge how rarely contemporary books on acting want to encounter the greater questions of aesthetic (rather than technical) issues that acting invokes. If Stanislavski's system appeals for the most part to our logic, his description of the demands of Maeterlinck's poetic visions will resonate with us (if it does at all) largely intuitively. It demands that we recognize how much of the human experience is NOT reducible to logical comprehension. And for that reason I think that this is Stanislavski at his best. As the man who has most exhaustively, most systematically attempted to outline the ways in which we can accomplish the credible imitation of a human being onstage, this description is almost a minor defiance of the whole of his earlier work.[49] Surely the creation of a theatrical piece that could make perceptible for us the 'barely visible contours beyond the clouds of reality' would be the result of a combination of our visionary, intuitive and imaginative faculties even more than our logic.

Stanislavski speaks often of the imagination but most generally in ways of *imaginatively representing the world to ourselves as we know it* (how would I behave *if* my uncle had killed my father; how can I use my imagination to believe that I am *actually* searching for a pin?). But in the passage about *The Blue Bird*, he speaks of imagination as *something more than representation* – perhaps, just perhaps, this is what it takes to move beyond the realm of the credible imitation and to become a beautiful actor.

The beautiful actor

No, I don't mean George Clooney or Penelope Cruz. I mean beautiful here in a larger, more 'old-fashioned' way. I mean beautiful in the sense of works of human creation that inspire us, that strike us as profound and perceptive and moving, and speak to us in new or even just more unexpected ways. I mean, in the deepest ways possible, work that appeals to us aesthetically. But I've been using 'aesthetic' here in quite a specific manner. A common sense view of aesthetics is that it is an area of enquiry that concerns itself with art and beauty. But as Francis Sparshott points out:

> The word 'aesthetics' was originally coined to mean something much more specific than the philosophy of art and beauty. It was meant to form a sort of counterpart of logic. What logic did for analyzable symbols, aesthetics was to do for unanalyzable symbols: logic is to ratiocination as aesthetics is to intuition.[50]

All of which means, of course, that the language of aesthetics must proceed from something like our intuitive responses to work. In *The Blue Bird* quotation above, it seems to me that Stanislavski is addressing the aesthetic: he seeks to address the 'unanalyzable symbols' of Maeterlinck's poetry. And in so doing, he needs much more than a system of technique. He needs a counterpart to logic: he needs intuition.

We've based so much of our concern in the countless books on acting technique with asking whether a performance is truthful. But because of the ways in which we have come to think of truth as something we can all identify – despite the fact that a little deeper thinking very quickly unlodges this certainty! – we seem to have lost the bigger, more challenging and perhaps more ambitious criteria in our judgements about acting. We seem predisposed to imagining truth as something related to logic. But we seem less accustomed to imagining a relationship between truth and intuition. What if we decided, instead, to leave this problem aside and simply confess that what we wanted to see was BEAUTIFUL acting? Acting that appealed *intuitively* to our sense of the symbolic, the significant and the aesthetic? Acting that wasn't the result of purely logical processes (which we know is pretty hard to imagine anyway), or a tacit subscription to a simple kind of correspondence theory? Acting that moved us closer to spiritual realizations, to worlds we have yet to imagine, to possibilities we hadn't considered? Even though this kind of desire is very hard to speak of, *wouldn't that at least keep the difficulty of describing and judging acting always to the fore in our minds when we speak of it?* And might it be said that we've been giving ourselves the easy way out by condensing all the complexity of the art of acting and its appeal to our intuitive, spiritual side into a quick decision about true/false?

Michael Chekhov spoke, of course, of truth. Be he was also willing to talk about beauty, and indeed includes a few exercises in his book on technique concerned specifically with 'the Feeling of Beauty', and even outlines an exercise for the training actor – which is perhaps the most inscrutable in the book. The actor is to move simply, and to:

Resist the temptation to increase or stress the subtle vibrations of beauty. Let these vibrations radiate freely and 'fill the air around with beauty', to quote Byron. A noble satisfaction will arise in you if you are on the right track...This noble satisfaction keeps all selfish elements beyond the threshold. Selfishness on the stage kills real beauty.[51]

Chekhov believed that attention to beauty would allow even the ugliest of scenes to be 'uplifted into a sphere that is higher than that of mere naturalism'.[52]

In one class may be grouped experiments in merely technical progress, based on a materialistic conception of life. Its object is not to present the living soul or a person or a society, but rather to give instead a conventionalised or stylised symbol of it.

The other branch of change is in the opposite direction. Its aim is to give back to the theatre its spiritual content: at the same time using all the advantage and achievements of technique, insofar as this can be done without allowing mechanics to become the ideal and without sacrificing to technical effects creative human individuality.[53]

Stanislavski and Chekhov both suggest that for actors, close, detailed observation and respect for the natural world and its wonders will begin to open up the intuitive or the beautiful.

When I was visiting the Moscow Arts Theatre School in the early 1990s, one of the school directors asked my students if they knew the works of Turgenev. When they replied that they did not he advised them that they should certainly have read *A Month In The Country*, and asked if they would do so as their homework over the weekend. He told them that reading Turgenev's play would 'beautify your souls'. As I sat in a freezing rehearsal room contemplating his words I was struck by two things. The first was that we don't talk in these ways now in the West. And the second was that we've given up a lot by abandoning this kind of language, because it challenges us to expect greater things of ourselves and our art. With the rare exception of such passages as those above, we don't find much in acting books about 'beauty'. But simply because aesthetic questions are so complex and difficult to unravel, and because they immediately test our ability to talk about the sensuous, they strike me as finer places to centre a debate on acting than issues of self/personality vs. character/transformation or 'realist' vs. non-realist' approaches, or whether actors are just faking their emotions...

Summary

Philosophers sometimes like to modify language in a way that allows for complexity. For example one might talk about 'strong' or 'weak' materialism – indeed there are philosophers who talk about 'strong' or 'weak' psychological realism. Although they are using psychological realism in a different context, the modification of its meaning in this way makes me wonder how useful our general application of the term is when we're talking about theatre. Given the kinds of unspoken assumptions and problems of definition that arise when we begin to try and determine what we value in the art/craft of acting, or in how we mean to define truth, perhaps we might want to consider whether we need a way of talking about acting that allows more explicitly a respect for its complexity. And we certainly need more of that complexity to be reflected in acting technique books. That is what I glean from Stanislavski's extraordinary comments to his company for *The Blue Bird*. Perhaps it is best that we don't proceed from rules, but keep raising the questions – questions always keep complexity alive. And if we can't solve the tensions between logic and intuition when it comes to judging or performing, can we at least learn to entertain both without recourse to either/or thinking?

When asked if there are universal laws of theatre Ariane Mnouchkine practice spoke of her production **L'Indiade** and replied:

'How could a young French woman of 15 be moved all of a sudden by a particular scene of Nehru's?…We said that this was something specific to the theatre: the memory of the unlived. That is, a young Frenchwoman who has not lived is capable, by the grace of the theatre and the actor, to understand and recognise what she has in common with a 60-year old man who is from a country that has 400 million inhabitants and to understand his fear. We were happy about this discovery and we said that this is what theatre is all about. That is: when an actor succeeds in making the unknown familiar and making the familiar enchanting and moving […] You ask me 'what are the laws'? If I knew them all the time I would not have to ask myself what I say every day in rehearsal: 'Okay, now what is theatre?'[54]

Okay. Now, what is acting?

Notes

1. Jean Benedetti, *Stanislavski & The Actor* (London: Methuen, 1998), p. 9.
2. Sanford Meisner & Dennis Longwell, *Sanford Meisner on Acting* (New York: Vintage Books, 1987), p. 16.
3. David Mamet, *True and False: Heresy and Common Sense for the Actor* (London: Faber, 1997), p. 127.
4. Stella Adler, *The Technique of Acting* (New York: Bantam Books, 1990), p. 12.
5. William Esper & Damon Dimarco, *The Actor's Art and Craft* (New York: Anchor Books, 2008), p. 6–7.
6. Eric Morris, *No Acting Please* (Los Angeles: Ermor Enterprises, 2002), p. 2.
7. Bella Merlin, *The Complete Stanislavski Toolkit* (London: Nick Hern Books, 2007), p. 17.
8. Kathryn Marie Bild, *Acting From a Spiritual Perspective* (Hanover: Smith & Kraus, 2002), p. 45.
9. Moni Yakim, *Creating a Character* (New York: Applause Books, 2000), p. 4.
10. Michael Chekhov, *On the Technique of Acting* (New York: Quill, 1991), p. xxxix.

11. Constantin Stanislavsky, *My Life in Art* (London: Methuen, 1991), p. 466.
12. Stella Adler, *The Art of Acting* (New York: Applause Books, 2000), p. 35.
13. Richard Hornby, *The End of Acting* (New York: Applause Books, 1992), p.73.
14. George Lakoff & Mark Johnson, *Philosophy in the Flesh* (New York: Basic Books, 1999), p. 98.
15. Benedetti, *Stanislavski & The Actor*, p. 128.
16. Marian David, 'The Correspondence Theory of Truth', *The Stanford Encyclopedia of Philosophy* (Fall 2005 edn), Edward N. Zalta (ed.), <http://plato.stanford.edu/archives/fall2005/entries/truth-correspondence/>.
17. Lakoff & Johnson, *Philosophy in the Flesh*, p. 105.
18. Stephen Law, *The Philosophy Gym: 25 Short Adventures in Thinking* (London: Review Books, 2003), p. 48.
19. Sharon Marie Carnicke, *Stanislavski in Focus* (Amsterdam: Harwood Academic Publishers, 1998), p. 121.
20. *Ibid.*, pp. 66–67.
21. *Acting: A Handbook of the Stanislavski Method*, compiled by Toby Cole (New York: Three Rivers Press, 1983), p. 24.
22. *Ibid.*, p. 25.
23. Geoffrey MacNab, 'The Wild One Tamed', *Independent*, 15 June 2007. See also Richard Hornby's fascinating sustained polemic against the Strasberg 'method' acting approach in *The End of Acting*.
24. Michael Shurtleff, *Audition* (New York: Walker & Company, 1978), pp. 154–155.
25. Hornby, *The End of Acting*, p. 28.
26. Hornby, *The End of Acting*, pp. 105–106.
27. *Twentieth Century Actor Training*, ed. Alison Hodge (Abingdon: Routledge, 2000), p. 132.
28. Constantin Stanislavski, *An Actor's Handbook*, ed. & tr. Elizabeth R. Hapgood (London: Methuen, 1990), p. 152.
29. Chekhov, *On the Technique of Acting*, p. 157.
30. Eric Peterson, *A Semiotic Phenomenology of Performing* (PhD thesis, Ann Arbor: University Microfilms International, 1981), p. 64.
31. Phillip Zarrilli, 'Action, Structure, Task, and Emotion' in *Teaching Performance Studies* (Carbondale: Southern Illinois University Press, 2002), p. 146.
32. *Ibid.*, p. 147.
33. This passage from Zarrilli's article is somewhat confusing in that he seems to be suggesting first that the relationship between self and agency is part of what the actor and the audience are sharing in terms of value agreement – in other words, I, as an actor, am proceeding from the idea that there is an unproblematic relationship between self and the notion of agency, while you, as audience are also proceeding from the idea that there is an unproblematic relationship between self and the notion of agency. While this may be a fair observation, it's difficult to see how that follows on from observations about training in voice, etc.
34. *Ibid.*, p. 148.
35. Phillip Zarrilli, *Pscyhophysical Acting: An Intercultural Approach after Stanislavski* (London: Routledge, 2009), p. 24.
36. Zarrilli, 'Action, Structure, Task and Emotion', p. 150.
37. *Ibid.*, p. 150.
38. A.J. Ayer, quoted in 'Art after Philosophy' in Joseph Kosuth, *Art in Theory, 1900–1990* (Oxford: Blackwell, 1992), p .845.
39. Kosuth, *Art in Theory, 1900–1990*, p. 846.

40. *Ibid.*, p. 847.
41. Stanislavski, *An Actor's Handbook*, p. 135.
42. Constantin Stanislavski, *My Life in Art*, tr. J.J. Robbins (London: Methuen, 1991), p. 569.
43. It could, of course, be argued that the kind of non-psychological approaches promoted by Brecht or Artaud can be seen as different and perhaps superior forms of realism which do more, in their symbolic way, to render the reality of the human condition than a representation based on psychological detail.
44. Anton Chekhov, quoted in *On the Technique of Acting*, intro. Mel Gordon (Quill: New York), 1991, p. xxiii.
45. Chekhov, *On the Technique of Acting*, p. 155.
46. Chekhov, *On the Technique of Acting*, p. xxiii.
47. *Acting: A Handbook of the Stanislavski Method*, comp. Toby Cole, pp. 265–266.
48. *Ibid.*, p. 266.
49. Although it is certainly the case that Stanislavski himself insisted throughout his life that his system was a living, evolving thing. He once apparently said to Joshua Logan: "Oh, I see you've read my books. Well,[…] we have extended past that. Now that's for the bathroom." [Carnicke, p. 168]
50. Francis Sparshott, *The Theory of the Arts* (New Jersey: Princeton University Press, 1982), p. 17.
51. Chekhov, *On the Technique of Acting*, p. 56.
52. *Ibid.*, p. 57.
53. Chekhov, quoted in Jonathan Pitches, *Science and the Stanislavski Tradition in Acting* (London: Routledge, 2006), pp. 146–147.
54. Josette Feral, "Building Up the Muscle: An Interview with Ariane Mnouchkine", *TDR*, Vol. 33, no. 4 (Winter, 1989), pp. 88–97.

Chapter 2

What Was I Thinking?

This book is concentrated on realistic acting styles, because as Robert Leach observes, we live in an age 'dominated by the naturalistic acting styles of Stanislavski, Strasberg and their followers'.[1] There are of course acting theorists who specifically set out to approach actor training from a different perspective: Vsevelod Meyerhold and Jerzy Grotowski come to mind. Meyerhold and Grotowski were looking at the overall art of theatre and emphasized areas other than psychological realism and representation as the focus of theatrical performance. Growtowski's focus is ultimately a kind of spiritual/anthropological project. Meyerhold was a child of the symbolist/constructivist/expressionist (and of course, Soviet!) era and his approach to acting was very much rooted in the physical. Theorists like Artaud and Brecht had very specific ideas of what theatre should be achieving in a larger political or social sense and so although an extension of that interest did touch on ideas about what role the actor played in this larger political or social activity, their work was not focused quite so exclusively on general advice to the players.

That the great majority of work we see or produce is rooted in psychological realism may have much to do with the fact that these days a large percentage of that work is experienced as film or television acting. The intimacy of these media have perhaps dulled our senses a bit in terms of the kind of dimension we either attempt or demand from stage actors – and of course it needs to be remembered when reading the works of Stanislavski or Michael Chekhov or Meyerhold and others in the early twentieth century that they were indeed working to find ways to bring new methods to the practice of *live* theatre events. But as we've seen, for all its dominance, psychological realism remains a kind of troublesome category for us in terms of what it is we mean when we talk about psychology being 'real' either in terms of a subject of study or in terms of what we infer when we observe human behaviour.

Of course we have our 'common sense' ideas which we explored in the last chapter, but if we look at the idea of psychological realism in terms of other disciplines – cognitive science, philosophy or psychology, we immediately see the larger problems within this most problematic of descriptions. The very idea of 'psychological realism' must emerge from the idea that psychology can be 'real' in some sense. It assumes that as actors we can consider and represent simulated states of mind (as in the simulated mind of Lear or Juliet), and determine whether these simulated minds have the qualities that we might decide seem 'real'. The more you look at this language, the more unsettling it all gets. It's worrying enough just to consider what seems 'real' in our own minds.

We know, of course, that there is much debate about the mind, particularly in terms of its relationship to the body and its physiological functions, and its relationship to the brain and its neurological functions, and of course in its overall relationship to the world. Briefly, some of these debates might be summed up in a series of questions – all of which have stimulated philosophical debate for centuries, and all of which are of critical concern to the actor:

Is the mind distinct and separate from the body? Surely as they have significantly different properties (minds have no weight, no measurable dimension, no physical presence; bodies have weight, are measurable, physically present, etc.) we must allow that they are significantly different entities? Does the mind exist independent of the brain? In other words, is the whole concept of 'mind' too complex and vast to be reduced to just the neurophysiological functioning of the brain?

Does anything exist outside of the mind? Is the external world just an illusion of the mind? If we can only perceive the world around us through a sensory apparatus that is regulated through the mind, how can we ever 'know' the world?

How can I understand the nature of the 'flow of thought' through my mind? How many thoughts can I hold in my mind at any given time and actually be conscious of them? How much of my thought is conscious thought?

Can all mental states be explained rationally, through scientific explanations of physiological processes? Are depression, euphoria, sexual pleasure, laughter simply a question of 'brain chemistry' and the varying combinations of chemicals? If so, is there any possibility of having some kind of 'will' that directs our feelings?

How exactly do we think? Is all thought a function of language? Is it possible to think outside of language? If we could, how could we ever describe it?

Is thought an identifiably 'progressive' process? In other words, is there first a sense impression: *I see an object*, then a process of categorization: *that object is square and made of cardboard – it is a box*, then a process of conceptualization or understanding: *if I carry on walking in my current direction the box will block my path*, and then an action: *I will walk around the box.* Or is there an unmediated action: I swerve around the box, and then thoughts, feelings, follow in the wake of the action? Or does the entire action take place unconsciously? If much of what I do is unconscious or if thought isn't progressive, what am I talking about when I refer to a 'thought process'?

Are thoughts the same thing as feelings, or is there something distinct in the experience of thinking about the answer to 89 + 17 and in watching a loved one smile? How do/can we distinguish between mental states and/or feelings?

What makes up the sense of an 'I'? When I refer to myself, what is it that I am referring to? Are our minds made up of a stable, 'core' ego that responds to the name of 'I', or are our minds a jumble of chemistry, a collection of experiences and scraps of memory? Is there an unchanging 'I' or does the whole notion of an unchanging 'I' exist just as a kind of safety-blanket against the random flux and uncertainty of a non-unified identity or series of 'subpersonalities'? How much of my mind is open to my own rational introspection?

It is a partial list only, but even in its partial and simplified form, we must admit that every question here is one that actors must contend with if they are to think deeply about the process of acting. If we meditate upon this list for some time we will undoubtedly find ourselves asking yet more questions, and perhaps doubting the ability of humans ever to understand their own cognitive processes. Indeed, philosopher Colin McGinn has put forth just this thesis: that consciousness is not actually something that it is within the ability of the human intellect to comprehend. So what might be the *practical* use of these questions?

In the first place I think it's helpful to meditate on them if only to realize how often in our work (and in many of the books written about our work) these questions go unacknowledged and how often the nature of our minds (and how they work) is somehow 'assumed' – an idea perhaps proven by the fact that almost every acting teacher I've encountered talks about 'the actor's thought process' without ever really discussing what that means. For some great theorists of course, we have to admit on close reading that these questions were *right at the heart of their work*. Even a cursory meditation here should inspire us to keep these questions before us when we read or work and to demand a little more clarity (by which I probably mean a little more acknowledgement of the confusion) within our language about how an actor thinks, how a character thinks, how memory works and what is the relationship of our minds to our bodies, etc. But perhaps it will aid us in a practical way to look a bit more closely at the ways in which Stanislavski and Michael Chekhov talked about the actors' consciousness.

'Conscious' performance

Somewhat like Freud, who argued that there was a significant and unconscious part of our minds that motivated behaviour, Stanislavski described a structure of the mind that included both conscious and subconscious activity. Indeed, as we noted earlier, his description of the actor striving toward the unconscious in terms of creativity very nearly undoes all of the rest of his acting theory. But Stanislavski's mental division is NOT modelled on Freud's, and is in fact closer to a kind of nineteenth-century Romantic vision of the unconscious as the repository of creative energy and inspiration:

Our technique [is] directed…towards putting our subconscious to work (in the creation of artistic truth) and…to learning how not to interfere with it once it is in action…Our freedom on this side…is limited by reason and conventions; *beyond* it, our freedom is bold, wilful, active, and always moving forward…Sometimes the tide of the subconscious barely touches an actor and then goes out. At other times it envelops his whole being, carrying him into its depths until, at length, it casts him up again on the shore of consciousness.[2]

In other words, all of Stanislavski's endeavours to articulate both his aesthetic theories of theatre/acting, and his extensive writings on technique and practical work on the training of actors are not, in fact, able to help us reach this final great stage of acting artistry – instead his suggestion is that the actor must work consciously toward contacting the unconscious within him or herself. As Jean Benedetti notes, 'Stanislavski summarised the whole process as: *through the conscious to the unconscious*.'[3] Stanislavski himself can only, of course, *consciously* observe the work of the actor, and *consciously* respond to the

> …the high point of the actor's art occurs when we are tumbled under a wave of subconscious activity that, at length, deposits us on the shore of our *lesser* conscious awareness.

work of the actor and it is only through that consciousness that he can explain to an actor how to follow a method of his design which suggests that the actor become conscious of his/her own goal-directed activity.

Consequently, consciousness is a pretty hot topic (and a fairly undefined one) in acting books – specifically the ways in which we direct our conscious thoughts attentively. Cognitive scientists might refer to this ability to selectively control our attention as the 'executive function' of the brain. In nearly any acting book you will ever pick up you will generally find great emphasis on the importance of the actor's ability to concentrate. That 'concentration' can only mean the effort of marshalling our consciousness in a very directed and intentional way. In fact, wherever you look in the world of actor training books there are lots of conscious writers reaching out to hordes of conscious actors, and describing a number of exercises and games that can only be undertaken in a conscious, goal-directed manner. And yet, in the quotation above, Stanislavski suggests that the high point of the actor's art occurs when we are tumbled through the darkness under a wave of subconscious activity that, at length, deposits us on the shore of our *lesser* conscious awareness. Now it may well be (and it has been argued) that the translation from Russian into English is not helpful here, and of course we know that Stanislavski was not talking about the subconscious in a Freudian way. But still, he's talking about *something* beyond ordinary, conscious thought, or ordinary executive function as the cognitive driver of our selective attention.

But what are we to make of this whole description? Perhaps what Stanislavski is talking about is simply that we want to be able to access our deepest imagination. Although he talks about 'being enveloped by the subconscious' – which sounds like more than reaching deep imagination – but the more you think about this extraordinary description, the more mysterious it all seems. Unless, of course, we just insert the word 'inspiration' for the word subconscious in the excerpt above. All this might mean that Stanislavski was using the idea of the subconscious in a kind of common sense way – meaning that we don't know where inspiration comes from **but it doesn't come from a conscious process.**

Let us imagine that I have worked my way through Stanislavski's system with rigour and attention over a lengthy period of training/rehearsal. This would require concentration, advanced exercises in emotional recall, an understanding of the ways in which my physical movement affects my mental state, a very clear idea of the world of the text, a strong outline of the events of the play and a studied understanding of its conflicts, a thorough idea of what my character wants at each moment of the play but also an overarching sense of the 'superobjective' of my character, etc. – all of these require conscious processes. And let us suppose that in the midst of all this that I had the sudden 'inspiration' that my character, Lady Percy, is psychic. There is, of course, nothing in Shakespeare's text that would support this idea in the way of demonstrable evidence. And nothing in my preparation that would lead logically to this conclusion. And let us further suppose that no one has mentioned anything like this at any time during rehearsal. Let us imagine that I just arrived one day at rehearsal, flush with the excitement of this new discovery and found that it gave fresh impetus to the way in which I rattled off my description of Hotspur's utterances in his sleep. Perhaps now, as Lady Percy, I imagine that my husband is not actually SAYING these things in his sleep but instead, while he sleeps, I watch him and have a psychic vision. I can see vividly palisados, frontiers, parapets, basilisks, cannon, culverin and all the currents of a heady fight – indeed this vision is so strong I convince myself (as Lady Percy) that I have been on the battlefield with my glorious husband, and that I have now seen all that he will soon see for himself. And yet, just as I am about to see the outcome of the battle – everything fades. When I come now to the scene in the play where I ask him to tell me what he is thinking, I am really hoping somehow that hearing from him will help me to complete my psychic vision – and that I will 'see' him in my mind as victorious in this upcoming battle. This changes everything in the scene for me as an actor. Suddenly I feel much more connected with what it is that is driving Lady Percy's desire to make her husband talk with her, and why she feels compelled to describe every little detail in the scene.

But where might this Lady-Percy-as-psychic idea have come from? In the normal course of things no one would be surprised if I answered simply that the idea 'just came to me'. Is this what we might call inspiration? If it is, can we truly describe this as subconscious? What makes this a subconscious/inspirational thought? Of course I could always say that all the thinking I've been doing lately about Lady Percy simply meant that my conscious mind was working through all the possibilities and just came upon this one, independent of my own rational processes? But surely that is a contradiction – how can I have a conscious thought that I am not conscious of? How is it that we actually conceive of the way ideas 'come to us'? Do we really 'watch' our thoughts carefully to see from which direction they come? If the idea of Lady Percy being a psychic had come to me in a vividly remembered dream, surely that would suggest that it is a product of my subconscious, but if it came to me one night after rehearsal as I was walking home from the day's work – is that a subconscious process? Can we ever consciously determine when thoughts are coming to us from a 'subconscious' area of our minds?

Substituting 'inspiration' for 'subconscious' in Stanislavski's formula might make it clearer for us, but Stanislavski himself would be the first to say that he was NOT talking about inspiration. When Nazvanov – student of Stanislavski's alter ego, Tortsov – describes a good acting experience as 'inspired' Tortsov rejects the use of this word. As Carnicke explains:

> For Stanislavski, the word 'inspiration' implies a force from without; recalling the word's etymology, with its ancient Latin connection to 'breath', inspiration is Apollo breathing life into the artist. But Stanislavski wants to empower actors and banish ideas that displace them as the nexus of creativity. For him, the subconscious is inner 'poetry' that the actor consciously organizes through the 'grammar' of technique. Traditional ideas of 'inspiration' have no place in the System.[4]

Surely the more we think about something, the more possibilities we bring to bear upon it – but are all the possible solutions we find to acting problems conscious solutions? These questions are hard to answer – which makes it equally hard to know just what Stanislavski meant. His use of the word subconscious is not entirely unrelated to Freud's use of the term. Freud described that part of the mind that is hidden from our rational mental processes and which only ever 'escapes' through dreams, jokes, slips of the tongue, but which (in its often undiscovered way) drives our behaviour. But might we not also add 'inspiration' or sudden flashes of thought to the list of ways in which the subconscious 'escapes'? If so, then such 'sudden flashes' must be at least related to a Freudian model of the subconscious. That might help us locate 'inspiration' in an acceptable way for Stanislavski – it certainly locates inspiration within the actor's psyche – but it doesn't get us any closer to solving the mystery of his description of the 'oceanic subconscious'.

To compound matters, Stanislavski proposes yet a further division in the unconscious: he "takes from Yoga the obscure notion of the 'superconscious' placing it next to the 'subconscious'...", defining the superconscious as:

> a transcendent force that 'most elevates a person's soul, and thus most of all must be valued and preserved in our art.' Only with its help can the actor convey the 'life of the human spirit.' As he explains, 'the subtler the feeling, the more unreal, abstract, impressionistic, etc., the more the superconscious, that is, the closer to nature and further from consciousness.' He concludes by quoting from the book he owned on Raja Yoga, 'The superconsciousness begins where the real, or more properly speaking, the ultra-real ends.'[5]

He adds:

> Having worked wonders in the realms of sub- and superconscious, Yogis give much practical advice in these realms. They also approach the unconscious through the conscious, preparatory devices, from body and soul, from the real to the *unreal*, from naturalism to abstraction. And we, actors, must do the same.[6]

There is almost no end to the questions that we might have now about Stanislavski's model of consciousness, not the least of which might be just what he means in his opposition between nature and consciousness. He seems to be suggesting that there are somehow 'unreal, abstract' thoughts or feelings that arise 'naturally' in us but somehow slip through the cracks of language and conscious reasoning processes. It's difficult to know whether we can agree with this or not unless we can discover what exactly he means when he talks about the real, the 'ultra-real' and the unreal. One imagines that Wittgenstein might have a view on whether these things can be talked about sensibly, but clearly Stanislavski's leanings were toward metaphysics and well away from logical positivism. Still, trying to make sense of his consciousness/nature opposition poses a real challenge. But like much transcendental philosophy, there is an overall *sense* to Stanislavski's words that is somehow easier to grasp than their actual *meaning*. Certainly he is not amongst those who assert that thought is shaped by language, and indeed, it seems that for Stanislavski there is an ineffable 'unreal' that escapes the prison house of language altogether and is somehow allied to 'spirit' that transcends material experience. On a simple level it seems that what he is alluding to is an unseen spiritual dimension of great art, but over the course of his theoretical evolution his dual concerns with both the 'soul' and detailed concern with material 'given circumstances' (for example) result in a strange kind of metaphysics whose tensions can't easily be collapsed or solved.

We know that the whole question of the sub- or unconscious was a point of an early disagreement between Stanislavski and Chekhov. At issue in this disagreement was how conscious the actor was of all of his or her activity on stage, and whether or not at some points our 'rational' conscious action is in danger of giving way to 'irrational' (might this mean unconscious?) feelings:

> When we are possessed by the part and almost kill our partners and break chairs, etc., then we are not free and it is not art but hysterics. At one time in Russia we thought that if we were acting we must forget everything else. Of course, it was wrong. Then some of our actors came to the point where they discovered that real acting was when we could act and be filled with feelings, and yet be able to make jokes with our partners – two consciousnesses.[7]

Chekhov was, as we recall, a champion of the 'Divided Consciousness' – but not of just any old 'divided consciousness' – his notion was that one part of the 'divided' consciousness was a 'Higher Ego'. The idea of actors having a kind of mental schism is of course not new – it was indeed the very subject of Diderot's classic book of the eighteenth century – *The Paradox of Acting*. Diderot's well-known paradox was that actors appeared to be possessed of real feelings but were, in fact, not. Diderot's view is summed up by Aldo Tassi:

> What Diderot is in effect saying is that there are no acts of consciousness occurring onstage corresponding to the state of affairs we call anguish. The anguish which is expressed there is only a depicted anguish. It is not a genuine emotion presently being undergone by anyone. It does not exist as a state of consciousness but is instead the *object* being produced by the act of consciousness. The act of consciousness which exists onstage and is producing the emotion witnessed by the audience is the conscious state we call pretending. In other words, the consciousness that is crossing the threshold of the body onstage and is coming into the world is the conscious state of pretending which produces the simulated anguish that the audience sees.[8]

Indeed, this description of the mental states of actors is intriguing, and causes much debate amongst acting theorists. It is a difficult one because of course, when the process Tassi describes above is taking place, do we, as actors, actually EXPERIENCE it in quite the way that it is described? The description above is of a mind in which consciousness (*the thinking 'I'*) is directed toward an internal object (*a state of anguish*). The suggestion is that the 'thinking I' has some sort of internal sense of what a state of anguish is, and then sets about to express that externally. We are talking about something both immediately understandable in common sense, practical terms and a bit more challenging in philosophical or cognitive terms. We are talking about how the mind can spontaneously divide itself and set about to 'work' on an internal object such as the idea of 'anguish', which can only be a thought. In the language of many cognitive philosophers/psychologists, we're talking about metacognition (thinking about what we're thinking) and metarepresentation (thinking about what someone else is thinking) – ideas which we'll discuss in more detail later. But in describing these metacognitive or metarepresentational acts, are we leaving something quite critical out of the picture – like the relationship/difference between thought and feeling? And can we understand this at all without some idea of how we think in the first place?

Some of my favourite philosophical scenarios come about when philosophers set about trying to determine this. I like all the questions raised here, such as: what are psychological states? What are mental states? How do we perceive objects? What is the nature of representation or 'thought-objects'? These last questions are tough enough when we're considering objects like the coffee cup on a table, but of course, far trickier when we're talking about how we perceive a 'state of anguish'. And of course, in the case described above we're not merely talking about perceiving a 'state of anguish' – which we might say is an internal/external question of perception and representation – we're talking about perceiving a 'state of anguish' as a THING, upon which I, the actor, can work. We're talking about mental architecture. This whole area of research on 'higher-order thinking' is a fascinating kettle of debate and contradictory theory. Most human brains have the capacity to think about thinking and to represent the thoughts of others in our minds.[9] And in the case of a 'state of anguish', let's assume that we've come to the conclusion (the metarepresentation[10]) that Hecuba is in a state of anguish. As actors, we actively metarepresent Hecuba's state of anguish in our own minds, but we must always do more than metarepresent Hecuba's anguish – we must fashion action that may be based on or related to this anguish and that means we are also thinking about the anguish we're holding in our minds – which is an act of metacognition.[11]

If these kinds of distinctions in higher-order thinking are confusing enough when we come across them in cognitive studies,[12] they grow a lot fuzzier when it comes to acting theory. Because actors aren't just metarepresenting Hecuba's thoughts in their own minds. Nor are they just thinking about Hecuba's thoughts. They are actually attempting to physicalize metarepresentation and metacognition all at once. In other words, we're 'thinking' (acting) what someone else (Hecuba) is thinking, and we're thinking about that 'thinking' (acting).

Stanislavski, of course, never used this kind of language at all. His work was a systematic response to Diderot's idea that the actor was not 'in anguish' but was pretending to be in anguish. His system was designed to be a way in which actors could use their own emotional memories to recreate emotion onstage. But we aren't likely to conclude that Stanislavski's work was really leading the actor to the point of being 'in anguish' while playing the role. Perhaps this is what an American Method teacher like Lee Strasberg might liked to have seen actors come close to (although of course if an actor were truly in anguish it is difficult to believe that the acting performance would be very good...). But if Diderot offered one view on the actor's paradox – in which the actor who appears to be consumed with passion is in fact quite coolly going about *pretending* to be passionate – the references to the sub- or superconscious in Stanislavski's writings and the appeal to the Higher Ego in Chekhov's work seem to offer their own paradox: they seem to be suggesting that after all the *conscious* process work put into preparing a role, both the Stanislavskian and the Chekhovian actor must then hope that some *unconscious* process will bestow an element of inspired artistry upon his/her performance.

But maybe there are some simpler ways to look at this. One might be what some psychologists describe as 'flow' or 'zone' – a state which most high-performance athletes aim to achieve in competitive situations. Perhaps for Stanislavski the 'subconscious' process he refers to is more akin to this experience:

> Csikszentmihalyi (e.g., 1990, 1996) describes nine dimensions of the total state of flow: a balance between perceived challenges and skills; a merging of action and awareness; having clear goals; receiving unambiguous feedback; being totally concentrated on the task; having a sense of control over what one is doing; not being self-conscious; losing track of time; and experiencing high levels of intrinsic satisfaction from the activity.[13]

This kind of description seems very close to the sense ('All is forgotten around me when I act') that Michael Chekhov dismissed earlier as 'numbing' the actor's consciousness. It is a state that high-performance athletes positively aspire to, and therefore is the subject of much consideration by sports psychologists. The 'numbing' that Chekhov dismisses might be seen as a beneficial thing by sports psychologists, who would be happy to see a high-performance athlete whose concentration on vaulting over a pole is so strong that she is 'numb' to the rain, the crowd and the ache in her calf muscle. Ellis Cashmore speaks of a kind of 'automaticity, effortlessness and bliss…a state in which athletes lose self-consciousness, self-judgement and self-doubts and just allow themselves to be carried along by the performance'.[14] The inclusion here of a kind of 'automaticity' – the sort of 'reflex' activity that an athlete or an actor might build up over hours of practice/rehearsal – is a particularly interesting one in terms of how actors (and athletes!) divide and expend their mental efforts. If we look at Stanislavski's description above, could these descriptions of 'flow' or 'zone' not be particularly relevant to the optimal performance state for the Stanislavskian actor? Was part of what Stanislavski imagined simply this: a high state of 'automaticity' that would allow actors (like athletes) to forget about lights, lines, costume, set and simply concentrate on their psychophysical actions with a sense of blissful self-forgetfulness? It sounds like a good acting experience to me, and helps me understand why adequate rehearsal time (which increases the amount of performance activity that can be passed into a state of automaticity) always produces better performances.

Michael Chekhov had another model of the actor's mind altogether. His notion of the 'Divided Consciousness' is something quite different from the process Diderot described and which Tassi outlines above. Chekhov wasn't just talking about the fact that actors have to consciously objectify their own thoughts (metacognition), nor about the kind of conscious/subconscious division described in Stanislavski's formulation. He was suggesting something else – which involved not just metacognition or representing a state of anguish, nor attaining a state of 'flow', but in actually objectifying oneself, while in the process of acting. He states that:

> …the actor must…develop the habit of seeing himself objectively as an outsider…Patient and quiet exercise will lead the actor to experience one part of his being – his body and

voice – as an instrument belonging to himself. He will gradually experience the other part of his being as an artistic ego, as his Creative Individuality, as the possessor of the instrument.[15]

This is a curious kind of division, as Chekhov clearly values this 'artistic ego' as the higher form of consciousness, but he is fairly reticent to explain quite just what he means. In the 87 exercises that make up his *On the Technique of Acting*, some of which are highly imaginative and suggest that the actor evoke dream states or perfect 'psychological gesture', there is nothing whatever to help the actor with the 'technique' of achieving this Divided Consciousness. Of course in the everyday way of things, we commonly assume that the actor must have a divided consciousness or multiple cognitive/metacognitive abilities (indeed, we can postulate multiple divisions!), because in the process of performance the actor is simultaneously engaging both the imaginative and the practical.

As Mrs Lovett I gaze upon Sweeney Todd with a kind of rapture and gratitude as he swings me around the bloody cellar, and as we dance I realize, gratefully, that he isn't going to abandon or kill me. The music swells and we are indeed going to live together and be happy at last as we have overcome all of our enemies and all the terrible injustices of the past. I look rapturously into his eyes in the hope that I can once again rekindle the ability in him to love and to want me. We burst into song together, and just as I imagine that I see joy and love light up in his eyes I remember (as he flings me into the oven) that I must drop my head and gather my skirt to clear the door as the stage manager had explained to us during the tech that the construction crew didn't make the oven door quite high enough.

Similarly the actress playing Margaret wanders onto the stage in front of her horrified husband and has an emotional breakdown as she holds the bloody, severed head of her lover, Suffolk, who has been torn apart by an angry mob – but only after she has found the 'special' that lights this scene (yes, some actors CAN find their light).

While acting we manage to release our imaginations at the same time as we manage not to fall through trap doors, not to get hit by flying scenery, not to get knocked unconscious by battens or knocked over by scenery trucks as we run off stage in the dark. But how do we do that?

But is this what Chekhov is talking about? That ability to engage our imaginations in the playing of a role, but also to 'watch' where we are and what we are doing in a practical sense? Surely not – we can't imagine that a practical conscious awareness of the dangers of a set in live performance could possibly be what Chekhov was after – he was talking about something he called the 'Higher Ego'. Part of the reason for confusion here is that Chekhov clearly relates his idea of Divided Consciousness with his idea of the Higher Ego, but never entirely articulates the relationship between the two. According to Chekhov, the Higher Ego has four functions:

> First, individual interpretation of the plays and parts; second, the ability to distinguish between the powers of good and evil; third, the relationship of the actor to the time in which he lives; and last, the objectivity of humor through the liberation of the actor from his narrow, selfish ego. All this widens the mental outlook of the actor, sharpens his perceptions, and makes his artistic work more significant.[16]

This Higher Ego is, indeed, quite a busy mental character with wide-ranging interests from history to literary interpretation to moral philosophy. Chekhov later suggests that when 'the aim of the whole creative process, the true desire of the Higher Ego'[17] is realized, the actor then acquires the Divided Consciousness.

In terms of sports psychology we can see a world of difference between Stanislavsi's subconscious 'ocean' and Chekhov's Divided Consciousness. Stanislavski's actors might, like high-performance athletes, be aspiring toward something much more Zen-like and well captured in the words of Daisetz Suzuki: 'Childlikeness has to be restored with long years of training in the art of self-forgetfulness. When this is attained, man does his great works. He thinks yet he does not think.'[18] Chekhov's idea, on the other hand, is that our Divided Consciousness DOES think – it observes and sees our actions in context with the whole of our surroundings – it is a part of us that is objectifying and observing ourselves, and objectifying and judging the world around us. He doesn't, however, specify exactly what the aim of that observation is. Clearly Chekhov is talking about higher-order thinking with a twist. We might ordinarily expect that metacognition would be involved in objectifying and thinking about our own thought, and that it might serve to contextualize or categorize, amongst other things. What we would not ordinarily expect is that our metacognitive ability comes with its own sense of 'selfness'. Chekhov's Higher Ego seems to be a kind of second 'self' and is therefore something quite distinct from the more functional aspects of everyday metacognition. And if this is so, then perhaps when we read Chekhov we need to be armed with some theory of the 'self'. These days, of course, 'dual process' mental structure is a highly popular subject,[19] but theories about dual process thinking tend to describe functional mental architecture, or cognitive styles – they do not posit dual 'selves'.

Chekhov's description of consciousness remains a mystery for me, but it does foreground the tendency in both Stanislavski and Chekhov to write about acting in a way that extends beyond technique – they clearly want to grapple with much more profound and interesting questions about consciousness and the art of acting. It may be that by looking a bit more closely at the workings of the brain in terms of 'flow of thought' and automaticity we'll come a little closer to finding some answers.

The actor and the 'swing thought'

Let's go back to the third question at the beginning of this section:

> **How** can I understand the nature of the 'flow of thought' through my mind? How many thoughts can I hold in my mind at any given time and actually be conscious of them?

And the ninth:

> **What** makes up the sense of an 'I'? When I refer to myself, what is it that I am referring to? Are our minds made up of a stable, 'core' ego that responds to the name of 'I', or are our minds a jumble of chemistry, a collection of experiences and scraps of memory? Is there an unchanging 'I' or does the whole notion of an unchanging 'I' exist just as a kind of safety-blanket against the random flux and uncertainty of a non-unified identity or 'subpersonalities'? How much of my mind is open to my own rational introspection?

In their book *Philosophy in the Flesh*, George Lakoff and Mark Johnson start from the fact that *most* of our thought is not conscious thought. 'It is the rule of thumb amongst cognitive scientists that unconscious thought is 95% of all thought – and that may be a serious underestimate.'[20] Given the vast amount of thought that we can recognize in any given day to be conscious thought, this is quite a profound statement.[21] We know that in everyday life we experience a 'flow' of thought or a stream of consciousness. It's been said that the average number of thoughts in a 24-hour period is somewhere between 12 and 50,000. It's clear that much of our thought is not *concentrated* thought and no doubt this is why so many acting classes and acting technique books start with concentration exercises. Presumably most of us know how easily we are distracted, how many half-conscious thoughts mingle with and disrupt us when we are trying to concentrate and how easy it is to allow the flow of thought simply to take its own course. Most acting theorists and teachers believe that before all else, actors must gain control over the wandering mind. When Johnson and Lakoff speak of unconscious thought, they do so not in a Freudian sense, but in the more general sense of the way in which living beings operate:

> Consider, for example, all that is going on below the level of conscious awareness when you are in a conversation. Here is only a small part of what you are doing, second by second:

> - Accessing memories relevant to what is being said
> - Comprehending a stream of sound as being language, dividing it into distinctive phonetic features and segments, identifying phonemes, and grouping them into morphemes
> - Assigning a structure to the sentence in accord with the vast number of grammatical constructions in your native language

- Picking out words and giving them meanings appropriate to context
- Making semantic and pragmatic sense of the sentences as a whole
- Framing what is said in terms relevant to the discussion
- Performing inferences relevant to what is being discussed
- Constructing mental images where relevant and inspecting them
- Filling in gaps in the discourse
- Noticing and interpreting your interlocutor's body language
- Anticipating where the conversation is going
- Planning what to say in response[22]

For me, the fascinating thing about this list is that most, if not all of these unconscious thought/actions are handled by the actor in rehearsal, or already done by the playwright or the director. So when an actor is engaged in a conversation on stage, theoretically they should have quite a lot of free space on the 'hard drive'.

But of course, actors are holding an immense amount of other information in their heads at any given time, and using a number of distinct brain processes/areas. First, they are straddling a couple of time frames:

- The past: they need to have a strong memory of what they have learned and rehearsed over the last three or four weeks (involving the part of the brain that lays down and stores long-term memory).
- The present: they need to be concentrated in the 'here and now' since anything may happen that could disrupt or impede the progress of the play (involving the part of the brain that negotiates working memory).
- The future: they need to be anticipating what may happen (involving the language and reasoning part of the brain and all the 'somatosensory' regions).

They are also (depending upon the size of the part) holding a substantial amount of text in their heads (which involves the long-term memory and the part of our brain involved in memory retrieval, but there is 'bonus' information included because memories themselves come with additional contextual information 'coded' into them[23]).

Along with this in any given scene the actor is (probably) holding a running thought process of their character in their head, which both during and in-between lines might go something like this (although not in the neat and linear way written below, as thought doesn't quite work like this, and indeed may not even be 'articulated' in our heads as language):

BENEDICK: Lady Beatrice, have you wept all this while? *My god she looks more beautiful than I've ever seen her looking. Her eyes are like glass and her lips are trembling. Beatrice look at me – just look at me, and you'll trust me.*

BEATRICE: Yea, and I will weep a while longer.

BENEDICK: I will not desire that. *I could put my arms around her and comfort her. I want to touch her. I want to tell her that I love her. I don't want to frighten her, she's so distressed. Her eyes are beautiful...Beatrice, if you will look at me I can make you trust me.*

BEATRICE: You have no reason, I do it freely.

We must also acknowledge that what the actor DOESN'T want to have in their head is still unfortunately often present, which adds yet more to the mental bulk , and much of which takes the form of the actor **trying to forget** (but will probably still find its way in):

- that my mother/boyfriend/teacher is sitting in the audience
- all of my director's notes about relaxing, about finding a more 'neutral' body, being under-energized, being over-energized, gabbling, babbling, strengthening my action on 'Not for the wide world!', etc.
- that the audience is there (or, depending upon your point of view, REMEMBERING that the audience is there)
the sound of my own critical voice as I perform ('that was terrible', 'why didn't they laugh?', 'I got that wrong', 'this isn't clicking', etc.)

This kind of thought can feel like a Freudian 'return of the repressed' – the more we try to push it away consciously, the more it returns with a vengeance. This phenomenon in sports psychology is described by Aidan Moran as a 'rebound' experience:

> ...whereby the suppressed thought becomes even more prominent in consciousness. This tendency for a suppressed thought to come to mind more readily than a thought that is the focus of intentional concentration is called 'hyperaccessibility' and is especially likely to occur under conditions of increased mental load.[24]

Along with the things we've already mentioned, there may also be any number of specific technical things which the actor must at least have within his sphere of consciousness during the scene, such as:

- Don't step on the hem of her dress when you cross to her
- If she has missed the special (as she did in rehearsal), gently lead her downstage right
- Tilt your sword hilt so the point doesn't hit the ground when you get on your knees
- Ignore the chalice accidentally knocked over by Hero – the DSM will clear it

The list, we must admit, is considerable. But in the ordinary course of any production, most actors can and will do all of this. But some will do it better than others. It seems reasonable to assume that some of the ones who 'do it better' are better at concentrating or marshalling their attention to somehow process and prioritize all this information in a really effective way.

Attention – what it is and how it works – is a pretty widely debated subject in the areas of psychology. On one level, it would seem like a relatively non-controversial idea: when we want to focus our attention, we make a conscious decision though the executive function of our cognitive process to filter out distraction and bring our senses to bear, fully, upon the object of our attention. But a little deeper thinking raises some interesting questions about this process. Neuroscientist V.S. Ramachandran describes the sort of minefield we're approaching when we talk about attention:

[A]ttention is a loaded word, and we know even less about it than we do about neglect. So the statement that the neglect arises from a 'failure to pay attention' doesn't really tell us very much unless we have a clear notion of what the underlying neural mechanisms might be. (It's a bit like saying that illness results from a failure of health.) In particular, one would like to know how a normal person – you or I – is able to attend selectively to a single sensory input, whether you are trying to listen to single voice amid the background din of voices at a cocktail party or just trying to spot a familiar face in a baseball stadium. Why do we have this vivid sense of having an internal searchlight, one that we can direct at different objects and events around us?[25]

Ramachandran's observations inspire further questions. For example, at a cocktail party, why is it that we're so often able to hear our names mentioned in a conversation all the way across the room, when we were focusing so squarely on the fascinating person we've just met? The second is, if we've decided to focus our attention like a powerful searchlight beam on a given target, why is it that we so often misdirect the beam and aim it at a wrong/distracting target? In other words, what process *controls* the direction of the beam – and should we be focusing instead on *that*? Philosopher Alfred North Whitehead made the point that full attention is a precious resource and should be recognized as such. Perhaps he had in mind certain Eastern philosophies when he wrote:

It is a profoundly erroneous truism…that we should cultivate the habit of thinking about what we are doing. The precise opposite is the case. Civilization advances by extending the number of operations that we can perform without thinking about them. Operations of thought are like cavalry charges in battle – they are strictly limited in number, they require fresh horses, and must only be made at decisive moments.[26]

Sports psychologists spend a lot of time analysing the components of attention and how athletes can learn to control concentration. Robert Nideffer outlines four kinds of attentional focus (broad, narrow, internal, external) and imagines that over the course of training, athletes will move from a broad focus to the narrow focus of performance.[27]

The right training processes, in his view, lead to a confident narrow focus in performance that is 'the zone'. He talks about altered states of consciousness between being 'in the zone' and 'choking'. Nideffer's descriptions are very similar to the ways in which actors might describe their best and worst acting experiences. Physical 'zone' feelings (we might think of this as a peak acting experience?) include: loose, relaxed, solid, strong, effortless, balanced. Psychological 'zone' feelings include: controlled, confident, powerful, easy, clear, focused. Physical feelings when 'choking' (we might think of this as a bad acting experience or stage fright?) include: tight, tense, shaky, unsteady, choppy, awkward. Psychological feelings include: scared, panicked, weak, rushed, confused.[28]

Most sports technique books, like most acting technique books, spend much time advising neophytes to focus their concentration and discipline the number of thoughts they entertain while playing. For example, golfing instruction manuals regularly advise beginning golfers that they can only hold 'one swing thought' in their minds as they approach and hit the ball. Presumably this is because too many thoughts would move the focus to the area Nideffer describes as BROAD focus. And of the many 'swing thoughts' the golfer may have, the advice is fairly consistently NOT to let the swing thought be about mechanical things like 'keep your elbows low', which would also move attention into the BROAD internal analysis area. Could this advice work for actors? Given the list above of things to remember onstage, are we really able to hold only 'one swing thought' in our minds as we approach the ACTION that comes with the line 'Lady Beatrice, have you wept all this while?' For that exact moment can I, as the actor, manage to concentrate on one thing and one thing only: *to get Beatrice to look at (and therefore trust) me?* Surely if I have the power to marshal and control my thoughts, this would be possible *if we assume that a great deal of what I've just described above has now passed into the category of automaticity*. In other words, if we get it right, of the thirteen or so simultaneous mental tasks described above, could twelve theoretically attain the state either of automaticity or 'low priority', which would allow us to place all our 'attentional focus' on the thirteenth ultra-important task of getting Beatrice to look at me? This is no small question when it comes to trying to understand what's going on in our minds when we're acting, and I have found it very helpful to look at the work of cognitive scientists whose research concentrates in the area of the dynamics of learning.

The short-term memory of the average human being is:

> …seven bits large and that the brain can process at 18Hz, this yields an interface capable of processing 126 bps (Miller, 1956). A typical task, such as listening to another person speak, can take up to 40 bps of memory. The brain must therefore demonstrate efficiencies in recognition, retrieval, and action in order to allow the person to effectively deal with the external environment in a timely manner.[29]

Okay, perhaps the prose style isn't sparkling, but the point is that we do have a finite capacity in our immediate processing of information. And because we have that limited capacity for processing information, we have to be efficient. That is, we have to be able to learn to the state of automaticity, which is the state where 'a task can be performed with little or no conscious attention'.[30] The question for the actor is how much of our stage activity in performance has been covered so completely in rehearsal that we rely to a large extent on a kind of automaticity? Clearly we can identify a large amount of activity that falls into this 'automatic' zone – and we can also identify the part that doesn't.

Let us imagine that we've just landed the role of Marchbanks in George Bernard Shaw's play, *Candida*. The director has decided that we have to master a meticulous RP accent. If we put a significant amount of work into mastering that accent, scientific research would seem to assure us that we can measure the success of our mastery over the accent by measuring what Flor and Dooley would call the 'resource dependence' or the 'resource insensitivity' of the task.

Tasks that require a large amount of my conscious effort or attention are 'resource dependent'. In the early stages of learning RP, there is a large amount of conscious effort needed to master all the various elements. As I learn, however, I grow more efficient and some of the RP begins to feel 'automatic'. It becomes, in other words, 'resource insensitive'. In the ideal state I would think most actors would hope to acquire/practice the RP accent to the point of its execution being completely 'resource insensitive' – in other words, the actor can then do it without expending any effort thinking about it. This leaves mental space and energy to concentrate on their actions and on the characters around them. It also alleviates the sense of self-consciousness about the accent.

The longer we meditate on this idea the more things we can probably place under the categories of 'automaticity' or 'resource insensitivity' when we go back to look at the list of things an actor may be thinking of in performance and also, critically, at the first list laid out by Lakoff and Johnson. If we can agree that most of Lakoff and Johnson's list (which covered a simple activity like everyday conversation) as well as all of our decisions about movement, place, action, time, etc. should have passed into automaticity through adequate rehearsal, this must mean that actors are operating in a 'cognitive space' that differs significantly from the cognitive space of everyday life – if only in terms of how much of their performance activity should be on the low end of the resource-intensive spectrum. I begin to wonder if this 'greater space' leads to two things: either (1) we have now created an immense amount of conscious space that will allow the repressed 'rebound' thought and all other manner of self-consciousness to creep in and paralyse our performance, or (2) if we are successful at suppressing these 'rebound' thoughts, perhaps we're into a completely different kind of cognitive space altogether from our usual, commonplace mental experience.

Of course this will vary in the individual actor – some actors will say that they reach a state we might now describe as automaticity with their lines. In other words, they don't struggle at all to remember lines while they are acting. For some this is a question of degrees.

Most would probably *aspire* to the state of automaticity where lines are concerned, but not all rehearsal processes allow sufficient time for the actor to attain this. Obviously the greater the number of things that we can perform in a 'resource-insensitive' way, the greater our chances of being able to have the 'one swing thought': ***'Lady Beatrice look at me!'*** (or whatever, in our wisdom, we decide that Benedick wants from Beatrice at this point), or to be 'in the zone'. And perhaps it is in the free space of 'the zone' that we find our ability to free the imaginaton.

And now, the Philosophical Actor begins to wonder what the relationship between sports psychology, 'hard science' and the theories of Stanislavski and Chekhov might be...? Could it be that once the actor has attained a state of automaticity in some areas of performance, that state then allows us extraordinary levels of concentration and imagination in performing a single action – which in itself might FEEL so unlike ordinary thought that we feel inspired/lost/floating above ourselves and observing? If our ordinary flow of consciousness feels chaotic and distracting, might it be that this extraordinary combination of automaticity and concentration allows us to feel as if we're acting in a 'space' so different from that everyday chaos that we suddenly feel more receptive to the kind of thought that feels 'intuitive' or inspirational rather than the kind of thought that is the result of everyday rational conscious processes? If so, this could be what Stanislavski is suggesting in the connection between all the conscious processes he outlines – all that rehearsal and exploration; all that research and experimentation; all that studio training and analysis – and that act of 'crossing the threshold of the subconscious'? Could it be that a meticulous Stanislavskian preparation condenses so much 'actorly' thought into the

> **Could meticulous preparation condense so much 'actorly' thought into the category of automaticity that the actor has mental space for concentrated action and is therefore, more susceptible to 'inspiration'?**

category of automaticity that the actor suddenly has immense mental space for concentrated action and is perhaps, therefore, more highly susceptible to 'inspiration' or the ability to really inhabit an imagined world?

Understanding Chekhov's Divided Consciousness in these terms is still challenging, but his description seems to me to accommodate a fairly wide range of experiences, not all of which must be manifested in the sense of watching oneself perform. In his summing up of the stages of acting he seems, like Stanislavski, to be talking about 'inspiration', and even equates these two at one point when he writes: 'Fourth Stage: Inspiration. Divided Consciousness.' And he goes on to elaborate:

> Using our method the actor puts aside physical and psychological obstacles in his nature, thus freeing his creative powers. The actor should never worry about his talent, but rather about his lack of technique, his lack of training, and his lack of understanding of the creative process. The talent will flourish immediately of itself as soon as the actor *chisels away all the extraneous matter* that hides his abilities – even from himself.[31]

If the state that the Chekhovian actor aspires to is one of chiseling away at all extraneous matter, it sounds very close to the state of attaining a high level of automaticity or 'resource insensitivity', which allows the kind of extraordinary focus that sports psychologists refer to as being 'in the zone':

> Once in the zone, athletes feel no pressure and need no encouragement; they have no fear, stress or restraints as they strive for excellence….[s]ubjects reported feelings of harmony and oneness in which 'total self is integrated physically and mentally' and fatigue and pain disappear. The experiences are noncritical and effortless, meaning that the athletes surrender themselves to the experiences rather than exerting themselves. In sum, the peak experience constitutes a 'higher state of consciousness'.[32]

Of course Chekhov was not describing 'oneness' or a sense of 'integrated self'. But the rest of this description of 'the zone' certainly feels close to the spirit of Chekhov's quotation above about how the actor might 'free' creative powers and allow talent simply to 'flourish'. And it also seems very close to what Stanislavski may have been describing when he talked about crossing the threshold of subconsciousness.

But perhaps the theory that best accommodates both Stanislavski and Chekhov is one based around some relatively new research into creativity that has begun to look very closely at relationships between the cognitive, the extracognitive and the metacognitive. We consider the cognitive to be those things that we are aware of thinking, including functional things like reason and logical problem-solving, or just general things that we're thinking about. In the actor's case this could be trying to work out just what it is that Benedick wants from Beatrice at this point. And we consider the metacognitive to be the act of thinking about our thinking (which is this case could be many things, such as thinking about how we came to our decision about what Benedick wants; or thinking about how our decision seems to be working as we play the role). We can consider the extracognitive to be that which falls outside of that realm of logic, conscious 'intelligence' or reasoning – which in this case might include the intuitive or the inspiration that all Benedick needs is for Beatrice to look at him (which, of course, has no logical or textual basis, but which might seem to us as actors to have a kind of elegance about it).

Some of the most interesting study in this area looks at the relationship between the cognitive, the metacognitive and the extracognitive in exceptionally gifted, creative or 'high-achieving' human beings. The extracognitive, especially, seems to be a significant part of what sets high achievers (like Nobel Prize winners) apart. These extracognitive aspects in their work are often things like intuition – particularly in terms of a kind of 'feel' for the direction of thought, or whether a problem or solution is worth pursuing, or a keen sense of the 'aesthetics' of an idea – such as the harmony or beauty of an idea. Inventor Jacob Rabinow, interviewed in Mihaly Csikszentmihalyi's study on exceptionally creative individuals, was asked how he knew when an idea was bad and his response moves quickly from the cognitive to the extracognitive:

It doesn't work, or it's old, or you know that it will not gel. You suddenly realize it's not good. It's too complicated. It's not what mathematicians call 'elegant'. You know, it's not good poetry.[33]

In their work on extracognitive phenomena in Nobel Laureates, Shavinina and Seeratan identify some specific components of extracognitive phenomenon as 'scientific taste', 'elegant solutions', 'feelings of being right', 'feelings of beauty', 'feelings of direction' and specific intellectual beliefs and preferences. They consider a number of responses from scientists who have made breakthrough discoveries and find that the importance of intuitive input was often cited:

You may object that by speaking of simplicity and beauty I am introducing aesthetic criteria of truth, and I frankly admit that I am strongly attracted by the simplicity and beauty of the mathematical schemes which nature presents us. (Werner Heisenberg)[34]

There is another aspect that I would add to it, and this, I think, is taste. Taste in almost the artistic sense. (Paul Berg)[35]

He who has once seen the intimate beauty of nature cannot tear himself away from it again. He must become either a poet or a naturalist and, if his eyes are good and powers of observation sharp enough, he may well become both. (Konrad Lorenz)[36]

Shavinina and Seeratan go on to argue that there is a strong relationship between the extracognitive and the metacognitive:

The phenomenon of the extracognitive contributes to the development of a person's metacognitive abilities. We would even add that the extracognitive lies somewhere in the heart of metacognition and, consequently, allows psychologists to better understand its anatomy and, hence, its nature. In its turn, metacognition leads to the further development of the extracognitive, strengthening and crystallizing its components in an individual's intellectual functioning. For example, the individual with developed metacognitive abilities will be more open to his or her own feeling of direction, feeling of beauty, and intuitive process.[37]

It strikes me that this way of separating out these cognitive functions allows us to kind of 'map' some of Stanislavski's and Chekhov's theories. We could locate much of Stanislavski's discussion of the spirit or the subconscious within the area of the extracognitive. We could similarly locate much of Chekhov's Higher Ego function in the area of the metacognitive. And if Shavinina and Seeratan are right, then these two areas overlap in a positive way. Perhaps Stanislavski and Chekhov are not as far apart in this area as they might have looked at the beginning of this section?

We're still not sure how we marshal attention and that needs some consideration. And of course, in a pretty significant way I have so far sidestepped the issue of the relationship between spirituality, extreme concentration and the meditative state – all of which seem to infuse the works of Stanislavski and Chekhov. That omission will, I hope, be understandable because it is not coincidence that the meditative state is aligned with spiritual practice (when it isn't, it is generally aligned with practice in hypnosis, and linked to a goal-directed kind of deep concentration). The true meditative state is generally considered to be a conduit for connecting with 'spirit' or a greater power/consciousness of some sort (although there is still much to be considered about acting and the meditative state, which we'll look at in the last section). No doubt both Stanislavski and Chekhov had this in mind but never detailed their own spiritual views beyond making it clear that they had them. My own beliefs aside, my argument here is a more mundane one – and one which centres on the simple idea of the actor's 'zone' – or that space which feels cognitively open and different enough from day-to-day conscious communicative experience to allow for more unconscious (even dreamlike) intervention and other cognitive states (extra- and meta-) to inform and inspire work. The difference here is perhaps the same as that between those more spiritually inclined folk who see the near death experience of 'seeing the light' as a kind of epiphany and those more empirically inclined folk who see it as REM 'intrusion phenomenon' or a sudden release of adrenalin. The effect is the same – we see the light – whichever source you identify.

We can't come to any hard conclusions about the ways in which Stanislavski and Chekhov outlined the actor's consciousness, and the suggestions here can only have the force of illuminating the subject rather than explaining it. But it seems important to keep raising the difficult questions about consciousness and the acting process, and to encourage some tolerance of the tensions we might encounter when trying gradually to work our way through just how to conceive of the actor's 'psychophyiscal' state.

Who am I anyway?

The second question from the beginning of this section was:

> **What** makes up the sense of an 'I'? When I refer to myself, what is it that I am referring to? Are our minds made up of a stable, 'core' ego that responds to the name of 'I', or are our minds a jumble of chemistry, a collection of experiences and scraps of memory? Is there an unchanging 'I' or does the whole notion of an unchanging 'I' exist just as a kind of safety-blanket against the random flux and uncertainty of a non-unified identity or 'subpersonalities'? How much of my mind is open to my own rational introspection?

The challenge is to describe or to understand what it is that makes up the sense of ourselves as an 'I'. This question now grows more interesting in light of what we've been looking at in terms of achieving the kind of optimal state for acting that transcends technique and becomes something extraordinary. If the theory is that we can attain a level of extraordinary mental clarity, which gives us the ability to think in extremely focused ways, surely we still have to ask the question: 'who is actually in control here' – who is the 'I' who is acting? And perhaps more significantly, following on from Richard Hornby's polemic against the tendency of actors to 'play out of self', the ability to understand who or what that 'self' is seems critical. As is, of course, the relationship of that 'self' to the character being played.

The issue of who the controlling 'self' is remains an area that always seems pretty weak when I read acting books. Let's start with some pretty big statements from some acknowledged masters:

The first sparks of inspiration may come at any moment in any stage of the work. If they come they must be welcomed and no conscious application of the method should interfere with such moments.[38]

In…separate moments, or even throughout whole scenes, you feel yourself inside your role, in the atmosphere of the play, and some of the sensations of the character you portray come very close to your own…This merging with your part we call the achievement of a sense of being inside your part and its being inside of you.[39]

A great disservice was done to American actors when they were told that they had to experience themselves onstage instead of experiencing the circumstances. You must not take yourself and put that into Hamlet. Hamlet is a royal prince of Denmark. Therefore, the truth of the character is not found in you, but in the circumstances of the royal position of Hamlet, the character you are playing. All action of Hamlet…has to be put in his circumstances, not yours.[40]

And one teacher/student dialogue:

'Keep up the repetition until something happens to you, something that will come right out of you. Right?'
'Right.'
'But to ask your partner questions continuously, as you did, is using your head, and what I'm trying to do is get you out of your head. Do you follow?'
'Get me out of my head,' Lila says.
'Into what?'
'My emotional life…You're trying to get me away from using my logic to using my…'
'Your impulses…'[41]

All of these quotations seem to me to lead to some interesting questions:

IF I get out of the way so as not to 'interfere' with inspiration, does that idea suggest that I am no longer controlling my work as an actor? How do I reach that point and is that the point I'm aiming at? When will I know when I have to take over again, consciously applying 'the method'? How can I recognize this inspiration when it comes to me?

How do I actually KNOW, as an actor, when I achieve the state of the character 'being inside of me' and of 'me being inside the character'? Does the conscious act of being aware of this not immediately destroy my sense of 'being inside the character'?

If I can never truly be a Prince of Denmark in the 'real world', how – except through my own imagination, research, sense of belief, etc. – can I ever comprehend Hamlet's circumstances? If comprehending Hamlet's circumstance through MY imagination, sense of belief, etc., are the preconditions for my comprehension of Hamlet's circumstances, doesn't that mean that I MUST take myself and put it into Hamlet? Who else could I take?

Perhaps these questions all lead us to a more fundamental one: what is the relationship between the actor and the character? And how can we understand this relationship?

In his book, which is based on Stanislavski's work, Jean Benedetti talks about a 'Real I' (the actor) and a 'Dramatic I' (the character) and starts with the admission that the actor cannot actually be someone else. 'The only feelings or thoughts or impulses I can have are my own. I cannot actually experience anyone else's emotions any more than I can eat and digest anyone else's meal.'[42] This much seems clear but where does the Real I go when the Dramatic I is working? Surely the Real I doesn't disappear – so how are we to describe or understand the relationship between these two personas? Let us take emotion as an example.

If we believe that good acting involves the expression of emotion, then isn't it MY emotion that is being stirred? And even if I fake it, isn't it MY fake emotion I'm portraying? Or should I stay out of this and let my imagination somehow create another kind of 'mind' that exists alongside of mine – Benedetti's Dramatic I – and should it be the Dramatic I that experiences all the emotion? Is the ideal state for me the one in which every now and then the Real I and the Dramatic I seem to have one of those 'mind melds' that Mr Spock on Star Trek used to have – where suddenly the contents of another's mind becomes lucid and available to my own – I am 'inside the character' and the character is 'inside me'?

If we were to describe the 'optimum' performance sensation would we say that we had mastered two things: the kind of 'zone' or state of 'flow' described above and,

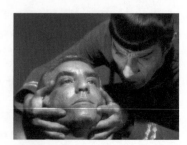

Courtesy CBS.

simultaneously, we had achieved 'mind meld'? As much as I really like this last idea, it doesn't actually solve much for me. Perhaps that is because before I start to build my 'second mind' – what Benedetti has called the Dramatic I – and go on to achieve my 'mind meld' won't I need to have a pretty good idea of who the Real I is and how that mind works? Uta Hagen thinks so:

> Your own identity and self-knowledge are the main sources for any character you may play. Most human emotions have been experienced by each of us by the time we are eighteen, just as they have been by all human beings throughout the ages…We do not have to get psycho-analytical or delve into Freud, Jung, Reich or Adler to learn to understand ourselves…[43]

She makes it sound pretty simple, but of course there are a lot of debates about identity and self-knowledge that range across many areas, including psychology, philosophy and cognitive science. But it seems worth our time – given that the 'Real I' must be the raw material of everything the actor does – to try and pin down whether – or how – we experience a sense of our 'own identity'. What is it that gives us the sense of being an 'I'? It can't simply be a list that describes us because that would only be a combination of observable fact (I was born in the USA) and observable behaviour (I am not a patient person). But what is that inner sensation of having an individual personality? Julian Baggini suggests that there are no real contents and compares the state of 'I' to that of a 'contentless centre around which experiences flutter like butterflies':

> [I]f we ask what the self is, the answer is that it is nothing more than the sum of all the experiences that are connected together by virtue of sharing this one point of view. The self is not a thing and it is certainly not knowable to itself…That doesn't mean we don't exist, but it does mean that we lack a constant core of being, a single self that endures over time…[44]

We may understand what Baggini is saying here – but nevertheless, in the common sense way of things, most of us have the sense that we are a single self, enduring over time. We grow and develop and sometimes change, but we do have (unless we're prone to some specific psychological or neurological problem) a sense of self that endures over our lifetime. This sense of self is strongly connected to memory and it is probably within the part of the brain that stores long-term memory that something like a 'core of being' or a 'single self' resides. We can test this quite simply through our imagination. Suppose we were to wake up tomorrow morning with no memory whatever. What would we have to call our 'self'? If no other neurological symptoms appeared, we would be able to look in a mirror and see what we look like. We could make some judgments about the kind of person we see in the mirror, but our judgments could only be neutral ones. If the clothes we found ourselves in were black, for example, we might conclude that we are not inclined to wear flashy clothes, but lacking any memory would mean that we could not connect the black clothes with any context (such as the recent death of a loved one, or our love of 'goth' fashion). We could not know what kind of person we were based simply on feelings because we would have no memory against which to test our feelings in other contexts and no way to compare the way we feel at the moment with ways we have felt before. In other words, we would have to begin again and once we've done that we would have to conclude that, unless our memories were suddenly miraculously restored to us, the person we are now will not necessarily be a continuation of the person we used to be. It is very hard, in fact, to imagine anything about our sense of 'selfness' that does not depend on our memory.

But perhaps Baggini's idea of a lack of a constant 'core of being' is useful for actors – because if we can't specify a content to the sense of self, then what is it that we're talking about when we refer to the Dramatic I? Is it just a point of view? Does that mean when I'm acting, I'm simply shifting my point of view? That sounds promising, but how does it work? Of course again, in a common sense way, we have a strong notion of ourselves as having a solid identity, a personality. And although we don't generally like to describe ourselves as having a 'character' we do routinely recognize within ourselves certain persistent patterns of thought and behaviour that we might come to think of as 'typical of me'.

One of my favourite exercises to explore with first-year actors is to ask them to choose someone in their lives that they are close to and know well. I ask them to come up with five words that describe that person as completely as possible. They do this in silence and it tends to be a concentrated silence. Because I ask them to write out their list, they think that I am going to ask for their five words. Once they have finished this list I ask them to make a second list. This is to be five words that describe their own personality as completely as possible. Invariably the class will find this suggestion outrageous. It generally meets with smiles or looks that suggest that I cannot possibly be serious.

I always ask them why this seems such an absurd request when they have just happily written the list of five words describing someone else's personality. The answers vary, but essentially they boil down to this: we don't like to be pigeonholed or confined by descriptions – not even our own. We like to think of ourselves as pure possibility. We know our own habits, thoughts and behaviours – for better and for worse – and we like to think that we are not trapped by our history. We like to hope that despite what we may always have done, we may yet do differently tomorrow.

I hope that this exercise demonstrates for them how difficult (but also how important) it is for an actor to avoid confining the characters they play by opting for simple descriptions and by failing to acknowledge that as human beings we live through hope, and some of that hope is concerned with changing ourselves, our lives, our circumstances for the better, no matter what the history of our past may tell us.

Although we know that memory plays a huge part in creating the sensation that we have an identity, we also know that we are much more than a collection of memories. We are indeed also those thought patterns and behaviours and other mental features, which may feel persistent but are not necessarily so. We know, for example, that severe mental trauma can result in the permanent alteration of behaviour. We also know that severe physical trauma can result in the permanent alteration of behaviour. In either of these cases memories can remain unaltered while behaviour is changed. Personal identity is many things and our minds can seem as infinite as space. So how could we ever begin to articulate an answer to the questions we looked at above about the geography of our mental space and whether there was enough room in there for both Hamlet and me?

I know that I can't actually BE Hamlet and myself. As V.S. Ramachandran points out:

Actually experiencing two selves may be logically impossible, because it would raise the question of who or what is experiencing the two selves. True, we sometimes speak of 'being in two minds,' but that is nothing more than a figure of speech. Even people with so-called multiple personality disorder don't experience two personalities simultaneously – the personalities tend to rotate and are mutually amnesiac: at any given instant the self occupying the center stage is walled off from (or only dimly aware of) the other(s).[45]

However, Johnson and Lakoff take things like 'figure of speech' VERY seriously indeed, consequently unlike Ramachandran they view the metaphor or figure of speech (such as 'being in two minds') as having real force. Indeed, they view metaphor as the basis for most of our conscious thought and the ways in which we accede to and make sense of the world around us. In their view, there is something clearly indicated in metaphor that distinguishes between a Subject (perhaps we could think of this as the executive function or the decision-making sense of ourselves) and a multiple number of Selves:

In the general Subject-Self metaphor, a person is divided into a Subject and one or more Selves…The Subject is that aspect of a person that is the experiencing consciousness and the locus of reason, will and judgment, which, by its nature, exists only in the present… The Self is that part of a person that is not picked out by the Subject. This includes the body, social roles, past states, and actions in the world. There can be more than one Self. And each Self is conceptualised metaphorically as either a person, an object, or a location.[46]

This can pretty clearly be seen in any number of metaphors that Johnson and Lakoff provide as illustration: 'I *held* myself back from hitting him', 'I've been *pushing* myself too hard', 'I'm *out of it* today', 'I've been *observing* myself and I don't like what I *see*.'

Viewed in this way, it's easy to understand why Johnson and Lakoff start with the statement that 'we do not have any single, monolithic, consistent way of conceptualising our inner life…'[47]

Given the difficulties of 'conceptualising our inner life', it is little wonder that the actual mechanics of the relationship between the actor and the character is never terribly clearly delineated by acting theorists or those who write books on technique. Because when we start talking about our minds, it's tough to talk with much clarity or precision. But leaving aside for the moment exactly how we do describe or experience our own inner life, one thing is clear: the relationship between the actor (Real I) and the character (Dramatic I) isn't an equal one. The 'Real I' comes equipped with a full and organic sense of self, built through our arsenal of memory. We know ourselves to some extent: we are hopeless romantics, or easily fooled or genuinely loved or incredibly lucky – we only have to look at the last few years of our lives to know these kinds of things about ourselves. And even if we aren't very good at judging ourselves, at least our own deluded sense of ourselves is a genuine one. So surely the 'Dramatic I' must be a rather thin and gangly thing compared with the robust and muscular fullness of the 'Real I'. And I would suggest that for many actors it is this imbalance that brings on much of the anxiety of creating a role: how am I to sustain the fragile imagined 'Dramatic I' against the naturally pushy tendency of the 'Real I' to take over my mental and physical space?

Most acting theorists suggest various things like experimenting with voice and body in the creation of character. Nick Moseley suggests starting with stereotype, then observing and working gradually toward a kind of well-observed and non-clichéd character that we can impersonate or embody.[48] Michael Chekhov starts with the 'psychological' gesture, which may give us many clues to the relationship between the physical and the psychological in the playing of character. But how do we 'try on' these things without feeling as if they are somehow external to us?

As an actress, I often found that somehow through the rehearsal process I would discover things – some very odd and rather tangential – that led me to sense of feeling as if the character I was playing was at once both 'within' me and also very distinct from me. Playing the character of Mrs Hardcastle, for example, seemed to centre on the breath. She struck me as a breathless character who was probably confined by corsets and stifled by the dullness of country life, and who felt as if she could never quite get enough air. Once this occurred to me I found playing her very easy. I 'felt' her running through her large country house, spying and planning and enjoying her intrigues, and the pace and sound that comes with a slight breathlessness seemed to define her for me and within me so well. Playing Aldonza the whore came somehow through the idea of what her world smelt like and how much the earth was a part of her reality. Lying on the ground, walking barefoot most of the time, cleaning and clearing and scrubbing in her vain attempts to keep the dirt at bay and the constant stench of men, and mules, and ale seemed somehow to suggest a hardness and wariness that she expressed by breathing in a rather shallow way and being very careful about where she stepped.

But the more I work to describe these processes, the less I think I can quite capture the experience. I know what it felt like for me, and I know that the impressions and ideas that went into the playing of these very different women were not well analysed or even ever articulated during rehearsals. But somehow these impressions gave me the sense of seeing the world as these women saw it. I've been teaching actors for more than two decades and in all that time I don't think I've ever advised an actor to think in quite these ways. Perhaps 'finding the key to the character' is just too deeply personal in terms of how each actor approaches it to be taught with any certainty or clarity?

In the maelstrom of all the questions we asked earlier about the 'I', we probably have to admit that the last question (how much of my own mind is open to my own rational introspection) is the critical one to answer before we go any further. In other words, if we want to know how to control our sense of self well enough to create and nurture a 'Dramatic I' or simulated sense of a 'character' self, shouldn't we know if there are limits or a particular shape to the content to our 'Real I'? In order to do this, can we just have a long look inside our minds and describe what we see there? If we could do that, how much of our minds could we see? We know that cognitive scientists estimate that far less than 10 per cent of our brain's activity is conscious activity, which limits our 'field of vision' considerably. If we happen to take a Freudian view, we might see the subconscious part or our mind as a heaving, swelling mass of desires and thoughts that we cannot access.

But even if we're not cognitive scientists, or sympathetic to Freudian theory, we must surely admit that our everyday experience – from strange and vivid dreams, to suddenly remembering things we were just a moment ago struggling to remember – it is clear that there is much of the mind and its activities that won't be obvious in those moments when we decide that when we want to know what is in our minds, we'll just have a good long look inside there. There are, of course, other even more unnerving things that arise from this contemplation.

For example, if I can't access my entire mind, who is in control here? And who is controlling the character I'm playing? We tend to have the common sense feeling that WE are making the decisions in our lives based on our own rational consideration of all the facts. But one of my Philosophy 1A teachers once put this problem on the board:

A is the medical fact that cigarette smoking contributes to mortal illness.
B is the general agreement that life is worth prolonging.
C is the number of people who would acknowledge the truth of statements A and B and still decide to smoke.

HOW CAN WE EXPLAIN C?

I think one of the hard facts of our lives is that we have to spend so much time **trying to 'explain C'** (*Why did I get so angry about such a stupid thing? Why am I eating this rich chocolate* *cake when I'm on a diet? Why was I unfaithful to my husband when I love him with all my heart?,* etc.). And of course, the actor has to 'explain C' not just for himself, but also for the character he is about to portray (*If I want to kill my uncle to avenge my father's murder, why the hell don't I just get on with it? If Falstaff has been like a father to me why would I humiliate him like that?*). This is not to say that there are no rational answers to these questions – just to suggest that some of the motivation behind what looks like contradictory behaviour in the face of what we profess to believe or want is very likely linked to that part of our minds that we can't access.

Well, assuming that we agree that not all of our mind is open to our own inspection – what does that leave us in terms of how we understand the ways in which we can distinguish our own conscious sense of self from that of our character's conscious sense of self? After all, this is the part of our minds we bring into rehearsal every day, and presumably, it's also going to be critical in our desire to create the sense of Iago's self that tells those outrageous lies. We might start with imagining the point in our mind 'where it all comes together' to create a sense of self. Surely this point – where all our senses come together to create something that feels like a rational, sense-perceiving, decision-making self – is the point we need to identify in order to imagine how that self can be distinguished from a character 'self'. But, as we might expect, this 'coming all together' point of 'selfness' is hotly debated by philosophers and others.

Some go with the Cartesian Theatre idea (a very neat idea for a book on acting). In this model, the mind sort of 'sits' in front of a theatre or cinema screen watching images come in, and making response decisions: 'Food coming toward me. Salivate. Pick up fork', etc. Many philosophers object to this idea because it has to proceed on the idea that there is a little mind controlling our mind (a 'homunculus' – Greek for 'little man'), which then leaves us, of course, with the problem of how to explain the mind of the homunculus. Some more empirically minded folk – rather like Baggini – see the mind as a collection of things; mostly chemicals and neurons and synapses, which can all be explained through scientific research and see the sense of a unified 'I' as an illusion of sorts. Some see consciousness as inseparable from language. Daniel Dennett agrees that explaining how we get to this 'fine point' of selfness where it all comes together to create the illusion of a rational, decision-making, goal-oriented self is the great challenge for anyone who wants to put forth a comprehensive theory of the mind. His theory is complicated but basically concludes that there is no final 'high point' of defined thought or 'selfness' but instead, like an anxious undergraduate continually revising an essay, we simply keep creating 'multiple drafts' of mental judgements as new and better information keeps informing us through our senses to consciousness. Perhaps, if Dennett is right, this is why our 'selfness' can feel so undefined and messy – it's the product of constant revision!

But suppose we just forget right now about trying to define what 'I' is, and just agree that while some may find Benedetti's description of the 'Real I' and the 'Dramatic I' useful, it certainly isn't an accurate description of our inner selves. What if, instead, we refocus our interest away from the 'how' part of our sense of self toward the 'what' part of our sense of self? What is it that we can examine if we want to determine the 'contents' of a self, or a character? In psychological terms, we have three options.

First, we might go the route of the introspective psychologist, who is concerned with the contents of the conscious and unconscious mind and how these affect behaviour (Freud and Jung would come into this category).

Second, we might adopt the method of the behavioural psychologist – this school of psychology more or less rules consciousness itself out of bounds (placing it in an impenetrable 'black box' since we can't actually know what is in there!) and concerns him/herself with the study of behaviour only. Lately behavioural psychology has evolved into, well, evolutionary psychology which considers the ways in which our minds have evolved in the interests of the survival of our species.

The third approach is the cognitive science approach – in which the subject of study is basically the ways in which the mind processes information. It covers everything from emotion to behaviour, but focuses exclusively on mental processes.

It is entirely possible that your first response to these three approaches is to conclude that actors and directors (whose rehearsal efforts by and large lie in understanding Hamlet's – or Hecuba's – behaviour) must be spontaneous behaviourists. After all, our business is in representing the thoughts, actions and behaviours of these characters. We're not interested in analysing how their minds work, or whether they suffered some deep childhood trauma – are we? Well, I would suggest that it all depends on what you mean by analysing how their minds work, and on whether knowing about their psychological peculiarities or imagining the effects of childhood trauma will in any way help us to understand the character we're about to 'create'.

In graduate school I once directed a rather strange piece called *The Effect of Gamma Rays on Man-in-the-Moon Marigolds*. I had the privilege to work with some very talented actresses and Gwen, who played the eccentric mother, Beatrice, was herself quite an eccentric actor. I learned much from watching the way she approached the study of Beatrice's mind and the resulting decisions about the character's behaviour.

One day she came into rehearsal, rummaged around in her capacious cloth bag, and located a large peanut butter jar filled with scraps of paper. She placed the jar on the set kitchen table and smiled at me as I sat out in the house. We were about to start rehearsal on a scene in which Beatrice calls the school principal to talk about her daughter. Gwen sat at the table and contemplated the jar for a moment then explained to me: 'She knows how important these phone numbers are. But her brain is the kind that just scatters things, and information, everywhere. That's why the house is so chaotic. I think she knows that she has to actually capture and keep certain important things like phone numbers. She captures them and keeps them – like bugs in a jar.'

It was that kind of observation and detail that made Gwen such an exciting actor to work with.

I'm not sure, however, that we could fairly conclude that actors are entirely behaviourists in their approach. Most of the interesting ones I've ever encountered LOVE to theorize about what's in that BLACK BOX called consciousness. Many of them also find the possibility of imagining how Hamlet's childhood thoughts of Mummy-Daddy-Me have massively affected the behaviour he might now display around the Mummy-Uncle-Me triad. And there are a many who, in the throes of the closet scene, find themselves becoming spontaneous Freudians.

Whatever psychology we may employ in analysing our characters, we're still left with questions about how we create and live within them (or is that 'how they live within us'?) Of course, in one way, we're back to the old problems of 'real' acting and 'character' acting. For actors who always 'play themselves' there is, of course, little need to talk about distinguishing self from character. But for actors who like to make big, bold character choices the relationship between self and character is a critical one. But to speak this way suggests that we accept the idea of these two kinds of actors in practice. Surely even the 'playing-out-of-self' actor must occasionally encounter roles that require some distinct character traits and ideas.

I will be bold enough to suggest (based on my own experience and talking with other actors) that when we are concentrated and living imaginatively within the story and within the world of a play, and focused on what we're trying to achieve in that world, our mental state is much more like what we might imagine Mr Spock's 'mind meld' would feel like – we're aware that we're on stage, but we're kind of 'at one' with our character, which doesn't necessarily feel like something foreign. Perhaps this is because – as Johnson and Lakoff suggest – we already accept the notion of an 'executive Subject' and plural Selves (as revealed in statements like 'I can't control myself around casting directors', 'I'm going to make myself get to rehearsal early tomorrow').

But do we more routinely think of the 'Dramatic I' as a parasite – existing on the 'Real I' as host, borrowing memory, emotion and sense of self?

Often when I am working on a play I ask the actors to use their time outside of rehearsal to do three kinds of familiar improvisations. The first is a 'situation' improv which we do early in the process just to kind of cement the 'road map' of the scene and its events. The second is a 'character improv' in which the actor can work alone in simply choosing some music or a book or painting that the character might love and want to have near them or in their home. The last is a 'memory improv' in which the actors spend as much time creating memories through improvised shopping trips, meals at a restaurant, days out in the park or having a dreadful argument. I think the point of the last two improvs for me has always been the attempt to help fill out the thin gangly life of the imagined character and to try and anchor the imagination in some real memories and passions that might bolster the sense of the 'Dramatic I'. But is there any point in these exercises? If it is true that a better way to conceive the relationship between the actor and the character is not as two parallel mental states running alongside, but rather as a kind of host/parasite relationship, do these exercises in imagined memories or passions actually serve any practical use? Is the problem after all simply that I've been posing the question in the wrong way? What if we stopped seeing the 'Dramatic I' and 'Real I' as distinct? What if the self and character are not conceived as 'different but parallel', but instead as being intertwined in ways that are similar to our everyday Subject/Self model?

Suppose we replace the Real I vs Dramatic I with a host/parasite metaphor – how would that relationship work? It seems clear enough that a character we play must draw heavily on our own memories and emotion, and could not in fact be something that altogether effaces or replaces our own sense of self. To do this would be impossible. But if we accept that when I play a character like Roxie Hart, and that character is in some senses parasitically 'living off' my own memories and emotions, it still doesn't entirely answer the question of where that 'Roxie Hart' character comes from and how I make her both distinct and sustained in my own mind. For some actors the 'access' to the Roxie Hart character might be as mysterious and personal as my own were to either her (she 'thinks' with her hands – she's always grabbing things and grasping at life) or Mrs Hardcastle or Aldonza.

I've come to wonder if the beginning of an answer may lie in a slowly growing school of psychology – psychosynthesis – that asserts that our personality is made up of 'multiples'. These psychologists hold that while most of us have a sense of our 'major' self, we also have a number of 'alternate' or 'minor' selves. For all its difference, this idea has some interesting similarities to Lakoff and Johnson's Subject/Self model that we've been looking at in this chapter. On one level, we might find this a little less bizarre if we simply consider the ways in which we all, whether we are actors or not, continually manipulate our own behaviour. We suppress or inhibit; we rearrange or enhance behaviours all the time, according to the various contexts and different people we find ourselves in and with. Around a potential employer we perhaps enhance the sense of our respect for organization, time-keeping, strategic thinking, etc. We might think of this as our 'business self'. On a first date we might curb our naturally more robust responses to things, and perhaps enhance our sense of interest in miniature trains or stamp collecting, if that's what our new date is into. Perhaps this is our 'dating self'. Under the watchful glare of a policeman we inhibit our tendency to mouth off, giggle or make bad jokes, etc. – perhaps this is our 'serious self'.

We wouldn't necessarily feel that this 'manipulation' of our own behaviour is *fake*, or even that we're 'acting'. The potential for us to act out many different kinds of behaviour exists within all of us and we do it quite spontaneously. We are not necessarily lying when we say we'd love to play a game of tennis when we meet a drop-dead gorgeous tennis player. We are probably just exaggerating that desire a bit if, in fact, we've never played a game of tennis in our lives. But when we look into the dark seductive depths of the tennis player's eyes, are we feeling 'fake' as we swear that we'd love to play a game? Even though in a sense, we're playing a 'role' here, I don't think we are feeling 'fake' – we seem to be marvellously elastic beings in terms of what feels real to us and what doesn't, and we are extremely good at fooling ourselves about what we want or desire, depending upon the context in which we want or desire things. In that sense – do we have 'multiple

> **Perhaps those, like Richard Hornby, who argue against the school of 'personality' acting are not worried about actors not 'creating a character', but about the fact that such actors are not tapping into enough *various selves* within their own personalities.**

selves' that are capable of handling different situations? While the idea of multiple selves might be a bit too far out for some, I think most of us have grown comfortable with the idea of our minds having lots of different instincts or 'voices' and at various times we go with one or the other. I'm aware that this conclusion assumes a kind of 'central executive' or Subject, who is controlling the show here – and of course the exact workings of this aren't entirely clear (think back to our consideration of where/how the 'self' comes together).

But in a sense this all comes down to whether we actually view the notion of 'personality' as a unified thing. Perhaps those, like Richard Hornby, who argue strongly against the whole school of 'personality' acting are not really worried about the actor not 'creating a character', but about the fact that such actors are not tapping into enough *various selves* or enough *extreme selves* within their own personalities. He explains, 'Finding the character…is direct and intuitive, a displacement of your sense of self.'[49] This is not a particularly transparent description (and I would argue that we can't really displace the 'central' or 'Subject' sense of ourselves, although perhaps we can alter the way we experience ourselves), but it sounds to me like he might have a notion of a shifting, possibly multiplicitous, personality.

Lakoff and Johnson are not alone, of course, in identifying a sense of multiple selves. For Rita Carter – whose book, *Multiplicity,* suggests that our personalities are always already 'multidimensional' – it all begins with an observation of some rather dull medical colleagues at a conference who participated in an evening's entertainment featuring a hypnotist. She noted that:

> A prim-looking woman did an excellent imitation of Mick Jagger, a knee man relived his sixth birthday party, and a distinguished liver consultant seemed wholly persuaded that he had come out by mistake in his pyjamas. Each one performed like a seasoned comic, including the ENT doctor who became a Martian invader who happened to have landed on a nudist beach…Apart from how funny it was (you had to be there), the thing that really riveted me about this spectacle was the utter transformation of the performers. It seemed for all the world as though the banal patter of the hypnotist had released in each of them a previously hidden personality…Could it be that we all have an uninhibited entertainer within us, capable of acting out any role that is suggested? If so, where are they lurking when not on show? Do we have to be hypnotised to release them, or might we switch from one to another in other circumstances too?[50]

The interesting thing about this apparent display of fascinating behaviour from otherwise less-than-fascinating people is that the behaviour was induced by hypnosis. Hypnosis is simply an extreme narrowing of attention, a heightened state of concentration, accompanied by an openness to suggestion. It has been theorized that while in this state of extreme attention, our ordinary barriers to accepting suggestion are dismantled, and we are therefore less likely to object to external suggestion as our concentration is elsewhere. In this extremely concentrated state, Carter (drawing on work done by French physician Pierre Janet) proposes that we may also be able to 'switch off one personality and switch on another'. This claim only makes sense if you buy the idea that we have a multitude of personalities that we carry around in our heads. The whole notion brings to mind popular films like *Three Faces of Eve* or *Sybil*, which were about multiple personality disorder (MPD), but in fact what Carter (and some others) are referring to is the notion of personality as a conglomerate of many different 'ego-states' or 'subpersonalities'. This is a fairly common sense observation, which we can test for ourselves (as we did earlier) simply by imagining how we behave at work in relation to how we behave home or at party, or whether we see a difference between our 'sexual self' and our 'responsible self'. What we might want to note here is that a state of extreme concentration is needed for both hypnosis AND acting, so perhaps the way in which the 'prim woman' imitated Mick Jagger and the way in which an actor plays Hamlet are more closely related than we might think, and deserves some serious consideration.

Daniel Dennett takes a kind of cognitive philosophical view, inspired by research into the area of 'split brain' subjects.[51] Dennett concludes that in light of the ways in which it appears that split brain patients can solve set problems in separate hemispheres of the brain (without the other side knowing), there must be a kind of innate human ability to put a 'face' on the disunity of our brains:

> We try to make all of our material cohere into a single good story. And that story is our autobiography.
>
> The chief fictional character at the center of that autobiography is one's *self*. And if you still want to know what the self *really* is, you're making a category mistake. After all, when a human being's behavioural control system becomes seriously impaired, it can turn out that the best hermeneutical story we can tell about that individual says that there is more than one character 'inhabiting' that body. This is quite possible on the view of the self that I have been presenting; it does not require any fancy metaphysical miracles. One can discover multiple selves in a person…[52]

One of many psychologists who write about our minds as being structured in multiple rather than single ways, John Rowan defines a 'subpersonality' as '*a semi-permanent and semi-autonomous region of the personality capable of acting as a person*'.[53] As Rowan points out:

Most of us have had the experience of being 'taken over' by a part of ourselves which we didn't know was there. We say 'I don't know what got into me'. This is generally a negative experience, although it can be positive too. The way in which we usually recognise the presence of a subpersonality is that we find ourselves, in a particular situation, acting in ways which we do not like or which go against our interests, and unable to change this by an act of will or a conscious decision. This lasts as long as the situation lasts – perhaps a few minutes, perhaps a few hours – and then it changes by itself when we leave the situation and go into a different one.[54]

The quotation above sounds as if Rowan's theory is quite different from Johnson and Lakoff's in that the 'will' or 'conscious decision' is unable to manipulate the behaviour of the subpersonality. But in fact, it is not. Lakoff and Johnson point out that the relationship between the Subject and Self(ves) is not unilaterally a master/servant one:

> In the Master-Servant case, the standards of behavior are set by the Subject, the Master. In the case in which the Subject has an obligation to the Self, it is the Self that sets the standards of behavior for the Subject. We can see this in the minimally different cases 'I was disappointed in myself' (Subject sets the standards) versus 'I disappointed myself' (Self sets the standards).[55]

Rowan's interesting twist here is that the subpersonality is something that responds to context rather than to our own conscious direction. This would mean that for Rowan, an actor would only be able to tap into a 'subpersonality' for character work if the context more or less demanded or encouraged it. Perhaps this makes sense when we're talking about character – I am sure that I am not the only actor who has felt that the act of creating and sustaining a 'large' character was immensely aided by knowing that my fellow actors 'bought into' the big character choices I was making or exploring in rehearsal. The idea of context creating the conditions for character to emerge is certainly interesting, but there are some pretty dark conclusions to be reached if we embrace it wholeheartedly.

In *The Lucifer Effect*, Philip Zimbardo considers the ways in which people respond in unexpected (and frankly disturbing) ways to context – even imaginary ones. Zimbardo once famously conducted a student experiment at Stanford University in the 1970s, where he divided the student participants into 'prisoner' and 'guard' roles. Although the imaginary experiment was planned to last for two weeks, it was called off after six days once it emerged that the students who took the 'guard' roles began to exhibit such abusive and degrading ways toward their 'prisoners' that the 'prisoner' students were no longer deemed to be safe. So convinced is Zimbardo that context drives personality that he became a witness for the defence of one of the Abu Ghraib guards, arguing that the context of the prison drove and determined the guards' abusive behaviour, and in effect brought out abusive subpersonalities (although he never actually uses that term). Like so many others who work in cognitive science or psychology Zimbardo is fascinated by the actor's relationship to the 'character' and puts forth his own take on the relationship between the 'Dramatic I' and the 'Real I':

> When actors enact a fictional character, they often have to take on roles that are dissimilar to their sense of personal identity. They learn to talk, walk, eat, and even to think and to feel as demanded by the role they are performing. Their professional training enables them to maintain the separation of character and identity, to keep self in the background while playing a role that might be dramatically different from who they really are. However, there are times when even for some trained professionals, those boundaries blur and the role takes over even after the curtain comes down or the camera's red light goes off. They become absorbed in the intensity of the role and their intensity spills over to direct their offstage life.[56]

The way in which Zimbardo describes an actor's 'professional training' makes me wonder whether it is true that acting teachers really approach this subject of the relationship between self and character quite so frontally. Certainly in my experience this whole area is rarely talked about in the way he suggests. Still, his point about context being a critical part of driving character is intriguing and certainly we can imagine that the context of rehearsal and performance, and the heightened imagination required in rehearsal exploration or performance might be the kinds of external situations in which something like a 'subpersonality' as Rowan describes it might emerge. It seems even more possible that the ability to maintain a strong sense of character is deeply dependent NOT simply upon the individual actor's sense of purpose and belief, but upon the actor finding themselves in a context wherein their portrayal of King John is reinforced and even heavily influenced by others recognizing and responding to King John. In other words, character might only emerge, fully, in the context of a collectively imagined world where each participant reinforces the character of all the others.

Rita Carter also suggests that actors do (in their narrowly focused state of attention on stage) switch from one personality state to another:

> Some actors wear their roles externally, but others absorb them to the extent that the adopted character ousts the actors' other personalities, even beyond the duration of the performance. The British actor David Suchet, for example, had a long stage run in *Timon of Athens* during which he found it increasingly difficult to flip back into his own major [personality] when the nightly performance ended. One evening a psychiatrist friend visited him backstage and observed that he seemed still to be acting like Timon. Suchet dismissed his concern, at which point the psychiatrist shot at him a number of questions such as: ages of your children? Phone number? Date of birth? To his own consternation, Suchet found he had to work hard to retrieve the answers – the 'Timon' personality he had created was so firmly in charge that his major [personality's] memories were temporarily irretrievable.[57]

Was Suchet's temporary difficulty in retrieving information really about 'switching' between one ego-state and another? If so, it would suggest that if an actor works in this way there is no distinction between the actor and role – there is in fact simply a kind of suppression of the 'major' personality, and a temporary dominance of a (created) 'minor' or subpersonality. This minor or 'sub' does not emerge from nowhere, however – presumably it is related to various possible personality states that we have access to within our own sense of ourselves.

Uta Hagen comes close to the idea of personality 'multiples', though her words strike me as more metaphorical than those employed by Carter or Rowan, but she emphasizes contextual events being a significant part of what inspires 'subpersonality' to emerge:

> The more I discover, the more I realize that I have endless sources within myself to put to use in the illumination of endless characters in dramatic literature; that I am compounded of endless human beings depending on the events moving in on me...[58]

I find Hagen's willingness to deal with the issue right from the start refreshing. Most acting theorists don't really grapple with the mysteries of the constitution of our personalities. Perhaps it is fair to say that this issue lies both right at the heart and also slightly outside of the actor's concern. I begin to think that we need to be much clearer about this when we think and write about the acting process. It may NOT be the case that we tap into 'subpersonalities' when we're acting – there is much more research and thought to be done in this area and especially on the whole idea of subpersonality. But there is certainly something resonant here in terms of the ways in which we play roles both on- and offstage that seem to present some very distinct parts of ourselves.

In her recent book, *Beyond Stanislavski*, Bella Merlin gives an account of some interesting and sometimes mystical explorations in the Russian approach to mental and physical processes involved in creating character. Although there is constant reference to 'psycho-physical' actions, it is more difficult to intuit anything here about the psychological part of all the work in terms of actor-to-character relationship. She does, however, refer to one of the Russian directors, Albert Filosov's, view:

> Filosov's directive to the actors at this point in the programme had been: 'Don't think about the character, just start from zero. It's only interesting to be yourselves and to play for each other, like children play for each other and not for the audience.' The argument was that, without starting from zero and working through your own personality in the early stages of preparation, characterisation could so easily be superimposed rather than organically discovered.[59]

This refusal to think early on about character might, the book suggests, encourage 'elements of the character [to come] to the fore', and we are advised not to suppress them. When Merlin has difficulties later with the character of Sonia in *Crime and Punishment*, she is simply advised by Filosov to 'lighten her vocal timbre'.[60] He further advises her not to be 'emotional' with the part. These seem extraordinarily superficial suggestions from an acknowledged Russian master but Merlin simply observes: 'Gee whiz, human beings are complex…'[61]

Writing well before so much psychological or cognitive research was available, Stanislavski saw things in a much more straightforward way:

I claim that all actors must be character actors…[but] this does not mean [the actor] must lose his own individuality and his personality; it means that in each role he must find his individuality and personality, but nevertheless be different in every role.[62]

For Stella Adler, similarly, the actor's job was pretty simple:

Define the difference between your behavior and the character's, find all the justification of the character's actions, and then go on from there to act *from yourself*.[63]

Joseph Chaikin considered that all acting was 'a demonstration of self with or without a disguise'.[64] For Sandy Meisner there was little consideration of disguise:

The first thing you have to do when you read a text is to find yourself – really find yourself. First you find yourself, then you find a way of doing the part which strikes you as being in character. Then, based on that reality, you have the nucleus of the role. Otherwise every shmuck from Erasmus Hall High School is an actor because everyone there knows how to read.[65]

Whatever his achievements or failings, you have to admire Meisner's ability to live with the unexplained!

When Helen Mirren is not playing a hard-drinking, tough-as-nails detective, casting directors seem to think that she should have been born with royal blood, as she plays queens quite a lot. If you contrast her Queen in *The Madness of King George* with her portrayal of Queens Elizabeth I & II, she demonstrates a marvellous range of 'queenly' behaviour. In *The Madness of King George* her predominant trait was to be subordinate to the king and to his needs. She was largely concerned with protecting him, but aware of her need of help in doing so. She was, in fact, helpless and vulnerable in the face of his illness and his tendency to play out his strange behaviours so publicly.

In her portrayal of Queen Elizabeth I, she was largely concerned with proving that she was in need of no one. She was aware of her power, her strength and her position and her response to that awareness was the demonstration of incredibly mercurial behaviour. Ready to dismiss or punish at the slightest offence and willing to forgive and overlook when it suited her. She manipulated those around her and exploited her power when it suited her needs or her strong, if largely unsatiated, sexual desires. She was fearless and frightened; independent and deeply needy; trusting and wary – she managed to capture the dizzying contradictions of a complex and powerful woman. As Queen Elizabeth II she was a study in suppression. The differences in her moods were subtle enough to be conveyed with a look or an extended pause. She was as emotionally buttoned up as her tailored suit jackets and incredibly inscrutable as she attempted to live her most public life in the most private of ways. Her suppressed pain, grief, confusion and anger are given vent only once during a moment of unexpected solitude in the Scottish highlands as she beholds the magnificent freedom of a stag.

Mirren's own ability to access and empathize with these three very different queens probably means that, like most of the rest of us, she is at various times helpless, vulnerable, subservient, powerful, mercurial, dismissive, forgiving, fearless, sexy, frightened, independent, needy, trusting, wary, suppressed, etc. Her three queens, while very different, might be considered 'character' roles, yet they all sprang from Helen Mirren's personality. She has only herself to draw on, so how did she distinguish her three queens so sharply? Was she consciously inhibiting parts of herself and boldly enhancing other parts of herself? Could her activity be described (as Carter and Rowan might) as temporarily unleashing 'subpersonalities' – in which a 'minor' personality temporarily overtakes the 'major' personality? Or could we, like Lakoff and Johnson, perhaps consider that the Subject (Helen Mirren) has the executive ability to create character through manipulating multiple Selves?

Perhaps the idea of 'subpersonalities' is not so far removed from Michael Chekhov's theories after all. In this passage he seems to demonstrate some sympathy with the idea:
'…in moments of inspiration…what happened to your everyday 'I'? Did it not retreat, give place to another I, and did you not experience it as the true artist in you?'[66] Despite Chekhov's hopeful tone here, we couldn't say with certainty that all inspired actors will necessarily have this kind of experience. Nor could we (if we adopt his theory that the everyday I 'retreats') very easily answer the question that we set ourselves early in this chapter about who is consciously in control of performance.

What are we to make of the relationship of context to personality (and context to character)? If we decide that the context can drive character and choices, does this mean that we must accept that there are always many things about our work as actors that will always be out of our conscious control? That conclusion might worry us unless we've spent some time really contemplating the notion that most of our thought *is* unconscious thought anyway. If we contemplate this idea deeply enough we have little other choice than to come to the conclusion that 'conscious control' is already a somewhat misleading phrase. Or we may, like Philip Auslander, believe that the actor's performance is produced *by the performance*:

> Theorists as diverse as Stanislavski, Bertolt Brecht, and Jerzy Grotowski all implicitly designate the actor's self as the *logos* of performance; all assume that the actor's self precedes and grounds her performance and that it is the presence of this self in performance that provides the audience with access to human truths…all posit the self as an autonomous foundation for acting…An examination of these theories of acting…reveals that…the actorly self is, in fact, produced by the performance it supposedly grounds.[67]

This is a challenging passage but we can roughly translate '*logos*' above as 'meaning' or 'basis' – which helps make Auslander's text a little clearer. He doesn't seem to see the phrases 'actor's self' or 'actorly self' as needing a bit more examination, and this certainly limits the force of his observation. But for all its apparent complexity, Auslander is really putting forward another version of the 'Dramatic I' – this time one which appears possibly spontaneously in the moment of performance and which is not produced solely through working memory or the detail of rehearsal (although both of these things will no doubt have influence). Auslander is proposing a complex version of Zimbardo's claim *that context sometimes produces surprising, unintended or possibly unmediated behaviour*, which is the result of the play of individual and environment. Wherever you stand on these issues, it seems to me that the questions raised by things like Zimbardo's experiments, are compelling and probably need much more serious consideration by actors and those who teach or direct. If it is true that personality responds to context to the extent that he suggests, then we would have to conclude that not all the choices facing an actor are made *by* the actor. *That puts a very different light on advice from most acting theorists.*

Whatever conclusions we finally come to, we have to recognize that the debates about method acting, character acting, 'playing out of ourselves', etc. have modelled the actor's mind in some discouragingly naive ways. This oversimplification has engendered some long-running arguments based on assumptions that simply don't stand up to scrutiny. Such things as assuming a fundamental unity of 'self' or metaphorically locating character in one space and actor in another, or worrying about 'character' as something that might efface the actor altogether (or the other way around) are not helpful in our quest to conceptualize the actor's process. It seems much more helpful to me to start with the metaphorical notion that actor and character are at least always occupying the same location or 'container' in an integrated way, and by acknowledging that the idea of 'self' may be a metaphorical 'face' (Dennett's words) that we create to provide the illusion of unity over a fundamentally multiplicitous psyche. That 'face' might be the way that we achieve 'integration, more or less effective, in the control system of a complex organism'[68] – the mind.

> **If it is true that personality responds so strongly to context, then we would have to conclude that not all the choices facing an actor are made *by* the actor**

Monkeys, mirrors, peanuts…

While there seems to be endless contradiction or at least confusion in the way that different acting theorists approach the relationship between the actor and the character, there are some simple and stubborn facts about it – most significantly that the actor's personality is involved in every aspect of the character played and must of course always be the basis of the work. That sometimes seems quite surprising when you encounter a very dull person who turns out to be a fascinating actor (or a fabulously engaging person who becomes very boring when they act) – and these encounters remind me of the dull doctors under hypnosis imitating Martians or rock stars. But the actor's work begins in understanding the role they are about to play. The actor's relationship with character begins when the actor finds a way to empathize with the character; to understand what the character is doing and hoping to do in a given situation. In other words, a 'felt empathy' with a character is fundamental for the actor playing that character. Simply reading the play – as Meisner points out – isn't enough. We need to bring to this activity some history of understanding the minds of others – we need to be able to predict how humans will behave and what drives their behaviour. We needn't be psychologists to do this – we've been predicting the thoughts and behaviour of others since we were born and we have an inbuilt skill for understanding through language, facial expressions and bodily movement how others are feeling, what they are thinking and what they might do next. We even come equipped with empathy for the thoughts and feelings of others. But exactly how do these abilities work?

Perhaps a little cognitive science might help us here. What V.S. Ramachandran has called the most important advance in brain studies over the last decade came as the result of a researcher, Giaccomo Rizzolatti, watching monkeys grab peanuts. Of course, when the monkeys grabbed peanuts certain parts of the brain's frontal lobes – where the motor command cells are – respond. None of this is new or surprising, but what happened in the monkeys watching this act *was*:

> One cell will fire when the monkey reaches out and grabs a peanut, another will fire when the monkey pulls something…These are motor command neurons. Rizzolatti found that some of these neurons will also fire when the monkey watches another monkey performing the same action. For example, a peanut-grabbing neuron which fires when the monkey grabs a peanut also fires when the monkey watches another monkey grab a peanut. The same thing happens in humans. This is quite extraordinary, because the visual image of somebody else grabbing a peanut is utterly different from the image of yourself grabbing a peanut – your brain must perform an internal mental transformation. Rizzolatti calls these mirror neurons…mirror neurons, instead of being some kind of curiosity, have important implications for understanding many aspects of human nature, *such as interpreting somebody else's actions and intentions.*[69]

It would seem that this mirror neuron system (MNS) is linked to the ability to empathize – and common sense would lead us to this conclusion. This would explain, of course, why when we watch someone cry, we sometimes spontaneously cry too, or why when someone goes through something particularly stressful we tense our muscles. We aren't just 'being sympathetic' – the mirror neurons in our brain are firing simply in response to the act of watching. The way in which the MNS works is through an 'embodied simulation' – which means that have a tendency to imitate internally the bodily sensation of an action that we observe, as explained by David Freedberg and Vittorio Gallese:

> Neuroscientific research has shed light on the ways in which we empathize with others, by emphasizing the role of implicit models of others' behaviors and experiences – that is, embodied simulation. Our capacity to *pre-rationally* make sense of the actions, emotions and sensations of others depends on embodied simulation, a functional mechanism through which the actions, emotions or sensations we see activate our own internal representations of the body states that are associated with these social stimuli, as if we were engaged in a similar action or experiencing a similar emotion or sensation.[70]

Could the discovery of a new kind of brain cell explain why quick empathetic responses might erase the sense of distance between the actor and the character?

These recent discoveries about the very 'embodied' ways in which we 're-experience' the experiences of others seem to me to be incredibly important in the understanding of how actors work. Freedberg and Gallese go on to explain that this embodied simulation of the activity or experiences of others is something that is 'pre-cognitive' – in other words, it happens before we think about it. We can, of course, reflect on our empathetic feelings and the ways in which watching someone's throat cut in a 'slasher' film makes our own throats feel incredibly sensitive or vulnerable, but we don't *need* that reflection in order to have these empathetic responses.

It seems to me that it might be theorized that the greater the strength of the MNS, in individual brains, the greater the embodied 'mirror' response. Given the many permutations and differences in individual brains, might it not be possible that some people actually do have greater strength of 'firing power' in these 'mirror neurons' than others – precisely in the same way that some brains have more facility for language, some more facility for drawing or for music or mathematics? Certainly it has been theorized that those with conditions like autism or Asperger's Syndrome may have deficient or less normally active MNS mechanisms. And if MNS is thought to be physiologically variable, surely that variability could lead to hyper-efficiency as well as deficiency. Such hyper-efficiency might one day be able to explain in neuroanatomical terms why some actors just seem like 'naturals'. Could hyper-efficient MNS account for why some actors can have an immediate (in Hornby's terms, perhaps, 'intuitive') understanding of what the character is going through? Might this be what allows that same actor to go on from there to bridge the sense of self and character through a 'felt' empathy via MNS in the brain? And once this is achieved, wouldn't an actor then feel 'at one' with the character? If so, this might explain quite a lot about why we talk about being 'inside' a character or the character being 'inside' us. If it is true that some people have greater strength in MNS, it might also be the reason why some people have a kind of strong and seemingly immediate emotional connection with a character. There is no doubt that the thinking part of the frontal lobe of the brain is responsible for helping us to understand the minds of others, and to be able, through bodily sensation, to comprehend what others have gone through in physical terms. The discovery of mirror neurons is quite new and there will no doubt be much research done in this area, but they may be helpful in our understanding of why quick empathetic responses can quite literally erase the sense of distance between the actor and the character.

Getting the trope/thought right

If we go back to thinking about what Johnson and Lakoff have to say about the Subject/ Selves model of consciousness, we can see of course that this metaphorical model is not, phenomenologically, REAL – it's a way of talking about our experience of having an 'inner self' – and we know that this is an area that we find difficult to talk about. But we also know that it's common to conceptualize our inner lives through metaphor:

> We are, of course, acutely aware that these modes of conceptualizing our phenomenological experience of the Self do not entail that the structures imposed by these metaphors are ontologically real. They do not entail that we really are divided up into a Subject, an Essence, and one or more Selves.[71]

The 'Essence' metaphor as they outline it is of particular interest to actors as it centres on various metaphorical ways in which we describe what we ordinarily take to be our 'true essence'. The fact that we often see this essence as difficult to pin down or express can be seen in many phrases gathered by Johnson and Lakoff: 'You've never seen what he's really like on the inside', 'She rarely shows her real self', 'That wasn't the real me talking yesterday', etc. We know that we commonly tend to characterize ourselves and others as having a kind of 'true core' that is really who we are. That true core may, as expressed above, be a hidden essence that is belied by our everyday behaviour – and the core may be anything from angelic to rotten. The ways in which we so often hear neighbours speaking about a murderer after the fact demonstrates how we sometimes see behaviour as something distinct from this 'true core' or essence. We may tend to think of behaviour as being in opposition to this true core, but if we think a bit more deeply about it we often come to realize that what seemed like duplicitous behaviour may also be an extension of that 'true core' – rotten or angelic. We often hear descriptions of murderers ('he was so quiet and kept to himself' or 'he was always very polite') or homeless people who die and give secret millions to charity ('he was always so quiet and kept to himself' or 'he was always very polite'), that the 'true core' of the person was not evident. But of course, we could equally argue that this 'true core' was making its appearance (in a sense) long before the murders or donations – the quietness and the politeness (devious/humble) were simply extensions of the *whole* (rotten/angelic) core.

It is our tendency in metaphorical descriptions to conceive of the human inner self as whole. Our metaphors of inner lives – even as manifested in Johnson and Lakoff's divided Subject/Selves suggest, ultimately, a kind of wholeness. Perhaps we sense that wholeness through the related actions of Subject/Self, which add up to a 'whole' or perhaps we see the Essence or 'true core' as ultimately being the (hard to describe) thing that makes up the wholeness of the polite murderer or the quiet millionaire. Even Freud's divisions of id, ego, superego were postulated as divisions of a whole psyche. When we do this, we're actively carrying out that fundamental operation of metaphor: we're transferring meaning from one realm or domain to another. In the case of wholeness, we are no doubt transferring meaning from the world of objects – which we can experience as whole, rounded, full, complete, etc., to the world of our inner self. We can metaphorically talk about ourselves as being 'centred', or 'scattered' or 'divided' or 'together' (and we have to have an idea of 'wholeness' in order even to talk this way) in just the way that we talk about objects, and overall we seem to pose the metaphor of our inner lives as ideally whole, or full, or rounded.

If this is the case, might it be that one of the things that we find difficult as actors is that we are attempting to graft a 'character metaphor' onto our already existing metaphor of self (a 'whole' Real I)? Might it be more helpful to jettison this 'character metaphor' altogether and substitute another trope – metonymy? Might we be much better off if we could learn to see a character we're playing as being in a metonymical relationship with our (already metaphorical!) sense of self?

Metonymy can be a confusing rhetorical device, and is often thought of as part of an overall metaphorical way of conceiving/describing the world. We're using metonymy when we refer to a part of something as representative of a whole thing – such as when we call people who work in management 'suits', or when we refer to farm workers as 'hands'. But metonymy works differently from metaphor in one very distinct way, which is summed up well by Hugh Bredin: 'metaphor *creates* the relation between its objects, while metonymy *presupposes* that relation.'[72] In other words, metonymy effaces the distance or difference between its objects. In that spirit, might it not be a healthier place for an actor to start the mental conception of the task involved in creating a character? If we begin metaphorically with thoughts like 'Hamlet is like me in some senses', we are already presupposing that Hamlet exists in a different location. If we begin metonymically, however, with thoughts like 'my introspective/intellectual/superior personality is Hamlet's introspective/intellectual/superior personality', then we are presupposing the relationship between ourselves and character from the start. If we add to this a sense of our own metaphorical conception of our inner lives as whole, or full, or rounded, we are then able to conceive of Hamlet as a constituent part of this wholeness, or fullness, or roundedness. It may seem a subtle shift of thinking but when I read acting books I am convinced that its effect is NOT subtle.

If it is true that metaphor is a mode of cognition, then if follows that the way in which we cast metaphor is a reflection of the ways in which we both perceive and conceptualize.

If we look at the ways in which acting books conceive the actor/character relationship we can see that there are some persistent types of metaphorical constructions at work. For example:

Character as container:
   Getting into the character
   Getting inside the character

Character as [different] location:
   'The background should lead you to your character'[73]
   'How do I get from a **Real I** to a **Dramatic I**?'[74]
   'Finding the character'

Character as Other (friend/potential enemy/picture or image)
   'As soon as you know your character, your character will give you attitudes…'[75]
   'When I confront the character I'm going to play…'[76]
   'Let us say that the actor has visualized the character in his imagination'[77]

Character as object/servant
   'Thus we master the character…We master his thoughts and feelings'[78]
   'You must master your characterization'[79]

My point in gathering these metaphors is not to suggest that the individual theorists do not go on to give valuable advice that actors may find useful, but only to point out some of the common ways we think of character as something other than a part of our whole selves which we put in service of theatrical creation; the whole selves from which we selectively present behaviours and appetites. Further, it seems to me that the metaphorical character-as-location/other/servant, etc. has done some disservice by *creating* a relationship between actor and character (which has added confusion) rather than *presupposing* one – which I think can make things clearer. If we presuppose that there is always already a part/whole relationship between actor and character – and therefore discard altogether ideas like 'character acting' and 'playing out of self' – then surely the real debate can come to rest on two simpler questions: the question of how bold or imaginative we are when making our choices and the question of how successfully we can *sustain* the choices we make as actors.

Summary

We've looked a lot in this section both at the ways in which our minds work and at the ways in which we conceive of those workings. Given all the complexity we've outlined here, it is surely surprising that really only the earliest of acting theorists (Diderot, Stanislavki, Chekhov) seemed to really want to grapple with the complexities of consciousness. On one level that's understandable – there are more than enough actors who wholeheartedly embrace Nike's 'Just Do It' attitude. And when it comes to performance time – as any good sports psychologist will tell you – the last thing we need is for our focus to go wandering around in the complexities of human cognition.

But when we're in reflective mode; in learning mode, there's much for us to ponder here.

We may never wholly understand what Stanislavski and Chekhov were trying to describe in their models of consciousness, but perhaps there is something more to think about in terms of the very different kind of cognitive space we have when we're really well rehearsed into a role. We might want to think more about the relationship between kinds of cognition (meta-, extra-) and the general limits of rational thinking when we're attempting to transcend the ordinary.

Along with rethinking the ways in which we talk about character, shouldn't we also contemplate what part context may play in inspiring or motivating an actor's process? That in turn might mean that in situations where we are training or directing actors, our concentration needs to remain balanced between our concern with individual choices that an actor may be making, and the ways in which we can continually enhance the strength of the imagined context – which will almost certainly (if strong enough) influence (perhaps subconsciously?) the actor's behaviour. **However we look at it, it is unlikely that we could put forth a single theory that would cover all the possibilities.** For every actor who feels that they are just 'themselves' when they act, there will be one who feels like they 'become' someone else. And some, like Bella Martin, who (like Michael Chekhov) do think of their minds as being 'split': 'All the time that I was involved in the scene, part of me was watching, enjoying wholeheartedly the satisfying feeling of "transformation".'[80]

Acting books filled with transitive verbs and twenty-step programmes may appeal strongly to our rational desire to 'solve the mystery' of good acting quickly. But rational approaches have limitations and quick rational approaches have severe limitations. Any approach to acting that fails to recognize this is probably naive. There's much more to be said about cognitive processes (some of which we'll look at in the last section) but the fact is, most acting books spend too little time looking at the ways in which we understand, conceptualize and create in the theatre. This is not to say that they don't impart technique – of course, they do. But they impart that technique as if we already understand how we think, how we imagine, how we empathize, how we remember...and as we know, these things are not just highly complex – they are a significant share of the actor's craft.

But they are not the whole picture because, of course, actors deal in emotion.

Notes

1. Robert Leach in *Twentieth Century Actor Training*, ed. Alison Hodge (Oxford: Routledge, 2000), p. 52.
2. Constantin Stanislavski, *An Actor's Handbook*, ed. & tr. Elizabeth R. Hapgood (London: Methuen, 1990), pp. 134–135.
3. Jean Benedetti, *The Art of the Actor* (London: Methuen, 2005), p. 125.
4. Sharon M. Carnicke, *Stanislavski in Focus* (Amsterdam: Harwood Academic Publishers, 1998), pp. 136–137.
5. *Ibid.*, p. 142.
6. *Ibid.* p. 140.
7. Michael Chekhov in *Twentieth Century Actor Training*, p. 83.
8. Aldo Tassi, 'Performance as Metamorphosis', *Consciousness, Literature and the Arts*, 1(2), 2000.
9. As we'll be considering later, there is much evidence that people with autism either have a diminished capacity for representing the thoughts of others or else no capacity for doing so.
10. To be clear, I'll define my use of metarepresentation here as: *X (actor) thinks Y (Hecuba) is in anguish*.
11. Here my formula is: *X is thinking about X's own thinking that Y is in anguish*.
12. Daniel Dennett isn't convinced that 'representation/metarepresentation' as a description of cognitive functions is clear enough ('we still do not know what we (all) mean when we talk about representation, and hence what we mean by metarepresentation'). See his 'Making Tools for Thinking' in Dan Sperber (ed.), *Metarepresentations: A Multidisciplinary Perspective* (Oxford: OUP, 2000).
13. Yuri L. Hanin, *Emotions in Sport* (Leeds: Human Kinetics, 2000), p. 141.
14. Ellis Cashmore, *Sports Psychology: The Key Concepts* (Leeds: Human Kinetics, 2002) p. 270.
15. Chekhov, *On the Technique of Acting*, pp. 156–157.
16. *Ibid.*, p. 25.
17. *Ibid.*, p. 155.
18. Quoted in Terry Orlick, *The Pursuit of Excellence* (Leeds: Human Kinetics, 2000), p. 155.
19. For a good (if complex) survey of contemporary literature in this area, see Evans & Frankish, *In Two Minds: Dual Processes and Beyond* (Oxford: OUP, 2009).
20. George Lakoff & Mark Johnson, *Philosophy in the Flesh* (New York: Basic Books, 1999), p. 13.
21. There may be, of course, another debate to be had here in terms of how we define thought and whether certain cognitive operations that might be described as autonomic can reasonably be rounded up under the term 'thought' in the common sense understanding of this word.
22. Lakoff & Johnson, *Philosophy in the Flesh*, pp. 10–11.
23. For example, some actors will 'see' the page from which the lines were learned, others will recall the feeling or look of the room in which they learned the lines, or how they were moving, etc.
24. Aidan Moran, "Attention in Sport" in *Advances in Applied Sport Psychology*, ed. Stephen D. Mellalieu & Sheldon Hanton (Oxford: Routledge, 2009), p. 202
25. V.S. Ramachandran, *Phantoms in the Brain* (London: Harper Perennial, 2005), p. 116.
26. Quoted in Robert Restak, *The Naked Brain* (New York: Harmony Books, 2006), p. 22.
27. R.M. Nideffer, *Psyched to Win* (Leeds: Human Kinetics, 1992) p. 21.
28. *Ibid.*, p. 21
29. Richard Flor & Kevin Dooley, 'The Dynamics of Learning to Automaticity', *Noetic Journal*, 1(2), 1998, p. 168.

30. *Ibid.*, p. 170.
31. Chekhov, *On the Technique of Acting*, p. 155 (italics are my own).
32. Hanin, *Emotions in Sport*, p. 269.
33. Mihaly Csikszentmihalyi, *Creativity: Flow and Psychology of Discovery and Invention* (New York: HarperPerennial, 1996), p. 49.
34. Larisa Shavinina & Kavita Seeratan 'Extracognitive Phenomena in the Intellectual Functioning of Gifted, Creative, and Talented Individuals' in Larisa Shavinina & Michel Ferrari (eds), *Beyond Knowledge: Extracognitive Aspects of Developing High Ability* (New Jersey: Lawrence Erlbaum Assoc, 2004) p. 85.
35. *Ibid.*, p. 85.
36. *Ibid.*, p. 86.
37. *Ibid.*, p. 96.
38. Chekhov, *On the Technique of Acting*, pp. 157–158.
39. Stanislavski, *An Actor's Handbook*, p. 121.
40. Stella Adler, *The Technique of Acting* (New York: Bantam Books, 1988), p. 32.
41. Sanford Meisner & Dennis Longwell, *On Acting* (New York: Vintage Books, 1987), pp. 47–48.
42. Jean Benedetti, *Stanislavski & The Actor* (London: Methuen, 1998), p. 1.
43. Uta Hagen, *Respect for Acting* (New York: Wiley Publishing, 1973), p. 29.
44. Julian Baggini, *The Pig That Wants to be Eaten* (New York: Penguin, 2006), p. 162.
45. V.S. Ramachandran, *A Brief Tour of Human Consciousness* (New York: Pi Press, 2004), p. 105.
46. Johnson & Lakoff, *Philosophy in the Flesh*, p. 269.
47. *Ibid.*, p. 267.
48. Nick Moseley, *Acting and Reacting* (London: Nick Hern Books, 2005).
49. Hornby, *The End of Acting*, p. 88.
50. Rita Carter, *Multiplicity: The New Science of Personality* (London: Little Brown, 2008), pp. xi–xii.
51. In particular, Dennett is considering studies done by Michael Gazzaniga, whose research area has been patients (split brain subjects) whose large connective tissue between the hemispheres of the brain (the corpus callosum) has been surgically bisected. This extreme treatment is on occasion used to allay particularly severe chronic seizures – usually in epileptic patients. You can actually watch Gazzaniga working with a split brain patient on YouTube (http://www.youtube.com/watch?v=ZMLzP1VCANo). The short film is about four and a half minutes long and makes an excellent introduction to the topic – I highly recommend watching!
52. Brie Gertler & Lawrence Shapiro (eds), *Arguing About the Mind* (New York: Routledge, 2007), p. 246.
53. John Rowan, *Subpersonalities: The People inside Us* (London: Routledge, 1997), p. 8.
54. *Ibid.*, p. 7.
55. Johnson & Lakoff, *Philosophy in the Flesh*, p. 288.
56. *Ibid.*, p. 213.
57. Carter, *Multiplicity*, pp. 107–108.
58. Hagen, *Respect for Acting*, p. 25.
59. Bella Merlin, *Beyond Stanislavski: The Psycho-Physical Approach to Actor Training* (London: Nick Hern Books, 2001) p. 178.
60. *Ibid.*, p. 216.
61. *Ibid.*, p. 57.
62. Stanislavski, *An Actor's Handbook*, p. 32.
63. Quoted in David Krasner (ed.), *Method Acting Reconsidered* (Basingstoke: Macmillan, 2000), pp. 4–5.

64. Quoted in Philip Auslander, *From Acting to Performance: Essays in Modernism and Postmodernism* (London: Routledge, 1997), p. 30.
65. Meisner, *On Acting*, p. 178.
66. Chekhov, *To the Actor*, pp. 95–96.
67. Auslander, *From Acting to Performance*, p. 30.
68. Gertler & Shapiro, 'What is the Self?', *Arguing About the Mind*, p. 207.
69. V.S. Ramachandran, *The Emerging Mind* (London: Profile Books, 2003), p. 43. [My emphasis.]
70. David Freedberg & Vittorio Gallese, 'Motion, Emotion and Empathy in Esthetic Experience', *Trends in Cognitive Science*, 11(5), 2007, p. 198. [My emphasis.]
71. Johnson & Lakoff, *Philosophy in the Flesh*, p. 288.
72. Hugh Bredin, 'Metonymy', *Poetics Today*, 5(1), 1984, p. 57.
73. Adler, *The Technique of Acting*, p. 72.
74. Benedetti, *Stanislavski & the Actor*, p. 4.
75. Adler, *The Technique of Acting*, p. 78.
76. Hagen, *Respect for Acting*, p. 152.
77. Chekhov, *On the Technique of Acting*, p. 95.
78. *Acting: A Handbook of the Stanislavski Method*, p. 79.
79. Richard Boleslavsky, *Acting: The First Six Lessons* (New York: Theatre Arts Books, 1965), p. 77.
80. Martin, *Beyond Stanislavski*, p. 222.

Chapter 3

How Am I Feeling?

Good question. The nature of emotion has puzzled philosophers, psychologists, physicians and cognitive neuroscientists for some time. The fundamental question of how we actually feel what we feel is also related to questions like:

What ARE feelings – are they thoughts or are they bodily responses?
How do feelings differ from cognition?
What exactly is the relationship between feelings and the body?
Are feelings and emotions the same thing?
What can we actually *know* about feelings and/or emotions?

When it comes to acting the questions have been (and remain):

Are the feelings actors generate *genuine* feelings? If so, how does the actor control those feelings?

How *do* actors 'generate' feelings?

Is the difference between an actor who is feeling genuine feelings and an actor with the ability to convince us that his/her feelings are genuine simply one of technique? How does that technique work, and can it be taught?

For me, when I read acting books, the questions are compounded even further – particularly when I read theories about 'affective memory' or 'trigger' objects, but the questions above are certainly enough to start with.

Writing in the preface of Diderot's book, *The Paradox of Acting*, the great French theoretician and teacher, Jacques Copeau, outlined his worries about the 'monstrous sincerity' of actors who use 'imaginary' or 'make-believe' feelings on stage:

The actor takes the risk of losing his…soul…which, having been too often upset by acting, too often carried away and offended by imaginary passions, contorted by artificial habits, feels irrelevant before reality…An actor's profession tends to pervert him. It's the consequence of an instinct which pushes a man to abandon himself and live a pretence.[1]

I'm always amazed at the passion with which acting theorists rail against…well…acting. Copeau's worries are all about the dangers of faking it. But whether we like to admit it or not we know that we are always faking it when we act, insofar as what is happening in Hamlet isn't *really* happening. I prefer the word pretending to the word 'faking' – despite the unfortunate associations that this word has in its cousins: pretence, pretentiousness, etc. But pretending was one of the great joys of childhood. And unless I'm seriously out step with the rest of the world, it remains one of the great pleasures of adulthood too. Even hardcore 'I-never-pretend' types will smile slyly in acting classes when I talk about the ways in which we pretend to have (or sometimes rehearse) heated conversations or arguments with someone – either before or after the fact – in which we are articulate, passionate and, more to the point, we say everything we mean to say and we win the argument.

But the subject has had acting theorists in a tizz for quite some time. Because, of course, this lies at the heart of the great debates about acting, and remains pertinent some 200 plus years on from Diderot's intervention. Richard Hornby gets right at the crux of the issue:

> The immediate inspiration for Diderot's essay was his acquaintance with the great English actor David Garrick who visited Paris in the winter of 1764–65. Garrick would entertain friends at private gatherings by putting his head through folding doors and, in a few seconds, express[ing] half a dozen widely ranging emotions. No one seemed to find this amusing exercise especially paradoxical, however, until Diderot came along. Garrick obviously could not have felt and *un*felt such a range of emotions so quickly, at least not at the intensity that they were being shown. Diderot, however, reached the conclusion that Garrick was feeling *nothing at all*, but was in fact controlling his face in an entirely mechanical way, as if by pulling strings.[2]

© National Museums Liverpool, Walker Art Gallery

Of course in describing this process as mechanical, Diderot did not have in mind what *we* would make of such a description. When we say that an actor is mechanical we tend to mean that his performance was stiff or wooden. Diderot, however, was positing a version of the 'Subect/Selves' distinction we looked at in the last section. He was suggesting that one part of our minds (Subject) can objectify another and 'mechanically' manipulate this other or Self. In Joseph Roach's description of Stanislavski's theories, Diderot is accounting for 'the complexit[ies] of higher organisms, including the phenomenon of double or multiple consciousness'.[3] As ever, when I read acting theory books on the subject of consciousness I am generally dazed – but I think the description of double or multiple consciousness is meant here to indicate the capacity of the brain to carry out a number of tasks at any given time, to think about more than one thing at once (simultaneous or parallel cognition) and to give itself directions (metacognition). For example – its ability not only to send 'action

> **Emotions play out in the theatre of the body. Feelings play out in the theatre of the mind**

impulses' to our bodies [*kiss her now*], but to be able to reflect on those actions at the same time [*her response isn't passionate enough – maybe I'm not such a great kisser?*]. In fact, the metacognitive process of doing and reflecting on what we're doing appear to happen so simultaneously that we think nothing of it – as any actor who is simultaneously acting and reviewing their acting performance as they go along will tell you. The neuroscience of it is more complicated, of course, and involves action and feedback signals travelling very quickly between the body and the brain. But that needn't concern us here – what concerns us is how the 'reflecting' mind may be able to manipulate or control the 'feeling' mind. But of course before we can consider this we have to try and figure out how to make sense of that last phrase – 'the feeling mind'. And in order to do that we have to have some idea about what feelings are.

We often tend to use the words 'emotion' and 'feeling' interchangeably, as if they are the same thing, but of course, for many people – for example, for some philosophers of the mind and some cognitive neuroscientists – these words describe different processes. For Antonio Damasio, the words are separate when we're attempting to understand the way they work:

> Trust Shakespeare to have been there before. Toward the end of Richard II…Richard unwittingly tells Bolingbroke about a possible distinction between the notion of emotion and that of feeling…he notes that the 'external manner of laments' expressed in his face is merely 'shadows of the unseen grief', a grief that 'swells with silence in the tortured soul.'
>
> My strategy for elucidating feelings capitalizes on this distinction…In the context of this book, then, emotions are actions or movements, many of them public, visible to others as they occur in the face, in the voice, in specific behaviours…Feelings, on the other hand, are always hidden…Emotions play out in the theatre of the body. Feelings play out in the theatre of the mind.[4]

In my experience most actors and directors consider these words to be synonymous and most of them use the words as if we all understand exactly what we mean when we use them. But do we? Damasio's point above is clear and his distinction between emotion and feeling seems to me to make sense where acting is concerned. For the purposes of our consideration here I'd like to maintain this distinction in terms of emotion being something that happens first, sometimes below conscious level (we'll look at all of this in more detail below), and feelings being the more immediately cognitive process that attends the emotions and consciousness. While this distinction might initially sound as if it might underscore the old mind/body split, it is in fact a repudiation of that. Given the speed and interplay of information passing through the body and mind, even if an initial emotional response is generated unconsciously, everything that follows along instantly and thoroughly entails conscious thought.

The whole of the history of acting theory – as laid out by Roach in his study, *The Player's Passion* – is about that 'elusive ideal of spontaneous expression' of emotion. Indeed, emotion, how we feel it, whether we are *really* feeling it, how we can sustain its 'spontaneity' over eight shows a week, is the whole business of acting studies. But when acting theorists talk about the ways in which actors work, including things like affectivity or emotional memory – are they talking about emotion or feeling or both? And when we get right down to it – when actors themselves talk about emotion, what is it that we're talking about?

Well, now we're like Eliza on the ice I'm afraid – desperately hoping for solid ground, but finding none. It's been many years since William James' iconic essay 'What Is an Emotion?', but despite radical advances in study since then, there is still little scientific certainty about how emotion works or even where it resides:

> Scientists have had lots to say about what emotions are. For some, emotions are bodily responses that evolved as part of the struggle to survive. For others emotions are mental states that result when bodily responses are 'sensed' by the brain. Another view is that the bodily responses are peripheral to an emotion, with the important stuff happening completely within the brain. Emotions have also been viewed as ways of acting or ways of talking. Unconscious impulses are at the core of some emotion theories, while others emphasise the importance of conscious decisions. A popular view today is that emotions are thoughts about situations in which people find themselves. Another notion is that emotions are social constructions, things that happen between rather than within individuals.
>
> A scientific understanding of emotions would be wonderful…But, as the above indicates, scientists have not been able to agree about what an emotion is…Unfortunately, one of the most significant things ever to be said about emotion may be that everyone knows what it is until they are asked to define it.[5]

I've quoted from Joseph LeDoux's excellent book, *The Emotional Brain*, extensively because his work makes clear how little we understand about emotion from a scientific point of view. The quotation above demonstrates the peril of concluding that Diderot's project was amenable to being described as a problem of mind/body split. Of course, it is exactly this old notion of 'Cartesian dualism' that attracts so much of Richard Hornby's ire in *The End of Acting*.[6] Hornby's understanding of Descartes is not a sophisticated one, however, and his real concern is with the problem of seeing the actor's mind and body as separate. He is certainly not alone in this, but by and large contemporary accounts of the workings of the mind (even more so contemporary accounts of the workings of emotion) have more or less displaced this 'dualism' altogether. As most philosophers and cognitive scientists these days would agree – *the mind is embodied* – which is to say, the more we study the mind, the more its holistic, physiological and psychological connection with the body is clear.

Still, we know little about emotion (although the science of it is growing rapidly); about its relationship to our cognitive processes or about whether feeling is not, in fact, wholly a cognitive process of sorts. And if we can't know these things, how can we know whether or not Diderot was right? In fact, when it comes to the way that actors, directors, acting teachers and writers of books on acting talk about emotion and acting, the only hard fact available is that we are all working largely through instinct and anecdote. We're NOT acting or teaching from a factual or an entirely scientific view because there isn't one.

Still, I feel more than ever convinced that actors and directors are continually working as researchers into the areas of emotion, memory and the body, and that in our informal ways we have come to know things that may take more scientifically minded researchers some time to explain. But there are a number of things that have advanced in the areas of researching how the 'emotional brain' works and some of these may be of use to us – not least because understanding the 'emotional brain' is the substantial concern of the actor.

Most actors I know would agree that emotion, memory and the body are closely linked in ways that we can't actively articulate. This link is demonstrated all the time in rehearsal rooms when actors find that a change in something which elicits a new feeling may temporarily cause text memory to fail. Similarly a late change in blocking can cause actors to suddenly lose lines that they've been confident with over the last two weeks of rehearsal. I've seen actors mistakenly jump to a different part of the text when something unexpected happens on stage, or if furniture is moved from a previous position, and seem not even to notice that they've jumped to a different part of the script. The mysteries of brain, body, memory and environment are a part of our work all the time.

And of course the most mysterious part of our work lies in why some people seem able to access what appears to be honest, spontaneous feelings in response to things happening on stage while others find this either difficult or, at the very least, inconsistent. Acting approaches vary enormously in the way that they view emotion in both aesthetic and technical terms, and in how they go about advising actors to access and use their emotions. I've found myself lately more attracted to books on mind science and the study of emotions and while they still acknowledge that there is much controversy over the whole of how emotion actually 'works', they offer much for the Philosophical Actor to consider.

On the whole, it seems that cognitive scientists and evolutionary psychologists are in some agreement these days about the fact that everyone possesses certain fundamental emotions. This was quite a controversial idea at one point, but sufficient field research suggests that there are a certain number of 'basic' emotions that cross cultures and geographical boundaries. Depending on which theorist you read, there may be as many as eight (Sadness, Surprise, Disgust, Anger, Fear, Acceptance, Joy, Anticipation[7]), or as few as five (happiness, anger, fear, disgust and sadness[8]). Of course there are many ways of looking at the problem, but essentially all of these researchers, in looking at 'fundamental' emotions, are trying to determine which emotions are 'hard-wired' into the brain. These theories are challenged by those who view emotions as psychological or even social constructions and not a part of 'biological hardware'. But on the whole, research into the idea that certain emotions are hard-wired is pretty convincing. How these 'fundamental' emotions add up to some complexity is a particular challenge for these scientists and one of the more interesting theories is put forward by Robert Plutchik, whose theory of basic and derived emotions begins with a kind of wheel of basic emotional categories:

Sadness

Surprise   Disgust

Fear   Anger

Acceptance   Anticipation

Joy

The idea is that within this 'wheel' of emotions, we can see how the basic emotions mix to produce more complex (or, in his language, 'derived') states. Plutchik describes how emotions mix in various ways according to their proximity in the 'wheel' above. The Primary Dyads (which are a mix of emotions above that are adjacent in the wheel) produce secondary emotions such as: 'joy + acceptance = friendliness' (although if we want to maintain Damasio's emotion/feeling distinction, we might perhaps decide that what Plutchik really means here is secondary *feelings*). Similarly Secondary Dyads (which are emotions once removed on the wheel,

> **Many theorists believe that emotions evolved as part of the '4F's' of survival – Fighting, Fleeing, Feeding and, um…mating**

i.e., sadness + anger = sullenness) and Tertiary Dyads (twice removed on the wheel: anticipation + fear = anxiety)[9] also produce secondary emotions (feelings).

As much fun as Plutchik's 'Wheel of Emotions' parlour game is, I only include it here to make the distinction between what we might consider primary and secondary emotions or feelings. Of course, for some theorists, surprise and anticipation ARE secondary emotions/ feelings. For these theorists, the difference seems to be one of connections between a particular emotion and our survival instinct. For instance, many theorists believe that emotions evolved as part of the '4F's' of survival – Fighting, Fleeing, Feeding and, um… mating. It seems simple enough to imagine how it is that these survival needs engendered survival emotions like fear, anger, disgust, happiness or sadness, all of which we can feel in our 'gut'. If this is true, we might all have different theories about how our emotions are connected directly to the '4F's' of survival, perhaps particularly about the ways in which display of happiness or sadness may have been responsible for securing social units that helped to ensure survival. But for the actor I think there are a couple of more interesting things to contemplate.

The first is whether really great actors are just better and more sophisticated at perceiving and 'mixing' the emotional wheel (above) and coming up with finer, more incredibly well-tuned feelings and nuances in their work, and the second is whether there is a difference in the way we represent emotion and the way we feel emotion naturally. In other words, if what distinguishes emotion from other kinds of cognition is the relationship that emotion has with the body, could we then say that all the emotions involve specific amounts/kinds of bodily response? Does this mean that we always need to focus first on bodily sensation when we're representing emotion? Does the fact that some emotions are generated through an unconscious survival instinct determine the likelihood of an actor's ability to represent that emotion with fidelity?

It certainly seems to me (on a purely subjective level) that the 4F emotions elicit the most powerful bodily responses. The wheel is – curiously – missing love, which is one of many other emotions that for most elicits strong bodily response, but perhaps the final 'F' is supposed to cover that, and all cognitive scientists are just a bunch of hard-nosed empiricists who realize that the love that leads to mating is primary, and the love we have for our grannies is something else.[10] In any case, the science of all this is still in a relatively early stage, but is advancing pretty rapidly. I think as actors and directors we have always known about the extraordinary connection between our bodies and our emotions. The science of that connection helps make clear to me why so many actors I've known (myself included) think that the body 'stores' the memory of feelings. In the first instance, this may be because in certain cases it does appear that the brain and the body do kind of 'side-step' the frontal cortex (the thinking and reasoning part of the brain) in our physical reactions.

Joseph LeDoux famously outlined what he terms the 'high road' and the 'low road' of emotional response. He's distinguishing here between two parts of the brain – the higher, cortical region (thinking, reasoning functions) and the lower, thalamic region, which doesn't bother with all that thinking – it just triggers response. LeDoux's research has uncovered 'a pathway that could transmit information directly to the amygdala from the thalamus'.[11] This might not sound immediately exciting, but the science of it is pretty fascinating in terms of where/how emotion is generated. LeDoux's discovery means that a particular stimulus (the sound of a twig snapping) in a particular circumstance (dark, lonely forest) could send information to the auditory thalamus (first stop for the auditory information in the brain), and that the auditory thalamus sends that information immediately to the amygdala. The critical point here is that the amygdala is responsible for much *autonomic* behaviour – that is, behaviour such as breathing, blinking, etc., which occur without our conscious control. So when the twig snaps, the amygdala will very likely cause us to freeze. Freezing is one of the primary responses to the fear of perceived danger – and we will respond by freezing at the sound BEFORE we *think* about freezing. Now why is this important?

First, in survival terms it's important because it would be better for us to freeze and assess our reactions to a possible attacker than to simply think about it – and thinking about it is precisely what we would do should we take the 'high cortical road'. As LeDoux puts it:

From the point of view of survival, it is better to respond to potentially dangerous events as if they were in fact the real thing than to fail to respond. The cost of treating a [twig] as [an attacker] is less, in the long run, than the cost of treating [an attacker] as a [twig].[12]

Second, in acting terms it may help us to understand why sometimes it feels as if emotion or the memory of emotion is 'stored' in the body – because at given times, and under given circumstances a subconscious brain process generates immediate physical responses prior to involving the thinking parts of the brain. Third, I think LeDoux's research goes some way toward proving what I would wager that actors have known for some time: that the traditional philosophical problem of the mind/body split is unsustainable – particularly in terms of the mind and the body being composed of different substances. If LeDoux's research teaches us nothing else it certainly demonstrates that when brain processes generate physical responses prior to conscious ones, it gets very difficult to determine how, exactly, we can theorize any distinction between mind and body.

But fear isn't the only emotion that 'knows' something before the conscious brain kicks in. In an experiment called the Iowa Gambling Task, Antonio Damasio and Antoine Bechara created a gambling game in which players were given four decks of cards and $2,000. The decks weren't distributed randomly though – they were set up so that two decks had many high payout cards but also much bigger penalties (as much as $1,250), and two decks had more low payout cards ($50) with very few penalty cards. Choosing from the latter deck exclusively would mean that the gambler would come out significantly ahead. Damasio and Bechara set the experiment up with the 'gamblers' heads and hands wired to machines that measured skin responses (of a type which signal anxiety or nervousness). It took the gamblers heads between 50 to 80 card draws to begin to draw only from the 'safe' decks, and also to explain why they were doing so. But there was an interesting twist to the tale: it took the 'gamblers' hands only an average of ten card draws to show signs of nervousness (skin response) when reaching for the dangerous decks. Clearly the 'gamblers'' emotions knew what was happening long before their conscious, logical processes caught up.[13]

Over the last two decades the area of emotion in cognitive science research has drawn much new interest, and this might be explained by a fairly revolutionary way of looking at what emotion IS. Le Doux explains:

> Like psychologists, brain researchers were strongly influenced by the emergence of cognitive science, and emotions were not part of the cognitive game plan. Emotions seemed more a matter of mental *content* than of mental *processing*, and were not pursued by those interested in the thinking process.[14]

This last sentence is significant because it points to a very fundamental change in ways of thinking about emotion. What LeDoux is saying is that recent research has revealed that emotion is *not* simply a question of content, but is instead more deeply connected to our actual cognitive processes. In other words, emotion is an instrument of cognition. This idea challenges much of what we read in acting theory, which has traditionally seen emotion and feeling as interchangeable, and largely as aspects of cognitive CONTENT, however mercurial and evanescent. But then again, perhaps theorists like Stanislavski, Chekhov and Meisner were far ahead of these advances in cognitive science when they sensed, early on, that the emotional part of acting could not be reached through the 'reasoning' part of the brain. Perhaps the question I asked earlier (does the fact that some emotion is generated unconsciously determine the likelihood of an actor's ability to represent that emotion with fidelity?) is the one that really challenges us. Even when, as actors, we get all the physical characteristics of terror right – can we represent that state faithfully if the proven internal generator of the state of terror is unconscious?

During a performance of *A Little Night Music,* I remember being on stage with Jennifer, a very young actress. I was playing Madame Armfeldt, and Jennifer was playing my granddaughter. I was directed to play the scene with a deck of cards – playing solitaire as I talked with the young girl. We had reached the end of the scene, at which point Desiree was to come stage and my granddaughter was to jump up to greet her. The moment for Desiree's entrance came and went, but no one appeared. Jennifer turned upstage to look at me and in those few seconds of silence I could sense her palpable fear. I picked up the cards and asked her if she would like to know how to tell fortunes with a deck of cards. 'Oh yes, Grandmother!' she replied, and I rambled on about cards, particularly the queen and king of hearts long enough for the actress playing Desiree to finally make her entrance (which she had missed by talking with the stage manager).

In the dressing room afterward we compared our experience of the scene and Jennifer related that she was so frightened that all she could remember was her mind going completely blank and the sound of her heart beating in her ears. She swore she didn't even remember saying 'Oh yes Grandmother!' Because one of my earliest experiences as an actress was working in a rep company where the one of the leading actors was an alcoholic (and therefore highly prone not only to forget lines but once or twice even forgetting which play he was in!!) I wasn't particularly frightened by being left on stage and having to improvise. I was quite used to doing so at that point and I simply remember thinking that there was a limit to the things one could do with a deck of cards. Looking back on this now it seems to me that Jennifer's response probably came straight from the thalamic region of her brain: from amygdala directly to body, where her fear responses (including freezing, increased heart rate, galvanic skin responses like raised temperature) became the only things she could remember afterward.

The neutral walk

One of the exercises I regularly do with actors is the 'neutral walk'. It's pretty common and certainly didn't originate with me. If you haven't encountered it, the basic idea is to ask all the actors to walk across the studio in groups of four or five. The direction given to the actors is to try and walk in a way that is absolutely neutral – in other words, to give nothing whatever away about yourself through this walk across the room. We learn a number of things in doing this – both in the walking and in the observing. The first is that it's very, very difficult indeed to do something like a 'neutral' walk that is being watched by others. It's difficult for the actors because the direction to walk in a 'neutral' way isn't much of a direction – there's not much for the actor to concentrate on DOING, there's only something for the actor to concentrate on NOT doing. In other words, the actors are playing a *negative* intention – a thing which most actors and directors will agree is not as powerful or as pleasurable as playing a *positive* intention.

The experience usually results in the actors trying the walk across the room two or three times and then concluding that it was an uncomfortable experience. While watching others, most of the actors are certain that they can see traces of something – anger, defiance, sorrow, fear. Of course the 'walking' actors deny all this. In other words, we learn that there probably is no 'neutral' state for an actor, even though many of us have worked with directors and teachers who talk to us about working toward a kind of 'neutrality' on stage. I have an innate sympathy with this instruction – especially since it is generally employed in cases where actors have extremely strong physical mannerisms that invade all of their work from Shakespeare to contemporary realism. But in practice, it's a pretty tough thing to achieve. This is because, like the neutral walk, the actor trying to achieve a neutral state is going to find 'being neutral' very difficult. What makes the 'neutral' attempts so interesting to me, in light of the brain science behind them, is that there is a very good reason why suddenly being asked to walk in a neutral way is so difficult. It's the same reason why, when we are asked to smile for the camera, we so often produce an uncomfortable looking grimace.

When we smile with pleasure at the sight of someone we love, that smile is produced by a very particular area of the brain (the anterior cingulate, the basal ganglia), which direct a series of complex signals to the facial muscles, producing a 'natural' smile. When someone asks you to smile (or, indeed to produce a 'neutral' walk or assume a 'neutral' stance), a distinctly different part of the brain is engaged – you will respond to their instruction with the auditory cortex and the language centres of the brain. Once received there, signals are sent to the motor cortex, which is the area of the brain that generates VOLUNTARY physical response. As noted brain researcher V.S. Ramachandran points out:

> Despite its apparent simplicity [natural] smiling involves the careful orchestration of dozens of tiny muscles in the appropriate sequence. As far as the motor cortex (which is not specialized for generating natural smiles) is concerned, this is as complex a feat

as playing Rachmaninoff though it never had lessons, and therefore it fails utterly. Your [requested] smile is forced, tight, unnatural.[15]

No doubt our difficulty with the 'neutral' walk and many other similar directions (from directors!) can be explained by the very different ways in which we process 'natural' movement and directed or requested movement. Surely brain area distinction is responsible for most of the stilted, forced and unnatural work we see in actors who are 'squeezing out' their emotions:

> Try to feel it. And I would try, and strain all my strength, and tie myself into knots and squeeze my voice til I grew hoarse and blood would rush to my head and my eyes would pop out of their sockets, while I tried to do what was required of me until I grew exhausted.[16]

Here, Stanislavski was responding to the direction: 'try to feel it' through the reasoning area of his brain and attempting to feel or move in a VOLUNTARY rather than an involuntary way. And there is a great distinction between the ways in which our brains process voluntary and involuntary movement – this difference is at the heart of what makes natural and 'unnatural' movement. As Damasio points out:

> We cannot mimic easily what the anterior cingulate can achieve effortlessly; we have no easy neural route to exert volitional control over the anterior cingulate. In order to smile 'naturally' you have only a few options: learn to act, or get somebody to tickle you or tell you a good joke.[17]

I find it interesting to contemplate what kind of actor Damasio is referring to here and where they might have trained. Surely Damasio's actor must be the kind whose imagination is so strong that they are able to represent fictional situations (and fictional emotional stimulus) to their own minds as real situations (or real emotional stimulus) with such strength that *natural* neural processing leads to *natural* emotional responses.

But I digress. We know actors who can 'fake' things pretty well though, so couldn't we just fake a 'natural' smile? The answer would seem to be yes, but ONLY if we run the smile through the correct brain pathways (such as Damasio's ideal actor would), because there are muscles involved in, for example, the 'natural' smile that we can't control:

> The contractions of the orbicularis oculi, which raise the cheek and gather the skin inward from around the eye socket, occur more frequently in genuine than in simulated happiness.[18]

As Damasio points out, this muscle (orbicularis oculi) cannot be controlled voluntarily.

While working on this chapter I happened to see an interview on television with actor Jon Hamm, who plays Don Draper on the television series Mad Men – a series I'm a real fan of and try to catch whenever I can. Watching Hamm's face during the interview was fascinating for me since I was aware that while he spoke his face looked physically very different from the face of his Don Draper character. Some of the interviewer's questions allowed him to talk about how 'surreal' the success of the show has been for him and how little he feels he has changed since the days when he was just another out of work actor waiting tables in Hollywood. Such memories inspired a kind of goofy (natural) smile from Hamm. The interview was intercut with scenes from the show in which his Don Draper character smiled.

Courtesy of Verena Von Pfetten.

And there, quite plainly written in his face, was the way in which a natural smile works muscles in the face so distinctly that they can literally change the way in which the face looks. It wasn't as if I wouldn't have recognized Jon Hamm in the interview as the actor who plays Don Draper, but he looked so different from his Mad Men character when he smiled that if someone had introduced him as Jon Hamm's brother I would not have been surprised.

But there is something even more interesting to look at in the complexity of the science around the voluntary and the involuntary control of muscles.

If we go back to the idea that gets talked about a lot in acting classes – the idea that the body 'stores' memory – what is it that we're actually talking about? In his book *Descartes' Error*, Antonio Damasio looks closely at the question. In trying to determine whether there is any evidence to support the claim that the body is actually able to *cause* feelings, he recounts a study done by Paul Ekman:

When he gave normal experimental subjects instructions on how to move their facial muscles, in effect 'composing' a specific emotional expression on the subjects' faces without their knowing his purpose, the result was that the subjects experienced a feeling appropriate to the expression. For instance, a roughly and incompletely composed happy facial expression led to the subjects' experiencing 'happiness', an angry facial expression to their experiencing 'anger', and so on. This is impressive if we consider that the subjects could perceive only sketchy, fragmentary facial postures, and that since they were neither perceiving nor evaluating any real situation that might trigger an emotion, their bodies were not exhibiting, at the outset, the viscera profile that accompanies a certain emotion.[19]

Damasio concludes that Ekman's experiment suggests either that a part of the body state we associate with a given emotion is enough to produce the appropriate feeling OR that this part of a body state triggers the remaining part of the body state, and *that* produces feeling. But there's an interesting kicker in his observation, because it turns out in these experiments that the subjects are not entirely successful in 'fooling the brain'. Because the subjects in Ekman's experiment were aware that 'they were not happy or angry at any particular thing' such expressions as smiles would have been generated differently than the 'natural' smile alluded to above. Damasio comes to a remarkable conclusion from this set of evidence:

> We cannot fool ourselves any more than we can fool others when we smile politely…This may also be the very good reason why great actors, opera singers, and others manage to survive the simulation of exalted emotions they regularly put themselves through, without losing control.[20]

From time to time in acting classes I conduct an exercise which I hope demonstrates the relationship between the body and emotion by turning out all the lights and asking students to just relax and listen. I then ask them to completely clear their minds, to approach the exercise with a kind of scientific objectivity and to go through a purely physical memory with me. I ask them to try to remember everything that they can about what happens to their bodies when they cry – but with the proviso that they should not cry or to think about anything sad. We start with the eyes, and I suggest any number of things that may happen to their eyes when they cry – perhaps a stinging sensation, a sense of blurry, wateriness, or a prickly sensation. I ask them to try and imagine this as strongly as they can, and they are free to physically do things if it helps to strengthen their imagination. We move on to the stomach, and feelings of tightness, or contraction, or leadenness, etc. We go through the breath and how it is working – shallow or tight or fast or high – again, I tell them they are free to try these things if it helps their physical memory. We then consider the feeling in our throats – tense, tight, slightly aching, etc., and the taste in our mouths, which can be slightly coppery, or bitter, or salty, etc. I always try to keep everyone's focus on the physical imagination and completely away from any emotional memory or physical reenactment, but actors being what they are, most of the students will actually begin to recreate physically what happens when they cry.

Invariably, of course, we must take a break right after this exercise, go get some coffee or go outside just to shake off our feelings. I am never surprised to find that many of them will be crying when the lights come on, and many of them will be incredibly sad. Although none of them will be able to give me a reason why they are crying or feeling sad, they are simply, suddenly, very, very sad…

How I wish that Damasio could take some electrophysiological readings of my acting students during the 'crying' exercise above. It would be interesting to know if students would say that they were fooling themselves, or attempting to fool themselves, but as we'll consider later, there are many weaknesses in the area of 'self-reporting' where emotion is concerned, so perhaps these reports wouldn't yield the knowledge we might hope.[21] I think Damasio's most controversial comment is his conclusion about opera singer Regina Resnik: 'Nobody would have guessed, watching and hearing her, that she was just bodily "portraying" emotion rather than "feeling" it'[22] – because this puts Damasio firmly back into Diderot's territory, and suggests that he thinks bodily 'portrayal' would not lead to the feeling of emotion. This would be a particularly unsympathetic conclusion to draw about Damasio, as further reading of his remarkable work in books like *Looking for Spinoza* certainly proves that his whole research project has been about demonstrating the intricate and utterly intertwined relationship between body and feeling and he goes on the define feeling as quite distinct from emotion:

> My hypothesis, then, presented in the form of a provisional definition, is that *a feeling is the perception of a certain state of the body along with the perception of a certain mode of thinking and of thoughts with certain themes*…If feelings were merely cluster of thoughts with certain themes, how could they be distinguished from any other thoughts?…My view is that feelings are functionally distinctive because their essence consists of the thoughts that represent the body involved in a reactive process. Remove that essence and the notion of feeling vanishes.[23]

Damasio's research also leads him to conclude that Rodgers and Hammerstein were not far off when they concluded – in their song *Whistle a Happy Tune* – that a demonstration of feeling through the body leads to a concomitant state of feeling: 'Psychologically unmotivated and "acted" emotional expressions have the power to cause feeling. The expressions conjure up the feelings and the kinds of thoughts that have been learned as consonant with those emotional expressions.'[24] This probably puts us immediately in mind of the differences between Stanislavski's careful attention to the building up of psychological detail and Michael Chekhov's 'Emotional Gesture'. Chekhov had a firm belief in the power of the relationship between movement, the body and psychological states (and so, perhaps, did the old schools of rhetoric and elocution who taught facial expression and stance). Of course, when we look at such things now – old works like Henry Siddons' *Practical Illustrations of Rhetorical Gestures* – filled with drawings of actors holding extreme examples of heroic or tragic poses, we might find them incredibly naive and out of date. But the fact is, ironically, these old rhetorical gestures and their proponents may have been on to something that it's taken some time for science to work out – which is that gesture, stance and expression can lead to feeling.

In his book, *Emotions Revealed*, Paul Ekman includes a photograph of a woman whose young son has been found tortured and murdered. The whole aspect of her intense, frozen grief is similar to the kinds of horrific expressions found in old books like Siddons', and Ekman goes on to help us try and achieve this precise look of grief, referencing the picture of the grief-stricken woman:

1. Drop your mouth open.
2. Pull the corners of your lips down.
3. While you hold those lip corners down, try now to raise your cheeks, as if you are squinting. This pulls against the lip corners.
4. Maintain this tension between the raised cheeks and the lip corners pulling down.
5. Let your eyes look downward and your upper eyelids droop.[25]

Like Damasio, what Ekman found – quite to his surprise – was that in imitating this expression of grief both he and his fellow researchers began to find that their own emotional states were affected. (Go on – try it. It made my skin tingle and my eyes go watery, and I felt a sudden sense of sadness.)

Of course this general kind of feeling in itself is not precisely the stuff of great acting, but I would argue that it might do every bit as much as Meisner's 'imaginary preparation', where he advises actors to 'go into a dark corner if you can find one' and either 'daydream' or imagine an emotional state that is appropriate to the beginning of a scene.[26]

Emotion and imagination

There has of course been research done in the area of 'felt' emotion and 'simulated' emotion. Perhaps most interesting for us is work done by a team of two Canadian researchers, Pierre Gosselin and Gilles Kirouac, using students from the Conservatory of Dramatic Arts in Quebec. Gosselin and Kirouac's study was specifically centred on how feeling is 'encoded' in facial expression and they wanted particularly to know if an observer could tell by looking at a video of facial expressions whether the emotion 'encoded' there was 'felt' or whether it was 'not felt' – in other words, this was a kind of modern-day scientific approach to Diderot's old question about the sincerity of displayed emotion:

Each scenario had to be acted out in two ways. In the EFE condition [their shorthand for actually 'felt' emotion], actors were instructed to use their training in the Stanislawski technique to feel the emotion they had to portray in the scenario. In the EUE condition [their shorthand for portraying emotion without actually 'feeling' it – in other words, faking it], they were instructed to portray the emotion without feeling it.[27]

In their various pollings of the observers there were some interesting responses. Before the experiment began, Kirouac and Gosselin predicted that the facial expressions produced by genuine emotional displays by non-actors would be close to the facial expression produced by the method actors' displays, and that the method actors' facial expressions would strike observers as 'genuine'. But on average, over all the categories considered, this prediction was right in only three cases: in the cases of happiness, sadness and anger.

The method actors did not fool the observers as often in the case of the other three emotions tested: fear, surprise and disgust. This leads Kirouac and Gosselin to conclude that 'although the Stanislawski technique has a fascinating effect on the production of realistic expressions, *this effect varies according to the emotion*'.[28]

I think there are a number of things to set us thinking here.[29] The first might be to question whether there are some fundamental differences in the kinds of emotions that they tested. If we look closely at their list: happiness, sadness, anger, fear, surprise and disgust, it seems to me that the latter three (the ones the actors found tougher to simulate in terms of facial expression) are what my friend Clare – who is a GP – calls 'straight to the amygdala' emotions. In other words, I can imagine those three (fear, surprise, disgust), when experienced genuinely, to be immediately and powerfully *embodied* – that is to say, 'taking the low road' in LeDoux's terminology, and resulting in emotions that are strongly felt in the body just immediately prior to our thinking about them. Whereas the other three emotions tested, happiness, sadness, anger – while all still clearly felt in the body – strike me as possibly more 'slow burn' emotions, which involve some thinking. This distinction is purely my own, and only a common sense observation, but if I am right, might it mean that the first three 'straight to the amygdala' emotions elicit body responses that are coming from natural neural pathways (where they stimulate involuntary responses) and are therefore harder to reproduce through the voluntary channels? Might it be that happiness, sadness and anger (the ones which might more readily involve the reasoning areas of the brain) can be more convincingly generated voluntarily? If this theory is right, it could account for why the actors using Stanislavski technique could fool people in only some cases. And if this is true, *is it then the case that actors should be meditating on **the differences** between emotions, rather than seeing all emotions in a rather 'homogenous' manner?*

Ironically, one of the ways in which categories of emotion have been tested has been precisely in the asking of subjects to do some exercises straight out of Acting 101. In his book, *The Primordial Emotions*, Derek Denton outlines the evolution of emotion from the primordial (such things as thirst, hunger, hunger for air, etc.) to the more complex. He describes the work of Antonio Damasio on 'self-generated' emotional states:

The subject is asked to recall and re-experience…emotional episodes. The point is that neurophysical organisation of the brain permits this to be done. The emotional concomitants of the memory accessed or the scene imagined can represent a very powerful experience. *By significant contrast it would seem that there is very limited capacity, if any, of the brain to be able to summon up to consciousness a full experience of the interoceptor[30] generated sensations such as choking with breathlessness.* Similarly there is limited capacity, at will, to bring to mind the full sensation of thirst [Denton does not count simple recall of physical sensation such as dryness of mouth, but is talking of the more holistic physical state of thirst]. The same may be said for conjuring up in the mind the full experience of being hungry or suffering severe pain arising from the skin.[31]

I would venture to guess that most of us would never think of thirst, hunger or pain as emotional states, although we would certainly know that they entail emotional states. The very fact that Denton and others consider these fundamental human needs to be 'emotions' reflects the ways in which emotion has recently come to be seen as something much more physical and elemental than simple 'mental content'. Denton, like Damasio clearly sees emotion as providing 'a natural means for the brain and mind to evaluate the environment within and around the organism, and respond accordingly and adaptively'.[32] But Denton's implication here is that there is something very similar between fear and hunger, anger and thirst, disgust and pain, and is specific to the fact that all these things are experienced as powerful physical sensations. His theory seems to be that a 'full experience' of fear, anger and disgust CAN be summoned up to consciousness. The question that remains for the actor is whether this is really true. Denton's challenge is an interesting one (I'm sure many actors, like me, will now try to summon up the 'full sensation of thirst'), because it gives us the chance to reflect on whether anger or fear do not pose exactly the same problems in simulation as thirst or hunger – in other words, I am willing to argue that the *full experience* of ANY of these states is unlikely ever to occur in a simulation.

Denton's elaborates on these 'primordial' emotions – which in more common sense language I think we might call instincts – and why they are more difficult to 'fake'. Each of these instincts, from sexual gratification to the overwhelming need for salt are connected very clearly to our survival. An ability thoroughly to re-present them to ourselves and our bodies means that we could in a very extreme case 'fool' ourselves into disaster of one sort or another, by perhaps becoming incapable of distinguishing a true hunger for food or air from a well-rehearsed and performed one.

But Denton's category of primordial emotions is distinct from that which most researchers consider primary (or universally recognized) emotions which, as we've seen, vary, but tend to come down to the six we considered above: happiness, sadness, fear, anger, surprise and disgust. There doesn't appear to be much agreement on which are primary, or secondary emotions, but let's agree for the sake of our analysis to call these six primary. And the central fact of these six primary emotions, Denton points out, 'is that they are hard-wired, and involve the basal areas – the arousal systems – just as the [primordial or "instinct"] emotions do'.[33]

If it is the case that we can successfully imagine, or 'self-generate' these primary emotions *to a degree,* and also that this successful re-imagining in the brain can trigger some bodily response – how do we do this?

Like the town of Brigadoon...

There is a story told (and written) often about the actress Eleanora Duse. It was originally commented upon by George Bernard Shaw and this is Sandy Meisner's (charmingly 'New York') version of it:

> Duse played in a play called Magda. There's a scene in the last act. When she's a young girl she has an affair with a guy from the same village, and she has a child by him. Twenty-five years later, or thereabouts, she comes back to visit her family who live in this town, and her ex-lover comes to call on her. She accepts his flowers – I got this from Shaw – and they sit and talk. All of a sudden she realizes that she's blushing and it gets so bad that she drops her head and hides her face in embarrassment. Now that's a piece of realistic acting! And Shaw confesses to a certain professional curiosity as to whether it happens every time she plays that part. It doesn't. But that blush is the epitome of living truthfully under imaginary circumstances, which is my definition of good acting. That blush came out of *her*. She was a genius![34]

So what can we say was going on with Eleanora Duse? Like the muscles controlling the orbicularis oculi, blushing is an *autonomic* response – in other words, it happens, but we can't **make** it happen. These responses, like breathing, blinking, etc. are regulated in a part of the brain that works beneath conscious control. So clearly in this case, Duse demonstrated the strength of her 'simulated' emotion. *But if her simulated emotion led to autonomic blushing, surely it cannot be said to have been simulated at all.*

If we know that the strength of our imaginations in recalling sensations of fear, anger, surprise, etc. can be powerful enough to trigger bodily responses, can we say with some certainty that it was this imaginary recall that was behind Duse's blush? Well, of course, imagination will have played a very significant part, but how it played that part all depends on what kind of actor Duse was.

Let's take two possible approaches from Uta Hagen and Sandy Meisner. The scene required of Duse some pretty complicated emotion – guilt, shame, pleasure, etc. If Duse had been working with Hagen, she might have searched her own past to recall a moment when she had felt something like this complex emotion strongly. She would then not have concentrated on the whole of that moment, but would have 'distilled' the memory down to an object – let us say a valentine's card. This object would then serve to trigger emotions like guilt, shame, pleasure, etc. If she had been working with Sandy Meisner he would have advised her to 'prepare' herself privately before beginning the scene. She could recall any number of her own past similar emotional situations and then perhaps exaggerate them or simply recall them as they were in order to bring herself into the scene with a sense of emotional reality.

But if she *was* using a technique like Uta Hagen's 'trigger objects' or Sandy Meisner's emotional fantasies, in which the actor is 'substituting' an emotional memory, or daydreaming about an emotional state prior to acting, rather than trying to allow the circumstances of the a play to induce a real emotion, then Duse's feat of emotional recall is impressive indeed.

'Substitution' or memory techniques require that the actor (let us say a young woman playing Blanche DuBois in *Streetcar Named Desire*) attempts to portray Blanche's fear of being assaulted by Stanley by flooding the mind with memory. Some actors find this kind of approach helpful – but I admit I've always discouraged it. This is because that when using Hagen's technique, at a critical point in Williams' play, the actor playing Blanche must be imagining a 'trigger' object related to a moment in her own life – an activity that is bound to remove the actor's much-needed attention from the task of fully taking part in pretending to be Blanche, afraid of Stanley. In Meisner's version, he advises actors to recall something that will put them in an emotional mood conducive to the scene *prior* to the playing of it. It seems to me that this activity, while perhaps 'priming' the emotional pump, is almost certainly going to force the actor into a kind of 'general' emotional state – in this case fear – which has originated from recalled circumstances that have nothing to do with Stanley Kowalski and – worse – could create a 'moody' and general performance.

Whichever way we decide to remember, it appears that we are often highly unreliable witnesses with regard to the memory of our own emotion:

> Daniel Kahneman and colleagues have shown, in a variety of ways, that what we remember about an emotional experience is an imperfect reflection of what was actually experienced. For one thing, people tend to remember how they felt at the end of an emotional episode rather than how they felt about the whole episode…Studies by Elizabeth Loftus and others have shown that memories of emotional experiences are often significantly different from what actually happened during them. She reports many instances in which vivid memories of crime scenes turn out to be inaccurate, if unintentionally so; sometimes again, unintentionally, they are completely fabricated.[35]

Of course, the accuracy of our memories is not at issue here – merely that we have some to use. But the inaccuracy that research has uncovered is interesting in that it demonstrates the strange and sometimes surprising relationship between emotion, cognition and memory, and certainly makes me wonder about the amount of time and energy that has been spent teaching, learning and debating the whole area of conscious emotional memory retrieval in acting work.

Meisner was not terribly worried about the emotional part of acting – which I think makes his work rather refreshing: 'If you have it [emotion], it infects you and the audience. If you don't have it – like Helen Hayes – don't bother; just say the lines as truthfully as you are capable of doing. You can't fake emotion.'[36] But either of these approaches, it seems to me, will constitute serious obstacles to the conditions necessary for an actor to enter imaginatively into the circumstances of the play, and to allow that imagination to make a fictional experience feel real enough to trigger some emotion naturally.

But suppose we DO subscribe to the 'substitution' school of emotional portrayal in acting – how does such substitution work? We know, of course, that emotional memory can trigger all kinds of things, including bodily responses. This has been proven by researchers like LeDoux and Damasio, and by any number of acting teachers up and down the land. But what actually happens when we recall emotion, or represent it in our minds?

The fact is that, if you're not an actor, most of the 'reliving' of emotional circumstances probably occurs unconsciously. Researchers distinguish two kinds of emotional triggers – 'natural' and 'learned'. Natural triggers occur, for example, at the sight of a predator. Research has shown that some of our responses to predators are hard-wired. This means that at first sight of an enormous alligator, our natural 'fear' trigger kicks in, even if we've never seen an enormous alligator before. And with it comes a host of physiological changes – increased heart rate, probable 'freeze' reaction, skin temperature changes, possible hair standing on end, etc. Along with natural triggers are 'learned' triggers – these can be lodged in our brains both consciously and unconsciously. For example, let us say that when you saw the alligator, someone in a nearby 4x4 truck honked the horn repeatedly in an attempt to scare the alligator away. If you survived the attack, it's likely that at some point, many years later, a car alarm of a repeatedly honking horn might suddenly bring back the conscious memory of the near-fatal alligator episode. However, research has shown that even if you DON'T remember the horn honking at the time of facing the alligator (and let's face it, at the moment you probably did have other things to pay attention to), your brain DOES remember it. And in this case it might send you into a mild panic, accompanied by increased heart rate, body temperature changes, etc., although you wouldn't know why this was happening. If you think about it, what Uta Hagen was talking about was the 'learned' emotional trigger. In her system, if you wanted to induce Blanche DuBois' fear, you would not focus on the alligator – instead you would identify a 'trigger object' – in this case a car horn.

Things get even more interesting when you consider some very recent research into fear responses in humans. A group of subjects were shown pictures both consciously (they were able to look at the scary pictures and reflect on them) and unconsciously (the pictures were shown so rapidly that some of the volunteers did not even report seeing them).[37] The results were that viewing frightening pictures activated two completely different brain pathways – one that was conscious and one that was unconscious. But the more startling conclusion is that the unconscious fear is more 'dramatic' and anxiety-producing than the conscious fear. This is because in cases of conscious fear the subjects can reflect on whether the pictures truly pose a threat or not. But the unconscious fear response does not have recourse to this kind of 'higher' reasoning – and therefore potentially remains within us – like an unsettling feeling.

But what happens when we are trying to follow Sandy Meisner's advice and consciously trying to recall an emotion? In order to understand that we probably need to look at what happens when we are trying to recall *anything*. As we've discovered in the case of emotion, it's certainly not as straightforward as it might seem. In the first instance our ability to retrieve memory is 'cue-dependent' (and no, I'm not talking about cue lines – but the principle is roughly the same – our ability to remember our lines often depends critically on our partner's ability to remember theirs). Cue-dependency is why, in either Hagen or Meisner's systems, it isn't enough to simply try to remember feeling sad. We can do this, but without specific cues (the death of the dear old family cat for example), general or vague 'attempts at retrieval are less likely to produce pattern completion'.[38] But what happens when we have the right cue (dead cat) – how do we actually summon up the memory of sadness?

In this case, the cue (dead cat) might immediately trigger in our minds a specific thing, perhaps the face of the cat. But of course, brains don't necessarily store 'pictures' the way we do. The image of the cat's face is distributed all over:

> There is not just one hidden formula for this reconstruction. [The dead cat] does not exist in one single site of your brain – she is distributed all over it in the form of many dispositional representations. When you conjure up remembrance of [the dead cat]…she surfaces in various early cortices (visual, auditory, and so on).[39]

These little 'building blocks' (okay, it's not exactly like that but the full explanation of 'dispositional representations' is more information than we need at this point!) of the memory's imagination exist in our brains in an ever-ready state, waiting to be called to service. Subject, as Damasio says, 'to activation, like the town of Brigadoon'.[40]

It's clear that some cues are better for memory than others. Context has a strong influence on memory, which is why you will recall more things about your childhood if you actually go to visit the old family home than you will just by sitting in a café and thinking about your childhood. But context also affects retrieval in another way. In one of their more frisky moments, a set of researchers decided to test a group of people by giving their test subjects two sets of words to learn. The subjects learned the words first under the influence of marijuana and were given a second set to learn without the influence of marijuana. The researchers found that the words learned under the influence of marijuana were best remembered if the subjects were once again given marijuana. And the words learned sober were best remembered sober. The conclusion is that the circumstances themselves in which we learn play a part in the retrieval of memory. This means that if you learn a set of information (let us say, your lines in a play) in a given context (let us say your bedroom), you will recall that set of information most successfully in the same context – i.e., your bedroom.

This begins to clarify many things for me – not the least being why we 'lose' lines in a studio rehearsal that we had down so perfectly when we rehearsed them in our bedrooms last night. It also begins to make clear why I always felt that asking actors to learn lines in rehearsal (insofar as they could) always seemed to me to be the way to keep the text in the actors' heads. It seems that aspects of our internal states can also affect retrieval. In other words, something we've learned in a particular emotional state will come back to us again most clearly when we are in that same emotional state again. Which is why changes in direction or interpretation during the rehearsal process so often causes actors to lose whole chunks of text.

But given all these things, how is the average rehearsal process affecting the way we learn? Doesn't this mean that if we (as Hagen and Meisner suggest we do) attempt emotional recall that is centred *outside* the given circumstances of the play – whether in rehearsal or performance – we're taking something of a risk? I would argue that it does. Research suggests that keeping context, *both internal and external*, as consistent as possible significantly aids memory. This is not to say that actors don't find themselves in different environments often during a rehearsal process (at their worst, a typical drama conservatoire timetable will shunt you around in up to three or four different environments in a single week!), but presumably there are enough other familiar contextual clues (the same actors, the same furniture, the same set configuration, etc.) to help the rehearsing actor retrieve both text and action. It is, however, a good reason for directors to militate against those dreadful timetables!

But what about the actor who isn't summoning up emotion by imagining past circumstances, but is instead 'living' the circumstances of the play in a fully imagined way? What can we know about the strength of imaginary emotional responses? Well, in the first place we know that they can induce bodily response. Damasio's tests proved this conclusively, as his subjects were being asked to imagine ('self-generate') emotional states, and their brain activity was measurable. We don't know exactly how imagined, or 'self-generated' emotional activity would compare exactly with the real thing (at least I've not been able to discover any research on this), but common sense would suggest to us that imagined emotion would be weaker than the real thing – although the case of Duse's blush might challenge this suggestion. The real thing – as we've considered earlier – can trigger subcortical activity between thalamus and amygdala and the body, setting off involuntary bodily survival alarms before the reasoning part of the brain kicks in. But is it likely that an actor would ever, truly lose contact with that reasoning part of the brain?

In graduate school I did a scene from John Ford's *'Tis Pity She's a Whore* in an advanced class in classical acting. It remained in my memory for many years. In rehearsals the actor I worked with (we'll call him James) played Soranzo and I played Annabella. We did the scene in which he discovers that Annabella is pregnant and the stage direction reads: 'He hales her up and down', and James' line was: 'Thus will I pull thy hair and thus I'll drag thy lust-be-leper'd body through the dust'. In rehearsals we went through some simple movements that looked threatening but in fact were not. In our class performance, however, things changed. I remember seeing James walk toward me as he began the line, and I realized that he looked very different than he had at that point in any of our rehearsals. Instead of the simple push and drag we had rehearsed (in which his part was to push lightly and my part was to stagger backward as if stunned by the sheer strength of the push), James pushed with the full force of his body – which was considerable as he was a body-builder who was at least 6 feet tall and probably weighed somewhere in the region of 225 lbs. I staggered backward in what would have looked like a particularly nifty bit of physical acting (had I been acting) and when I looked up again he grabbed me around the throat, instead of by the hair as rehearsed. At that point both classmates and I realised that James had lost control and thanks to some pretty quick efforts he was pulled away and immediately began to apologize profusely both to me and to the acting teacher.

It was a scary moment and it was a singular one. In the 30-odd years I've been involved in theatre it is the only time I've ever seen an actor really, genuinely lose control while acting in a manner that was clearly dangerous. I've seen actors break things in their simulated rage, I've seen them kick furniture across the stage and rip costumes, I've seen them knock things over in stage fights, and I've seen stage choreography go wrong in ways that resulted in unintentional injury. But I've never seen anyone actually attack another actor in the middle of the scene. While it certainly shook me up, I remained more curious than hurt and remain so now. James was a 'gentle' giant of an actor who was certainly strong (he went on to play in *Conan the Barbarian!*), but usually presented himself as a gentle person. He was not given to temper or even to the usual drama school jealousies/bitchiness. So what happened?

Without reconstructing the context it's impossible to know, of course. But given the fact that there are learned emotional 'triggers' that can operate beneath the reach of our conscious apprehension – might there have been something, either in the room, in a sound, in a given way that I or someone else looked at him in a very heightened emotional scene that set off one of these subconscious 'triggers'? Might it be that unconscious emotional memory is strong enough to temporarily override the reasoning part of the brain when in the process of acting?

We know that one of Michael Chekhov's great worries was that actors who employed Stanislavski's technique would grow hysterical ('When we are possessed by the part and almost kill our partners and break chairs, etc. then we are not free and it is not art but hysterics'[41]). Antonio Damasio, similarly, wonders how it is that actors are able to avoid giving way fully to their emotions, but decides that as long as actors' emotions are 'portrayed' and not 'felt', then we are 'generating different patterns of brain waves' and that it is this 'simulation of exalted emotions' that allows actors to work without losing control.[42] And yet, on the whole, we would have to agree that it's far from common to witness actors actually losing control of their emotions. Aren't the more interesting questions actually WHY – in these rare cases – actors *do* lose control? And why that loss of control doesn't happen more often?

Perhaps one answer lies in the pretty frequent involvement of the prefrontal cortex area of the brain, whose tasks, along with thinking and reasoning, are to keep the amygdala under control. In the case of consciously retrieving emotion (Stanislavski, Hagen, Meisner, etc.) it seems pretty clear that the very act of *deciding* to retrieve emotion would be one that involves the thinking and reasoning areas of the brain – in other words, we are responding to our own metacognitive direction to 'go fetch' an emotional memory which (like the photographer's request to 'smile!') is going to be processed first by the higher cortex. As V.S. Ramachandran points out, we don't laugh when we try to tickle ourselves – this is because 'your brain knows you're sending the command'.[43] In just the same way, as actors we know more or less what is coming. We are self-generating, reasoning and processing in ways that are already different from our everyday cognitive functions.

This may be connected to what Gregory Bateson would call a 'frame' – a kind of mental space in which we bracket 'play' off from the real world. 'Feelings expressed within this context of the playing frame would have a different meaning compared...to emotions in life outside of the frame.'[44] I am guessing (there is no research to draw on here) that this in itself would prevent the kind of fully embodied (and involuntary) emotional response that true fear, rage or disgust would, and would possibly therefore also create slightly weakened signals to the other parts of the body than true emotion would. The actor's remembered emotion then, even if embodied in our imagined state, might naturally be less potent than it would be had the stimulus come at us externally in the shape of a snake, an alligator or someone with a gun. **But perhaps there are actors (Duse) whose imaginations are so strong that this distinction is not so prominent?**

Still, if we look at the structure of the brain, it is curious that actors don't lose more battles in their imagined emotional states – not least because frequently, in the struggle between reason and emotion, the emotion often gains the upper hand. This is because the neural pathways from the amygdala to the cortex are more plentiful and better developed than the neural pathways from the cortex to the amygdala. This, Joseph LeDoux concludes, may be why psychoanalysis is such a prolonged process.[45]

But what about a more physical approach to triggering the kind of 'real' emotion that could include autonomic responses? We considered briefly, earlier, things like Chekhov's 'psychological gesture' and the ways in which a facial expression or particular physical stance might induce feeling. These approaches, while no doubt effective, are not as extreme as Alba Emoting – a technique which centres entirely on physically recreating the emotional state. The technique is so new that there is little written about it, but it seems to begin with the idea that actors cannot rely on what occurs on stage to trigger their emotions, so they must 'self-generate':

...there is no stimulus in the fictive world of the play beyond that provided by fellow actors (which may, in the best of circumstances, be considerable, but cannot be depended upon moment to moment); in Stanislavski's words, 'There is no such thing as actuality on the stage.' (Stanislavski, 1989:54). The attempt to fill the gap left by lack of genuine stimuli has been central to Western actor training (certainly, in the US) since Stanislavski and the birth of realism brought to the fore the idea of truth on stage. Most techniques – emotion memory (with or without physicalization of reexperience), 'magic if,' belief in circumstances, substitution, use of images, objects, and so on—attack the problem through cognition: the actor uses the mind to create stimulus for emotion.[46]

Because there is a 'stimulus gap' the actor must, according to Alba technique, bypass cognition and go straight to physical recreation of emotion. It seems clear that an actor COULD adopt a wholly physical technique approach to emotion, and that there is enough research to support the fact that we can induce a state of emotion through a self-induced physical state. On the home page of the Alba Emoting website, the basic philosophy is described:

> Alba Emoting identifies six 'basic' emotions from which all others derive. Each of the basic emotions, as well as emotional neutrality, has its own unique, identifiable set of bodily responses ('effector patterns') which are universal to all humans. By reproducing three aspects of these patterns – breathing, posture, and facial expression – an actor can experience and express genuine, organic emotion at will, without the use of memory or images.[47]

There are many questions that this claim raises for me – not the least of which is the scientific basis of the claim that the six 'basic' emotions have entirely body-based generators that will not engage either memory or mental imagery. But this aside, the method as described seems to me to underestimate profoundly the complexity of the actor's work, and doesn't answer the question of how a wholly technical physical approach could ever marry up with artistry. We don't work at any point ONLY with our bodies and the emotional responses they generate – even to think in such a way suggests a return to the old mind/body split. We don't work at any point ONLY with our emotions. And we shouldn't be working at any point ONLY with our cognitive reasoning processes. Surely the challenge of acting is that we work through all three at once. And in any case, Alba emoting could only really generate the most fundamental kinds of physical emotional responses – rage, fear, anger, disgust, happiness, etc., and acting demands much more complex combinations of feeling which in turn demands much more cognitive processing – which would surely negate the point of generating all the emotion through breath, stance, muscle tension/release, etc. However I look at it, I can only conclude that while imagination can certainly be stimulated by physical approaches as well as by memory – which means that the Alba approach would be as valid as Hagen's or Stanislavski's – there is little evidence to suggest that we can manage to imagine fully, in the complex ways that we need to when acting, through a wholly physical or wholly mental starting point.

Duse was a woman

There is any number of things that occur physically when we're experiencing strong emotions like fear, disgust, anger or sexual arousal, amongst them increased heart rate, dilated pupils, sweaty palms, raised blood pressure, etc., some of which can cause a temporary redness in the skin. But Duse's blush was – according to George Bernard Shaw's description –

brought on by the imaginary portrayal of a woman who was NOT connecting to these kinds of primary emotions or the physiological responses that accompany them. Instead, she was playing a woman who is confronting the father of her child, born out of wedlock, and her blush on glancing at him

> **Did Duse imagine a 'trigger' object (as Hagen might suggest), or think of something in her past that made her blush before the scene started (as Meisner might advise)?**

could have been the result of many things combined to create a very complex emotion: embarrassment/unseemly curiosity/the memory of their passion/shame/temporary fear or tongue-tiedness/renewed spark of attraction, etc. Without seeing the scene or seeing what it was that Duse may or may not have deduced in looking at her ex-lover, we can only speculate. But when we're talking about emotion this complex, we're a long way from Plutchik's 'primary' wheel or the six basic emotions we've been considering above. According to Shaw, Duse's blush began when she had the courage to raise her eyes to look at her child's father 'to see how much he had altered'. At that very moment, she began to blush. One of many interesting things for us to consider is that the emotion described above is what Damasio would classify as a social emotion, not a primary emotion, and these emotions are complex in their make-up: 'A whole retinue of regulatory reactions along with elements present in primary emotions can be identified as subcomponents of social emotions.'[48]

As actors, we can all imagine many things that may have combined to create the complex mix of emotions that induced the blush. These kinds of emotions/feelings work very differently from the primary emotions and require a more 'distributed complexity' in terms of the brain work involved. As Rita Carter points out:

> Complex emotions…are sophisticated cognitive constructs that are arrived at only after considerable processing by the conscious mind – an elaborate exchange of information between the conscious cortical areas of the brain and the limbic system beneath.[49]

This kind of elaborate 'neuro-exchange' does not, despite this description, take long, but it does require more conscious cognitive appraisal than primary emotions do. What Duse was clearly capable of was to intuit in the given circumstances of the play just how complex the emotional response of the character might be. So did Duse imagine a 'trigger' object – as Hagen might suggest – or think of something in her past that made her blush before the scene started – as Meisner might advise? Did she, as Stanislavski and many others suggest, simply imagine herself to be in the circumstances of the character and allow her emotions to follow on naturally? I would favour the latter hypothesis, because it seems clear to me that unless Duse was able to imagine thoroughly that the physical reality of seeing her ex-lover was 'real', it would be difficult to blush at this given moment. If she was using a kind of 'trigger object' memory, could that be strong enough to induce blushing? If she had simply 'gotten herself into the mood' as Meisner suggests – what mood would make her blush?

Both Meisner and Hagen recognize that emotion needs to be 'coaxed' somehow through memory. It can't, of course, be forced, as Joseph LeDoux notes:

> Conscious emotion is in a way a red herring: the feeling and behaviour it prompts are surface responses [that] the initial mechanism orchestrates…Emotions are things that happen to us rather than things we make happen. We try to manipulate our emotions all the time but all we are doing is arranging the outside world so it triggers certain emotions – we cannot control our emotions directly. Anyone who has tried to fake an emotion knows how futile it is. Our conscious control over our emotions is weak and feelings often push out thinking, whereas thinking fights a mainly losing battle to banish emotions.[50]

I'm fascinated by his idea of 'arranging the outside world'. In physical terms this could simply be buying fresh flowers and putting on our favourite music in order to trigger a sensation of contentment or happiness. I'm guessing that most of us would agree that this kind of 'arranging the outside world' is very effective. But when it comes to acting, what does it mean to arrange the outside world so that it triggers emotion? I think it can only mean that as actors, when we're working optimally, we have actually arranged our inner world (our imaginations) so that when we look at the outside world, it looks the way we imagine it does. I am suggesting, then, that Eleanora Duse looked at the actor playing her ex-lover and, through sheer imaginary strength, SAW HER EX-LOVER. I can't think of anything else both immediate and powerful enough to have induced an autonomic response like blushing.

Of course, Hagen, Meisner and Stanislavski were concerned with the use of past memory to aid the actor in understanding the depth or urgency of the dramatic moment. In rehearsals and discussions, past memory must play a part in the actor's ability to empathize with the character's situation and to truly understand what it might feel like to be in a given situation. But surely once we recall what it has felt like to us to encounter an ex-lover, and once we recall what it has felt like to us to keep a very guilty secret, then we have managed only the first step of playing the role. I would think that this first step plays a significant part in the next and most important step for an actor: the ability to imagine that just at this moment you have looked up into the face of the man you once loved and whose child you have born without his knowledge.

Should most of our training as actors, then, be much more focused in training the imagination and perhaps less centred on emotional memory? We certainly tend – no matter whose theories we're working through – to do a lot of imagination exercises when we're training, especially at the early stages. But in my experience we tend to do less of this as the actor progresses. Maybe much more attention should be placed on training imagination throughout our careers. How exactly imagination works is a fairly controversial area – the main disagreement is over whether imagination is really abstract thought, or whether it's something that comes to us, or works through, sensation. Of course, if imagination is primarily a function of abstract thought then the reasoning/conceptual part of the brain would be involved. If it is mainly a function of sensation, then the somatosensory areas of the brain would be most involved. It's easy to understand why this debate has posed the problem as a question between these two possibilities. So many things we might imagine (the feeling of flying, seeing someone we love deeply, winning an Oscar) seem to involve both abstract thought and sensory feeling in an interrelated way. It seems that research has not come much closer to solving this riddle, but perhaps it needn't be framed in such an either/or way. However we imagine – from mental pictures to really abstract, unvisualized ways – we know that it often involves a highly complex interplay of thinking and feeling, and we know that these things seem to reinforce each other as our imaginary world becomes more detailed.

We once did a 'lemon' exercise in class when I was an undergraduate student. We were asked to close our eyes and visualize a lemon. And then we were asked just to 'see' the lemon, and to 'see' what the teacher was describing without 'feeling' anything. The teacher first described the lemon – about the size of a tennis ball, dayglow yellow, with spongy, slightly pitted skin. He described picking up the lemon and feeling its juiciness by squeezing it slightly. He then described picking up a knife, piercing and then slowly cutting into the lemon and the way that the lemon juices ran onto the table and all around the knife. From the moment the knife punctured the lemon, the bright yellow flesh and seeds seemed to pop out from the skin. This exercise went on for some time, without the teacher at any point describing the smell or the taste of the lemon. Yet by the time he finished, everyone – without exception – claimed to have felt an incredible tightness in their jaw and an increase in salivation as they anticipated the sourness of the lemon. It was an interesting demonstration of the immediate ways in which the imagination can trigger autonomic bodily responses like salivation.

If we go back to Duse's blush, there's something really interesting in the way that George Bernard Shaw describes the moment. She blushed when she looked up and saw the man. *What did she see there?* We'll never know, of course, but we can probably surmise at least two things: (1) that Duse must have had a terrific imagination which was muscular enough to convince her autonomic bodily control system that what she was experiencing was real, and (2) that Duse was very good at reading and responding to complex emotional signals in her acting partners. The question for us must be how it is that some actors are very good at this and some are not.

Common sense would suggest that some of the skill of reading complex emotional signals is attributable to intelligence and to learning. It is not surprising that so many great directors spent their time at university reading philosophy and literature, rather than theatre. But is that skill of reading complex emotions, of being able to construct and to empathize with them something that we can all learn? If we think for a moment in terms of evolutionary psychology, we can see why the ability to read primary emotions is 'hard-wired' into the brain.

Evolutionary psychology concerns itself with the study of how the human mind evolves and adapts to circumstances over time in order to ensure survival. We can pretty easily imagine that the ability to read correctly states of sadness, anger, fear, disgust, happiness, etc. in the behaviour of other human beings would contribute greatly toward our survival – but how about the ability to read complex emotions and the subtle expression of them?

One of the great pleasures of acting has, for me, been in reading the subtle shifts of feeling/expression in acting partners as they make new discoveries in the course of rehearsal or performance, and in then allowing that new information to influence my own tactical acting behaviour. This kind of ability to read nuance and tone and subtle shifts in another actor's expression is what keeps performances alive and interesting. Yet surely this kind of fine skill is not comparable to the blunt tools made for reading primary emotions, which come factory-fitted for our survival. What makes one actor better at this than another?

The answer lies partly in a bit of sexism, I'm afraid, and in this area research evidence clearly favours women. The idea of breaking neurological research into gendered pathways is a relatively new one, and much more work needs to be done, but there are some interesting early findings.

The fact is that male and female brains are 99 per cent identical in terms of genetic coding – but that 1 per cent turns out to be pretty critical. It has always been known that the male brain is larger, but in terms of brain power, this is one area where, for men, size doesn't matter. Despite their physical differences, male and female brains have exactly the same number of brain cells – women simply pack them into a smaller space. But other differences, throughout most of the history of physiological, psychological or neuroanatomical research, have been largely overlooked. In the last two decades, however, some extraordinary differences in terms of male/female ability, neuroanatomy and behaviour have been discovered.

Anatomically, women's brains feature some significant differences from male brains, as described by Louann Brizendine in her book, *The Female Brain*:

1. Anterior cingulate cortex (ACC): weighs options, makes decisions. It's the worry-wort centre and it's larger in women than in men.
2. Prefrontal cortex (PFC): the queen that rules the emotions and keeps them from going wild. It puts the brakes on the amygdala. Larger in women, and matures faster in women than in men by one to two years.
3. Insula: the centre that processes gut feelings. Larger and more active in women.
4. Hypothalamus: the conductor of the hormonal symphony; kicks the gonads into gear. Starts pumping earlier in life in women.
5. Amygdala: the wild beast within; the instinctual core, tamed only by the PFC. Larger in men.
6. Pituitary gland: Produces hormones of fertility, milk production and nurturing behaviour. Helps to turn on the mommy brain.
7. Hippocampus: The elephant that never forgets a fight, a romantic encounter or a tender moment – and won't let you forget it, either. Larger and more active in women.[51]

These differences, as you are probably already concluding, add up to some significantly enhanced abilities in women, most of which make sense in terms of evolutionary psychology. Women aren't as big or as strong as men but in evolutionary terms, their enhanced abilities to empathize, bond with others, nurture and read even the most subtle of emotional signals in the face and tone of voice gives them advantage in the twin jobs of surviving and propagating the species. The male brain, as you might have guessed from the above description, is more 'hair-triggered' – it has less 'block' to the primary emotions than does the female's – and this is highly advantageous in terms of immediate response to danger or possible quick response for capturing prey. These gender differences are difficult for us to disrupt, as a great story from Brizendine's book illustrates:

> Common sense tells us that boys and girls behave differently, we see it everyday at home, on the playground and in classrooms. But what the culture hasn't told us is that the brain dictates these divergent behaviours. The impulses of children are so innate that they kick in even if we adults try to nudge them in another direction. One of my patients gave her three-and-a-half-year-old daughter many unisex toys, including a bright red fire truck instead of a doll. She walked into the daughter's room one afternoon to find her cuddling the truck in a baby blanket and rocking it back and forth saying 'Don't worry, little truckie, everything will be all right.'[52]

While Brizendine's list of brain differences accounts for much, it doesn't entirely explain why women should be so much better than men at emotional intuitiveness, expression, empathy and understanding. This may be because she leaves out of this initial anatomical survey the fact that the corpus callosum – the mass of tissue connecting the right and left hemispheres of the brain, and through which these two halves communicate – is larger in women's brains than in men's. Women also have more tissue in the massa intermedia and the anterior commissure – both of which are responsible for linking various areas of the two halves of the brain. These larger female 'conduits' are presumably capable of facilitating greater exchange of information between the (largely) more emotionally sensitive right hemisphere and the left side of the brain where language and logic dominate. These great amounts of connective tissue may mean that women have more effective hardware for linking emotion to language and to analysis, and could explain why women are so much more adept at perceiving, analysing and expressing emotion than men.

It occurs to me that it may also explain why there are always so many more women who want to act than there are men. This fact is borne out by audition and placement numbers in every conservatoire or acting programme that doesn't operate on a male/female quota system on intake. There is an interesting sidebar here in anatomical terms. In the 1990s it was discovered that the brains of gay men were:

> …structurally different from the brains of heterosexual men. The nucleus in the hypothalamus that triggers male-typical sexual behaviour was much smaller in the gay

men and looked more like that in the brains of women…[it was also discovered] that the corpus callosum differs between gay and straight men, too – in [gay men] it was found to be bigger.[53]

This research suggests that gay men, like women, may have enhanced hardware for facilitating hemispheric communication and may therefore be, like women, more adept at connecting language, analytic skill and emotion than straight men. Perhaps another mystery of the theatre explained?

The corpus callosum may have still more significance in terms of how great actors work. This is an area that needs much more research, but in just the same way that cognitive science advances by studying brains that AREN'T working, I would think that discovering whether an actor as skilled as Duse may have a neuroanatomical advantage might depend on looking at the neuroanatomy in cases where things like empathy, play and the ability to pretend (baseline tools for the actor) are not present. And that case could be autism.

'Mindblindness'

In an influential work, Simon Baron-Cohen put forth the idea that what distinguishes autism is an inability to understand what is going on in someone else's mind:

A theory of mind remains one of the quintessential abilities that makes us human…By theory of mind we mean being able to infer the full range of mental states (beliefs, desires, intentions, imagination, emotions, etc.) that cause action. In brief, having a theory of mind is to be able to reflect on the contents of one's own and other's minds. Difficulty in understanding other minds is a core cognitive feature of autism spectrum conditions.[54]

In Cohen's description, autism results in 'mindblindness' – an inability not only to understand other minds, but even to understand that other people have thoughts that are different from our own. There have been a number of tests devised by researchers into this area, and some researchers, like Alan Leslie and Uta Frith, see a connection between having a theory of mind and the ability to imagine or pretend playfully:

[Infant brains] are capable of forming copies, or *representations*, of people, things, and events. Representations bring the world into the mind. However, in the second year of life the infant appears to be able to go a step further, and can now form representations of what other people *intend* to communicate. The mind forms these powerful new representations through a presumably innate mechanism, which according to Leslie decouples representations from reality…Through decoupling, representations are free to be thought about in their own right and can be played with by the imagination…In autism, a failure in mentalizing could be due to a fault in the decoupling mechanism.[55]

In other words, we start out by representing aspects of the world around us in our heads, but we quickly move on from there to decouple those representations from strict correspondence with that reality and begin to perform any number of synthetic, imaginary associations which might form the basis of fantasy, playing and pretending. Researchers have come to think that the mechanism for having a theory of mind is the same mechanism for fantasy, play and pretending – both of which require that the mind have the ability to 'decouple' thought 'from its normal duties of referring to reality'[56] thereby allowing the synthetic process of combining thoughts and representations which can evolve into entirely new meanings altogether. Frith predicts that in future, neuroscientists may be able to determine where in the brain this 'decoupling' takes place and how, and that work could lead to describing the 'neural underpinnings' of our ability to predict what is in other peoples' minds.

In the time since Frith was writing there have been some advances in the science of how the autistic brain differs from the non-autistic brain and some of the findings centre around the size of the corpus callosum.[57] The corpus callosum, as we've seen, is responsible for communication and connectivity between the hemispheres of the brain, and for ensuring that there is some balance between the intuitive/sensitive/empathizing right brain and the language/reasoning/systematizing left brain. It has been posited that autism may be something like an 'extreme male brain' – in which the left hemisphere/systematizing brain activity dominates. It is logical that the smaller amount of connective tissue (in a smaller corpus callosum) between the hemispheres could lead to dominance by one side of the brain over the other. But why it should be the left side is less clear. What this suggests to me is that if an autistic patient displays a lack of empathy, or ability to 'self-project' into the minds of others or facility for pretending and play – in other words, if autism is 'mindblindness' – then might good actors be thought to possess something like '20/20 mindsight'? Certainly there must be a case for the good actor having strong systems of brain connectivity. This might not necessarily involve the corpus callosum, since brain connectivity happens all over the brain. But if, in autism, there appears to be deficient connectivity, could we not make the case that there must be some brains with hyper-efficient connectivity? Indeed, that is what a study on gender brain differences found, which determined that hyper-efficiency seemed to be a matter of size:

> Melissa Hines and her coworkers, then at UCLA, found that in a population of normal women, those with the largest corpus callosum, in particular, a subregion of the corpus callosum called the splenium, performed best on tests of verbal fluency. They hyposthesized that a larger splenium allows a greater flow of information between language centers in the left and right brains.[58]

There's a danger in concluding here that something like hyper-efficient connectivity in brain activity is likely to be neuroanatomical. But that may not be the case, despite these findings about size of splenium. As in variations of general intelligence, the actual physical components of the brain structure are not likely to be the significant differentiating factor.

As David Linden points out, 'Most of human cognitive variation is more likely to be manifest as changes in…the connectivity of brain cells, and the patterns of brain electrical activity.'[59] And if this connectivity is variable, then it seems logical to me that actors who happen to have high-efficiency connectivity are likely to be better actors, simply because the enhanced connectivity is likely to improve not only verbal fluency (as found above) but would also improve the fluency of connection between all the disparate areas of brain function.

From 'embodied thinking' to 'display'

It is clear that part of the actor's job occurs in the mental processes of perception, interpretation and analysis – both in the world of the play text and of the world in which we live. But the whole demonstrable skill in acting lies in how we express ourselves on stage. All of us have known or worked with or taught actors who simply seem to have a contracted or very limited palette of emotional expression. Many of these actors are perfectly capable of analysing a scene, or of articulating what they think is going on in the mind or heart of a particular character. They may also say that they feel a strong empathy with the character and know exactly what they want and how they hope to achieve what they need within the scope of the play. But the distance between 'feeling' and expressing that feeling can, for some actors, be unbridgeable.

In cognitive research terms, we're talking about the ability to 'display' and about the way in which 'display rules' can come to influence our spontaneous expression of feeling. In very rare cases, known as alexithymia, some people can feel emotion but are completely incapable of expressing that feeling through language. This inability probably results from a disturbance in the neural connections between conscious emotional processing areas of the brain and the areas that control speech and facial expression. The consequence can be a 'flat' sound in the expression. There may be degrees of this disturbance and Rita Carter points to former Prime Minister, John Major as an example of a 'mildly alexithymic voice.'[60] This characterization of Major's rather hollow sound and often unconvincing speech patterns puts me in mind of some student actors I've worked with who can talk cogently about their feelings but find it difficult to portray any of that feeling or to escape the dullness of their own natural speech patterns. It makes me wonder if there may have been some mild degree of alexithymia working in these cases – but until more is known about this condition it would be hard to say.

But there are any number of non-neurological factors that contribute to the diminishing of emotional display, from the way in which we are brought up to the way in which the society we live in either does or does not reward our open expression of emotion. And, of course, we know that the 'display rules' differ between boys and girls.

One fascinating study of emotional display compared the responses of a group of Japanese and a group of American men watching a particularly grisly horror film. Each group watched two different but equally horrible film clips – the first time thinking that they were not being observed and the second time knowing that they were being observed. While watching the first film clip (when they thought no one was observing them), both the Japanese and the American men displayed similar expressions of horror and disgust at what they were seeing. However, while watching the second film clip – and knowing that their responses were being observed – the American men displayed the same kinds of expressions of horror, but the Japanese men displayed little or no expression at all while being watched.[61] Such socialized 'display rules' mean that we often suppress emotional responses, depending on where/how we were raised and who we think may be watching us.

Of course, knowing that we're being watched stimulates its own kind of brain activity, largely involving the medial prefrontal cortex (MPFC). In a study cited by Richard Restak, participants were asked to switch their attention between two different objects. But while doing this, they were also told that their reactions would sometimes be recorded on video camera and sometimes not. Further, they would be TOLD when the camera was on and when the camera was off. As we might guess, during the 'camera-on' periods their brains exhibited very different activity than during the 'camera-off' sequences. Restak explains:

> During the camera-on periods your MPFC will activate, followed by deactivation during the camera-off segments of the experiment. At one moment you're concentrating on doing well in the experiment (camera off), and the next moment (camera on) you're concentrating on yourself – specifically, how you will appear to others who may be watching you on a monitor. The MPFC springs into action as you shift your focus from the word game to how other people may be judging your performance in the game.[62]

This is a particularly interesting brain response for actors to contemplate. Presumably all the work that we put into concentrating on our actions is designed to keep the 'I'm being watched' MPFC activation out of the performance picture. There is no doubt that in those moments when we can't manage to forget that we're being watched, we become aware of the very different *feeling* that the MPFC activation creates in our minds and bodies.

One of the earliest acting exercises we used to do at the Liverpool Institute for Performing Arts was one we called the 'head-to-head' improv. We always started these exercises with two chairs facing each other, all the other students sitting or lying on the floor very close by these two chairs and two actors in opposite corners of the room. The two actors would be primed secretly in each corner of the room, and the improv conflict itself was invariably irresolvable.

For example, Actor A would be told: *you have run away from home because your mother recently remarried after the tragic death of your father. She was so distressed after his death you thought she would never find happiness again, so when she found and remarried this new man you were initially happy too. But he began coming into your room at night attempting to molest you. You ran away and because you love her so much you didn't tell her why and would never tell her why, nor will you ever go home.*

Actor B would be told: *your daughter left after you remarried, following the death of her father. You know how much your daughter loved her father, and you think that she simply can't accept your new husband. You've spent months looking for her and have finally found her and you need to persuade her to come home as she is too young to be on her own. You have decided that in order to persuade her you will give her a letter from your new husband telling her that he loves her and wants her to come home so you can all be together again.*

After being given these instructions the actors walk to the chairs and sit down during a count of 5-4-3-2-1, at which point the improv starts. Because the conflict is so powerful and the immediate feelings/desires of both actors so quickly engaged, (and perhaps because the 'audience' is seated on the ground), inevitably after the exercise – which can be incredibly powerful to watch – both actors will report that they were completely unaware of being watched. They similarly report that their usual sense of self-consciousness while acting disappears during the improv and returns only once the exercise has finished. It seems clear to me that exercises like this would feel very different for young actors from their usual performances because – if their self-reports are correct – the actors may be working with a differently activated MPFC. The fact is, of course, that there must be many actors who have sufficiently developed concentration and imaginations that the MPFC activity while being watched doesn't affect their acting – but most actors, whatever their experience, know the feeling of suddenly being aware of being watched. And most would concur that this happens most often in classroom settings where the lack of lights, costume, darkened theatres and 'aesthetic distance' make us all too aware of our fellow actors (and acting tutor!) watching us. Does this mean that we're often attempting to teach actors when their MPFC activity could be at its highest?

Of course the MPFC isn't only activated by knowing that we're being watched, or monitoring ourselves from moment to moment – it's also extremely active in the whole area of intuiting the feelings of other people. According to Restak, the MPFC springs into action 'whenever we imagine ourselves in the shoes of another person.'[63] It follows, logically, that if we're employing some of that MPFC activity in worrying about how we look in front of others, we're probably able to employ less of it in the imaginative activity of putting ourselves 'in the shoes of another person' – say, Hamlet.

Given the many social and cultural influences on the ways in which we display emotion, the relative lack of attention to this in acting books seems curious to me. Much great work about acting (Stanislavski, Chekhov, Vakhtangov, Meyerhold) has been generated in Russia – a culture which is vastly different from that in America and may itself have much to do with why American adaptations of Stanislavski's works evolved in the way that they did. Robert Solomon looks at the issue of culture and emotions and concludes that there are 'evident differences in the overall intensity of the emotions or at least in the overt expression of emotions'[64] from culture to culture. These differences may be due to many things, but in Solomon's estimation they probably come down to seven variables:

1. There may be different 'display rules' – in terms of what overt expression is deemed appropriate or inappropriate by a given society.
2. The repertoire of emotions may vary from culture to culture.
3. The subtleties or nuances of emotion may differ.
4. The actual causes of emotion may differ.
5. The modes of expression and the times/places in which the expression of these emotions is appropriate may differ.
6. If emotions lead to action, the appropriate courses of action may differ.
7. The nature of verbal expression of emotion may differ significantly.

Solomon compares two cultures – American commuter culture and the 'Utku' Inuit in the Canadian Arctic. Where in the former culture, anger is frequent, easily provoked and often openly expressed, in the latter 'anger is a genuine rarity…Even in circumstances that we would find intolerably frustrating or offensive, the Utku do not get angry. Where most of us would be resentful or furious, the Utku are merely resigned.'[65] Solomon refers to a study by Jean Briggs on the Utku people, and acknowledges that it is, of course, likely that the Utku do get angry, but that as a culture, the expression of that anger is repressed. If we think in terms of individual expressions or displays of emotion it is one thing to consider the larger cultural differences (which would seem to be discernible), but something else again to consider the other kinds of influences that may determine why two actors raised in a similar culture can be so different in terms of ability to express a range of emotion.

As an acting teacher and director, this difficulty has often seemed insuperable. Trying to help an actor increase what appears to be a 'naturally' small or narrow expressive range is challenging and I've found that even extensive effort is rarely rewarded here. Perhaps if we add 'family' to the words 'culture' above we may be able to understand why some people have such a limited repertoire of expression or display – but that may not lead us any closer to solving the problem in class or rehearsal. As we know, we are genetically fitted with the capacity for having certain basic emotions. But we don't inherit the triggers for those emotions, and we don't inherit social contexts genetically. We have all witnessed the ways in which emotion is often expressed in what appears to be an uninhibited way with babies and young children. This happens because the parts of the brain that control primary emotions (perhaps anger or fits of giggles) take time to mature, whereas the parts of the brain that generate immediate emotional response are fully formed and working even at a very young age, and this means that learning to control emotions takes time. Children have an amazingly immediate connection to their emotions, as Susan Greenfield notes:

> Small children seem to live on an emotional rollercoaster. With miraculous rapidity, heartrending sobs give way to gurgles of delight at the sight of a chocolate bar or a cat walking past. Yet at the time the rage – or the laughter – seems so important and so definitive.[66]

The difference between the amounts of emotion a child experiences on a daily basis in comparison with an adult is remarkable. Research has shown that 'children laugh on average 300 times a day. By adulthood this number plummets to 50'.[67]

There are theories that suggest that the emotional 'control' centres in the brain can be developed and accelerated a bit by conditioning. Think of the difference in behaviour between a child who is raised by parents who continually reinforce the idea of emotional restraint by admonishing the child to 'calm down' or 'stop crying', etc., and a child who is raised by parents who don't want to inhibit the child's natural expression in any way, simply allowing them to express whatever they feel. We have probably all known people who have been raised in particularly repressive family cultures and some who have been raised in particularly liberal family cultures. Without offering a judgement on one over the other, it seems that it is the case that 'children who rarely activate the emotional control centre in their brains may grow up to be poorly controlled adults because the necessary brain equipment was not nourished during the most critical stage of development'.[68] In other words, the children whose parents more or less let them run amok emotionally may not always develop the kinds of inhibitory controls that will make them disciplined, responsible adults – but might it make them good actors?

I've often observed that some of the best actors I know are rather childish in the best (and sometimes most irritating) sense of the word. They jump quickly into pretending and they let loose emotionally when the pretence appeals strongly to their hearts. They often have a wide range of emotional expression and I never feel with them (as I often do with more intellectual, mature actors) that I am sometimes 'pulling teeth' in order to get some expressive range from them. Might our 'display' abilities then be a complex combination of both a high level of connectivity in the brain and also where/how we were raised? Might the development of our cortical 'control' centres be the key to how much we are willing or able to express what it is we feel? If this is true, is it this combination that accounts for why some people are simply better at acting than others? Does it mean that – like so many other areas in the study of acting – there is no single technical approach or theory that can accommodate all the variables when we get into the complex questions of emotion and display?

From primary to social

Emotion researchers and writers distinguish strongly between kinds of emotion and while some of these distinctions are of the 'fine tuning' variety, I find Antonio Damasio's three categories extremely useful for thinking about the process of acting. He lists:

- Primary emotions (the usual fear, anger, disgust, surprise, sadness, happiness). He notes that these emotions are generally cross-cultural and even cross-species.
- Background emotions, which are those emotions that are not particularly noticeable in our behaviour. Background emotions are something like the context of our behaviour – we might describe background emotions as 'moods', only much shorter in duration. These emotions are the result of our overall continuous monitoring of our own well-being and might manifest in subtle shifts in behavioural dynamics – such as tranquillity, edginess, unease or excitement – and are the result of the ways in which we continually evaluate our safety, security, well-being – in short our survival. These background emotions may not in themselves be the cause of any other given emotional response or action. In other words, much other, more specific behaviour, created by many other more specific feelings (lashing out, being affectionate, fighting, flirting, daring, etc.) could be imagined as taking place within the context of a background emotion.
- Social emotions (he includes sympathy, embarrassment, shame, guilt, pride, jealousy, envy, gratitude, admiration, indignation and contempt[69]), which are related to primary emotions, but are learned or socialized responses.

Social emotions tend to be complex and often regulatory – they sometimes mitigate or refashion our private primal responses into emotions more fit for social settings. Background emotions tend to be part of the 'cognitive unconscious' – which is to say that the brain clearly establishes background emotion without necessarily any conscious input. This can be seen clearly in the ways that we often wonder why we feel so impatient suddenly or why we're feeling a bit blue, or how it is that when someone asks us how we are we have to think about it for a moment if we want to elaborate on the usual 'fine, thanks!'.

For me these three distinct areas map well onto the ways in which actors often have to look carefully at the complexity involved in any given scene. And they make even more sense to me when mapped against the ways in which social contexts affect emotional display. To be specific, we could take a scene – let us use Act I, Scene IV, where Horatio, Hamlet and Marcellus encounter the ghost of Hamlet's father – and see how these areas map:

	Primary Emotion	*Background Emotion*	*Social Emotion*	*Display 'rules'*
Hamlet	Fear Disgust Anger Surprise	Grief Edginess Unease	Shame Contempt Indignation	High Status – may restrict display of fear but not anger or disgust
Horatio	Sadness Surprise Fear	Unease and Worry – if ghost doesn't show Hamlet may think he is lying	Embarrassment Sympathy	Mid-Status – Perhaps most free to display all emotion
Marcellus	Fear Surprise Sadness	Unease – a ghost could signal dangerous times ahead	Sympathy, possibly Embarrassment	Low Status & Soldier – restricts display of Fear or Anxiety

While acknowledging that the exact way in which primary, social and background emotions interact is highly complicated (and in everyday living experience cannot be neatly separated of course!), this map still helps me greatly in seeing some of the ways in which the intricacy of the overall emotional mix in this early scene is a symphony of mutually conditioning emotions, feelings and actions.

As I look at the chart above I am also aware of the ways in which complexity grows from left to right. And strangely, the first thing that hit me when looking at it was the possible explanation for why young actors are always so much more successful doing serious/tragic drama than style or comedy. The successful representation of primary emotion (especially in a limited run) is more likely, simply because in its raw state (as we so often encounter it in tragedy), primary emotion is less complex. It is more immediately 'embodied' and in that sense perhaps more immediately 'locatable' physically in representation. The sickening physical reality of hearing about your uncle pouring poison in your father's ear is so much more immediate and viscerally understood than the physical/mental excitement/arousal, wariness, attraction, 'anger', aloofness and desire to dominate that seizes Benedick upon beholding Beatrice when he first returns from war. Hamlet's response is primal whereas Benedick's immediate primal desire is heavily mediated through social display rules, and the background emotional 'noise' of previous encounters that have left him wary and edgy.

Summary

So are actors really 'feeling' emotion or are they faking it? I've come to believe that this question – as posed – makes no sense. We know that when we are simply thinking about feeling or thinking about emotion, we involve the very areas of the brain that 'light up' during the actual process of feeling emotion, so to that degree we are always closely connected through brain function to emotion or feeling, whether we are *truly* feeling or not. So how would we begin to judge whether somewhere, along the spectrum of thinking about and acting on those thoughts we are truly 'inhabiting' or feeling, instead of just thinking about 'inhabiting' or feeling? Wouldn't that judgement come down to 'self-reporting' whether we think we are feeling or faking and doesn't that leave us with two problems: (1) the lack of reliability in 'self-reporting' and (2) the general paradox of involving metacognition (thinking about thinking) in the process of actually feeling – which is a bit like that moment during a sleepless night when we suddenly wonder if we've managed to fall asleep and then realize that if we're asking ourselves the question, then the answer is probably 'no'. Of course we can always, as actors have ever done, rely on others to judge for us whether we were really FEELING our EMOTION or not, but as we know, this leads to another set of problems about individual perceptions, etc. We also know that human beings (regardless of whether they are acting!) tend to suppress feeling and that our only way to judge feeling or emotion in others is by expression. Surely this means that we can't talk about feeling or emotion without talking about expression and there is no way to guarantee the relationship between expression and feeling.

We also know that in the case of strong primal emotions like anger/rage, fear and disgust the 'cognitive unconscious' is so closely involved and wired up to instant bodily response that it's unlikely we could ever fully experience these emotions on stage without being a danger to ourselves and others and without slipping over from the 'metarepresentational' and the 'metacognitive' into cognitive and representational (i.e., NOT ACTING anymore).

In the case of social or background emotions, we've discovered that much of these are an often unconscious context for emotion and display of feelings rather than the focus of conscious attention since – as Whitehead points out – attentional thought is expensive and 'requires fresh horses'. As actors are particularly concerned with focused attention, is it likely that we would spend precious resources in these areas while performing?

In the case of feelings, it's far more likely that we can successfully reproduce these with enough training and observation, given that memory and empathy involve the same areas of the brain. Recent studies have in fact proven that brain areas activated in remembering what has happened, prospecting (imagining what will happen) and exercising our 'theory of mind' (guessing the beliefs, desires and actions of others) demonstrate a surprising convergence, largely involving the inferior parietal and medial temporal lobes. While this might help explain how we do all these things at once seemingly effortlessly, it doesn't do much to help us figure out why some actors generate stronger imaginative beliefs in a given situation than others.

But if we've learned nothing else, surely we've learned that the whole question of emotion, feeling and cognition is so complex that it is highly unlikely that we'll ever come to a single, satisfying answer about what it is great actors do when they manage to blush, apart from admiring their ability to pretend with such conviction. When that ability is teamed with a considerable range of expressive ability and a strong capacity to empathize with and understand the behaviour of others, then we surely have the constituent elements of a fine acting performance. But what about that latter ability? We've seen how mirror neurons work in terms of creating a neurally-driven sense of empathy, but beyond a physical sense of mimicry/empathy, how do we come to understand the aspects of the minds of others that AREN'T visible?

Notes

1. Jacques Copeau, quoted in *Twentieth Century Actor Training*, Alison Hodge (ed.) (London: Routledge, 2000) p. 58.
2. Richard Hornby, *The End of Acting: A Radical View* (New York: Applause Books, 1992), p. 102.
3. *The Player's Passion: Studies in the Science of Acting* (Michigan: University of Michigan Press, 2001), p. 206.
4. Antonio Damasio, *Looking for Spinoza* (London: Vintage Books, 2004), p. 27–28.
5. Joseph LeDoux, *The Emotional Brain* (London: Phoenix, 2003), p. 23.
6. See particularly pp. 107–116.
7. These are Robert Plutchik's 'basic eight' although Sylvan Tomkins proposed a slightly different eight: surprise, interest, joy, rage, fear, disgust, shame and anguish.
8. These are Philip Johnson-Laird and Keith Oatley's five, which are similar to Paul Ekman's six basic emotions: surprise, happiness, anger, fear, disgust and sadness.
9. You can find a nice rendering of Plutchik's wheel on the web: http://www.fractal.org/Bewustzijns-Besturings-Model/Nature-of-emotions.htm.
10. Richard Dawkins and some evolutionary psychologists have much to say about this – which we'll look at in the next chapter.
11. LeDoux, *The Emotional Brain*, p. 158.
12. *Ibid.*, p. 165.
13. See Jonah Lehrer, *How We Decide* (New York: Houghton, Mifflin, Harcourt, 2009), pp. 46–47.
14. Joseph LeDoux, *The Synaptic Self: How Our Brains Become Who We Are* (New York: Penguin, 2002), p. 201. [My emphasis.]
15. V.S. Ramachandran, *Phantoms in the Brain* (London: Harper Perennial, 2005), p. 14.
16. Constantin Stanislavski, *My Life in Art*, tr. J.J. Robbins (London: Methuen, 1991), p. 159.
17. Antonio R. Damasio, *Descartes' Error* (Oxford: OUP, 1994), pp. 141–142.
18. Pierre Gosselin & Gilles Kirouac 'Components and Recognition of Facial Expression in the Communication of Emotions by Actors', P. Ekman and E. Rosenberg (eds), *What the Face Reveals* (2nd Edn) (Oxford: OUP, 2005), p. 243.
19. Damasio, *Descartes' Error*, p. 148.
20. *Ibid.*, p. 149.
21. Elly Konijn ('The Actor's Emotions Reconsidered' in Phillip Zarrilli (ed.) *Acting (Re)Considered*) attempts to do just this – but the proven limitations of self-reporting are such that this study needs to be read with some caution.
22. Damasio, *Descartes' Error*, p. 149.
23. Antonio R. Damasio, *Looking for Spinoza* (London: Vintage Books, 2003), p. 86. Original emphasis.
24. *Ibid.*, p. 71.
25. Paul Ekman, *Emotions Revealed* (London: Weidenfeld & Nicolson, 2003), p. 95.

26. Sanford Meisner, *On Acting* (New York: Vintage Books, 1987), pp. 84–88.
27. Gosselin & Kirouac, Components and Recognition of Facial Expression', p. 247.
28. *Ibid.*, p. 258. [My emphasis.]
29. I confess to some reservations about Kirouac and Gosselin's knowledge of acting technique (their unusual transliteration of Stanislavski as Stanislawski is probably the first clue), and about acting training in general (at one point they bemoan the lack of actors trained in the 'Stanislawski' method: 'Because the drama schools only train 5 or 10 students a year, there are not many young actors using the Stanislawski method'). Given the prevalence of Stanislavski technique in most actor training programmes, perhaps the good folks over at the Quebec Conservatory were having a little fun at the expense of their scientific friends?
30. Interoceptors are those internal receptors of sensation (such as the desire to eat or to urinate) which monitor the body internally and ensure that temperature, feeding, etc., are all regulated efficiently.
31. Derek Denton, *The Primordial Emotion* (Oxford: OUP, 2005), pp. 178–179.
32. Damasio, *Looking for Spinoza*, p. 54.
33. Denton, *The Primordial Emotion*, p. 180.
34. Meisner, *On Acting*, pp. 14–15.
35. LeDoux, *The Synaptic Self*, pp. 202–203.
36. Meisner, *On Acting*, p. 87.
37. This experiment is reported in Eric R. Kandel's *In Search of Memory: The Emergence of a New Science of Mind* (London: W.W. Norton, 2006), pp. 387–388.
38. E. Smith & S. Kosslyn, *Cognitive Psychology* (New Jersey: Prentice Hall, 2007), p. 217.
39. Damasio, *Descartes' Error*, pp. 102–103.
40. *Ibid*, p. 104.
41. Quoted in Alison Hodge (ed.), *Twentieth Century Actor Training* (London: Routledge, 2000), p. 83.
42. Damasio, *Descartes' Error*, p. 149.
43. V.S. Ramachandran, *The Emerging Mind* (London: Profile Books, 2003), p. 112.
44. Arnold Modell, *Imagination and the Meaningful Brain*, (Cambridge, MA: MIT Press, 2003), p. 140.
45. Damasio, *The Emotional Brain*, p. 265.
46. Roxane Rix, excerpt from 'Alba Emoting: A Revolution in Emotion for the Actor', found at: http://albaemoting.org/_wsn/page2.html.
47. See: http://albaemotingna.org/index.html.
48. Damasio, *Looking for Spinoza*, p. 45.
49. Rita Carter, *Mapping the Mind* (London: Phoenix Press, 1998), p. 131.
50. Le Doux, quoted in *ibid.*, p. 155.
51. Louann Brizendine, *The Female Brain* (London: Bantam Press, 2007), p. xiii.
52. *Ibid.*, p. 12.
53. Carter, *Mapping the Mind*, p. 111.
54. Simon Baron-Cohen, 'Theory of Mind in Normal Development and Autism', *Prisme*, 34, 2001, p. 174.
55. Uta Frith, *Autism: Explaining the Enigma* (Cambridge: MA: Blackwell, 2003), p. 81.
56. *Ibid.*, p. 82.
57. See Egaas, Courchesne and Saitoh (http://www.ncbi.nlm.nih.gov/pubmed/7639631), whose study found evidence of reduced size of corpus callosum – particularly in posterior section – in 51 autistic patients (2006); also http://www.loni.ucla.edu/~thompson/PDF/CVidal-AUT-CC-BP06.pdf,

a study by a team a doctors which concluded that callosal deficits in autism 'suggest aberrant connections between the cortical regions [of the brain]' (2006); and Hrdlica, M. (http://www.ncbi.nlm.nih.gov/pubmed/18580841?ordinalpos=1&itool=EntrezSystem2.PEntrez.Pubmed.Pubmed_ResultsPanel.Pubmed_DiscoveryPanel.Pubmed_Discovery_RA&linkpos=3&log$=relatedreviews&logdbfrom=pubmed), on structural neuroimaging in autism, which concludes that existing research suggests a larger overall size of brain in autism but a reduced area of the corpus callosum (2008).

58. David J. Linden, *The Accidental Mind* (Cambridge, MA: Harvard University Press, 2007), pp. 159–160.
59. *Ibid.*, p. 26.
60. Carter, *Mapping The Mind*, p. 132.
61. See Erika Rosenberg in Ekman, *What the Face Reveals*, pp. 10–11.
62. Richard Restak, *The Naked Brain* (New York: Harmony Books, 2006), p. 75.
63. *Ibid.*, p. 74.
64. Robert C. Solomon, *True to Our Feelings: What Our Emotions Are Really Telling Us* (Oxford: OUP, 2007), p. 252.
65. *Ibid.*, p. 253.
66. Susan Greenfield, *The Private Life of the Brain* (London: Penguin, 2002), p. 51.
67. *Ibid.*, p. 51.
68. Carter, *Mapping the Mind*, p. 145.
69. Damasio, *Looking for Spinoza*, p. 45.

Chapter 4

What Were YOU Thinking?

W hen it comes to understanding the complex ways in which human beings behave, we certainly live in interesting times. And, as George Lakoff and Mark Johnson point out, in the light of a pretty explosive growth in areas like cognitive science, the whole landscape of philosophy is shifting:

The mind is inherently embodied.

Thought is mostly unconscious.

Abstract concepts are largely metaphorical.

These are three major findings of cognitive science. More than two millennia of a priori philosophical speculation about these aspects of reason are over. Because of these discoveries, philosophy can never be the same again.[1]

Not everyone agrees with Lakoff and Johnson – some think they overstate the case, and some have quibbles about the ways in which they argue the three main points above – but probably no one would argue with the fact that the rapid growth of firm scientific discoveries about how we think has changed the ways in which philosophers approach the subjects of knowledge and the ways in which human beings relate to the world around them.

Now this is all BIG STUFF and probably much more than the Philosophical Actor wants to contend with – still, whatever is happening out there in the world of philosophy and cognitive science may very possibly provide some interesting challenges and possibilities for the practical artist.

Perhaps nowhere so much as in the area of psychology.

Getting out of our heads…

…and into someone else's is at once both impossible *and* the very stuff of acting. We are always guessing about why exactly Amanda is so tactless around Laura, why Madame Ranevskaya just can't face the truth or why Lear thought it was such a good idea to give the kids their inheritance early. On the whole, this kind of psychological guessing game is right at the heart of the actor's art and craft. Thinking about the psychology of the characters we portray is something actors are expected to do, even if that consideration is largely done in the practical environment of the rehearsal room. What we don't tend to consider very often is the 'psychology of acting'. There are a lot of ways in which we could examine the relationship between acting and psychology, but in this section I want to consider that relationship in two specific areas: (1) psychology and actor training and (2) psychology and character.

Psychology and actor training seems to me to be an important area that gets little attention. Nearly everyone I've spoken to has a story – either of their own experience or someone else's – of the kind of 'psychological games' that some acting teacher somewhere inflicted upon either them or some hapless fellow student. At best, these games might be the kind of harmless things described by David Garfield in Strasberg's methods to 'unblock' students:

For Strasberg, freeing the expression begins with relaxation and concentration. David Garfield observes that to facilitate relaxation, 'Strasberg has the actor sit in a chair and proceed to find a position in which, if he had to, he could fall asleep.' The actor must relax before an audience, something not easy to do. Of particular importance is the relaxation of the jaw, an area of much concern for Feldenkrais practitioners. As feelings of relaxation increase and emotions stir, Garfield explains that the actor 'opens his throat and permits a sound from deep in the chest to come out, to make sure the emotion is not blocked'. The actor continues to emit sounds that help release tension and free creative expression.[2]

Garfield's gentle memory here certainly doesn't tell the whole story, however, as Jonathan Pitches explains:

Stanislavsky, we recall, abandoned the practice of open rehearsals when he was probing his actors' emotional resources. Strasberg, by contrast, taught the vast majority of his lessons in an open forum. In doing so, the diverse sources on which he draws in his teaching come into conflict…Strasberg adopts the tried and tested pedagogical technique of public analysis…But as a self-confessed reader of Freud, regressing his actors, even in the context of a relaxation exercise, such a public forum may be seen as inappropriate.

Actors Studio members differ in their response to this conflict. Kim Hunter, for example, believed that it was a safe space for experimentation whilst others (Eli Wallach, for instance) suggested directly to Strasberg that his sessions were closer to public therapy: 'you should not practise psychiatry without a licence.'[3]

It was noted that Strasberg's amateur psychological techniques were 'tougher on women than men',[4] which seems to have elicited the kind of response that Jean-Paul Sartre might term 'bad faith' – a bad faith that is uncomfortably evident in Sally Fields' conclusion about her studies at Strasberg's studio: 'I needed to be smacked around a little.'[5]

I've witnessed a fair amount of questionable practices in the teacher/student relationship in my time. At worst these kinds of things have taken the form of teachers insisting that students relive or relate some of their worst memories (of the 'No, Daddy, please, don't!'

What makes some acting teachers so sure that they know what is going on in their students' heads?

variety) or else take off some/all their clothes in front of the class. The common theme running through these approaches will be the need for the teacher/director to 'help' the student/actor get over some psychological 'block' or 'damage'. When I was at Central there was a conservatoire in London that was legendary for its psychological and physical 'strip the students' policy and many of us felt that we could always spot the students of this particular conservatoire, because they had a peculiar intensity. But what could be behind the behaviour of these acting teachers who feel that they must 'help' students overcome 'blocks'? Surely it can only be two things: (1) an absolute certainty that they KNOW what is going on in a student's head and (2) the certainty that whatever it is that is going on in an actor's head has direct bearing on the actor's ability. Now the idea that we know what someone else is thinking isn't aberrant belief – this very ability to 'mentalize' or have a 'theory of mind' is an important part of brain development. But the dubious practice inspired by it in acting classes surely *is* aberrant in some cases. What makes some acting teachers so certain that they know what is going on in their students' heads?

It is true that on many days of our lives we'll spending some time looking at someone thinking 'Why did you do that?' and then filling any number of minutes trying to answer that question. The 'theory of mind' practice of trying guess what is in other people's heads or what motivated their behaviour is common enough and indeed necessary to our very survival, and we do it every day. In philosophical terms, when we're theorizing what someone else is thinking, we're 'metarepresenting'. When we look at or think about our friend, Amy, we have the representation of Amy in our mind. But when we guess what Amy is thinking when she grabs an umbrella we have a 'metarepresentation' of her mind – and we may have the metarepresentational thought: Amy believes that it is going to rain today. But along with our ability to metarepresent other peoples' thoughts in our head, as actors we also need to have a theory of the relationship of minds to behaviour. In other words, I can't begin to make sense of someone else's behaviour unless I have a particular theory about how what's going on in their mind influences their behaviour.

Theories about the relationship between thought and behaviour can be extremely general such as:

1. all people learn from experience;
2. women are more interested in monogamy than men;
3. most people take on some of the values of their parents.

or it could be that I have a theory that includes slightly more specific generalizations such as:

1. people who are physically abused become physical abusers;
2. children of alcoholics are always neurotic;
3. actors are all attention-seekers.

Whatever our 'general theory' of how-minds-motivate-behaviour may be – and no doubt these are influenced by everything from our own experience to things we have witnessed or been told about – we all do HAVE a theory of mind and behaviour. It probably isn't something we think about much, but we can test its presence simply by making one sort of factual statement about the behaviour of someone we know (Robin finds it hard to throw anything away) and then asking ourselves what we think motivates that behaviour (Robin grew up in a poor household, so hates to 'waste' anything). In most cases, we will have some guess about what motivates the behaviour of others, and this guess will come from general sorts of theories that we have about the minds of others and the ways in which they work – not the least part of which is a general belief that behaviour IS motivated in some ways that we can predict.

This whole area – which may seem obvious or simple to us – has become something of a site of philosophical and scientific struggle recently. Stephen Stich explains that philosophers are particularly fascinated by:

> the ability to _describe_ people and their behavior (including their linguistic behavior) _in intentional terms_ – or to 'interpret' them, as philosophers sometimes say. We exercise this ability when we describe John as _believing that the mail has come_, or when we say that Anna _wants to go to the library_. By exploiting these intentional descriptions, people are able to offer _explanations_ of each other's behavior (Susan left the building _because_ she believed that it was on fire) and to _predict_ each other's behavior, often with impressive accuracy. Since the dominant strategy for explaining any cognitive capacity is to posit an internally represented theory, it is not surprising that in this area, too, it is generally assumed that a theory is being invoked.[6]

There are many ideas about how we begin to predict or interpret the behaviour of others – most of which we, as actors, are working through and discussing all the time. Indeed, the actor who asks 'What is my motivation?' is one of the great clichés of the theatre – but of course, this question presupposes that behaviour IS motivated in ways that we can consciously identify. But how do we link internal motivation with observable behaviour? One obvious approach is reason/fact-based. For example, when I see Linda twiddling with her hair, I might know (a) that Linda has a history of twiddling with her hair when she is nervous; (b) that she always twiddles her hair when she is flirting; (c) that she is unaware of twiddling her hair when she does it; (d) that she wants to break the bad habit of twiddling her hair. From this collection of facts, I might figure out any number of things about WHY Linda is twiddling her hair just at this moment, and I might also predict whether or not she's going to continue with this behaviour or whether she is going to stop.

Another obvious approach is 'simulation' – which would require no knowledge of Linda at all. Suppose we are in a library and we see a young girl twiddling with her hair. We can't draw on any history or facts about this girl because we don't know her. But we can consult our knowledge of our own history and behaviour and then make some predictions about the girl's behaviour. For instance, suppose I twiddle my hair when I'm bored, and that I find it comforting. I might then guess that the unknown girl is bored, and she will probably keep twiddling her hair until she is no longer bored. It should be clear, in these examples, that most theories of mind that allow us to predict behaviour or ascribe motive/intention to behaviour carry with them an assumption of rationality. In other words, we would ordinarily imagine that our predictions about another person's state of mind, or guesses at what was motivating their observable behaviour can be correct if we assume that the subject of our predictions or our guesses was rational and not, as Daniel Dennett explains, deranged:

> If we observe a mouse in a situation where it can see a cat waiting at one mousehole and cheese at another, we know which way the mouse will go, providing it is not deranged; our prediction is not based on our familiarity with maze-experiments or any assumptions about the sort of special training the mouse has been through. We suppose the mouse can see the cat and the cheese, and hence has beliefs (belief-analogues, intentional whatnots) to the effect that there is a cat to the left, cheese to the right, and we ascribe to the mouse also the desire to eat the cheese and to avoid the cat (subsumed, appropriately, under the more general desires to eat and to avoid peril); so we predict that the mouse will do what is appropriate to such beliefs and desires, namely, go to the right in order to get the cheese and avoid the cat.[7]

In this case, Dennett is describing something that might be both reason/fact-based (mice like cheese, mice will avoid predators, etc.) and could also possibly have an element of simulation (I know what I would do when faced with a choice between predator and dinner). I am probably safe in suggesting that we normally use a combination of these approaches when we're acting, since it doesn't seem to me that one necessarily excludes the other. But what approach are we using when we decide (as teachers or directors) that a student/actor needs to tackle their own 'emotional issues'? What approach was Strasberg using when he decided that in order to help actors, he needed to encourage them to explore their own traumatic emotional experiences?

Let us imagine that Guru A sees a young actor who is having some difficulty connecting with his/her emotion, Guru A might take the reason/fact-based approach:

1. when we get to the scene where his mother dies in the play, Young Actor X (YAX) can't seem to muster any emotional response at all;
2. YAX has mentioned in rehearsal that his mother died when he was young;
3. when we rehearse this scene, YAX never seems to want to refer to his own personal experience with this or to talk about how his mother died, whether he was present, exactly how old he was, etc.;
4. YAX seems to lose all his performance energy when we get to the scene where the mother dies.

Armed with this knowledge/history, Guru A might reasonably come to the conclusion that YAX has a kind of emotional or psychological 'block' when it comes to the issue of mothers dying and playing in scenes where a mother dies. However Guru A might also watch YAX's dull performance in the scene where his mother dies with no knowledge of YAX's history and might therefore simply consult his own history and behaviour: 'I find it hard to make emotional connections when scenes are too close to my own personal, still-tender, experience of something. YAX seems to be shutting down when we get to the scene where his mother dies – this is probably because there is something in the scene (death, death of mother) that YAX hasn't "dealt with" and is therefore emotionally "blocking"'.

We might find one of these ways of reaching the conclusion: 'YAX has an emotional block' more acceptable than the other. We might also, ordinarily, expect that this conclusion would more usually be reached by a combination of these two approaches: reason/fact-based and 'simulation'. But (as this is all about predicting the behaviour of others) what action would we expect Guru A to take in order to help YAX? Before we can answer this question (and we may already have jumped to any one of a number of tactics for confronting emotional blocks that we've either used or learned!) surely we have to ask ourselves whether Guru A is right or not. *Is YAX or is YAX not having a problem*? And how can we know this?

In an interview in 1964, Strasberg explained how he made judgements in cases like these:

Let's say the actor learns to relax and concentrate. He learns to arouse his imagination, which is his belief in the reality and logic of what he is doing; but then we find that the actor's expression of these things is weak. Often we see things going on inside that can't come out – the face contracts, the eyes contract – the emotion isn't let through. The actor feels at times like crying but he can't cry, he can't uncurl the muscles to permit the tears to flow. Such strong conditioning has been created against the expression of emotion. I would say that I have experimented with the whole problem of freeing the expression of the actor.[8]

We might be better able to accept Strasberg's logic (which goes something like this: a.)YAX can't express emotion; b.) actors who can't express emotion need techniques for freeing emotion; c.)therefore YAX needs techniques for freeing his emotion) *if we are already predisposed to believing that all actors must express emotion*. Well, this seems a commonplace, does it not? Of course all actors must express emotion. But WHAT emotion are we talking about (as we've seen this whole area is highly complex)? Is Strasberg after the actor's true emotion? Or a kind of 'theatrical' emotion that an actor can use in a 'technical' sense? Can we not reel off a list of successful actors who have never really 'expressed' emotion? As we might recall, this certainly wasn't a prerequisite for Meisner ('If you have it [emotion], it infects you and the audience. If you don't have it – like Helen Hayes – don't bother; just say the lines as truthfully as you are capable of doing.'[9]). So we may agree with Strasberg's logic only if we accept that all actors need to express emotion (assuming you know exactly what you're talking about here), or we may agree with Strasberg's logic only if we accept that actors need to be able SEEM as if they can free their emotion. And it would appear that Meisner didn't particularly agree with either of these assumptions, so we would have to conclude that these two ideas are not universally held.

Strasberg speaks with real certainty about the need to help actors 'free their emotion' and I would venture to say that in current practice it has become something of a commonplace to speak of actors whose performances are 'not fully connected', whose performances are 'not deeply felt'. I'm also aware of how often, when talking to other directors and acting teachers, it is common to hear of actors 'having an emotional block' or being 'unable to connect to their own emotion'. These statements all involve a judgement about the psychology of another person (the actor). They also imply that in order to help the actor improve, we need to help them deal with their own psychological issues. But we must surely wonder where the idea that we must deal with the actor's own psychology has come from? Apart from Diderot's very early intervention about the paradox of feeling/simulating emotion, the great early theorists like Stanislavski, Chekhov, Boleslavsky did not centre much of their concern on the individual actor's own psychological workings – indeed it is difficult to find anything in their works that refer to the individual actor's psychology.

They addressed relaxation, imagination, creativity, inspiration, spirit, physical and 'psychophysical' actions, objectives, sense and emotion memory, physical freedom and gesture, curiosity about the world and the behaviour of *others*, but there isn't much in any of these early works that could be said to be addressing the issue of the individual actor's psychology. And there is certainly nothing in the category of the 'how to release your emotional blocks'. This concern seems to me to be a relatively recent phenomenon. Of course, many trace this to the work of practitioners like Strasberg, whose influential teaching was both widely adapted and in some cases just as widely misunderstood. I would suggest that there was much other activity in the mid- to late twentieth century that inspired the search into the actor's psyche, in the works of influential practitioners such as Jerzy Grotowski. In *Towards a Poor Theatre*, Grotowski talks about the 'eradication of blocks', and of 'a psychic stripping away of disguises' and he set out the actor's objectives:

> To stimulate a process of self-revelation, going back as far as the subconscious, yet canalizing this stimulus in order to obtain the required reaction…To eliminate from the creative process the resistances and obstacles caused by one's own organism, both physical and psychic (the two forming a whole).[10]

But Grotowski (and others) were not addressing acting technique in terms of realist texts, of course, and the aesthetic drive in their vision of theatre was one which grew from a much more avant-garde tradition. Still, their work was highly influential in the educational curriculum of my generation and perhaps their ideas have come to be assimilated by many acting teachers. In any case, the quotations above are the first I have found that actually addresses the actor's psychological state in terms of emotional expression and the need to free 'blocked' or unexpressed emotion in individual actors. Most of the early texts refer rather indirectly at 'emotional freedom' by addressing physical and imaginative freedom, openness, awareness, concentration and the like.

I've been on a quest to find something that does address what I know has become a kind of 'commonplace' in terms of actor training, and in his book *Acting and Reacting* (published in 2005) Nick Moseley's approach includes from the very start a concern with the individual actor's psychology. I think the book makes an interesting example to consider, precisely because it is so recent. Moseley's approach is in fact rather gentle and humanistic but when addressing young actors about to enter a training programme his advice is curious indeed:

> In this context, the moment we begin to dismantle the structure of your fixed set of beliefs about yourselves and the world you live in, we find insecurity, panic and despondency. Yet we have to dismantle it, otherwise you will never be able to do more than 'pretend'.[11]

There are a number of things to worry about here – starting, perhaps, with wondering how it is that Moseley and his colleagues can have any certain knowledge of the 'set beliefs' in the minds of others. Where does one learn the skill of dismantling set beliefs? I can't find anything in the many classic texts of acting theory that addresses such a thing and of course it brings us back to our question of how we can know what is in another person's head. Clearly for Moseley there is little need to explain how he knows what is in his students' heads – we are meant to accept that he has trained enough students to KNOW WHAT THEY ARE THINKING. He knows that they have fixed beliefs, he knows that the fixed beliefs are hindering the students' progress and he knows that the fixed beliefs must be dismantled.

Here, we might guess that acting teachers like Moseley are operating on both the reason/fact-based approach in predicting the behaviour of others – but in trying to imagine how this reason/fact-based approach works here, things grow very tricky. We might we imagine that such teachers have:

1. a history of greeting young acting students who all had fixed beliefs that needed to be dismantled;
2. a history of helping to dismantle these beliefs in a training situation, and a knowledge of how to help dismantle these beliefs;
3. a history of observing that young actors become better artists once their fixed beliefs have been dismantled.

But surely all this only works IF the teachers in question have a level of self-knowledge that ensures that *they themselves do not have fixed beliefs that need to be dismantled* – because otherwise this whole enterprise will be undermined by the circularity of the argument: I believe that my students have fixed beliefs which must be dismantled but in order to prove this I can only refer to my fixed belief that my students have fixed beliefs…it all gets exhaustingly circular!

The other possibility, though, could be a simulation model – which in this case might be that a teacher has themselves observed the ways in which their own fixed beliefs have inhibited their own acting work. This, of course, does not constitute a reliable 'universal' rule for judging what young actors need, but I imagine that it serves as a start when guessing what might be going on in the heads of young actors.

This gets more difficult if we keep in mind Daniel Dennett's observation about the ways in which all theories of intention must assume rationality. Let us suppose that we all agree that some 'fixed' sets of beliefs could be necessary to our survival and are rational (for example, we might believe that flying in an airplane is dangerous or that having colon-cleansing therapy is necessary for our health). These are beliefs rather than fact in the sense that they may not be scientifically borne out either by our own experience or by statistical information, but they are still 'fixed beliefs' that we think will aid in our continued health and survival. We could at least agree that it is not necessarily irrational to hold these beliefs. So, if I hold these possibly rational 'fixed' beliefs, do they become part of the set of fixed beliefs that must be dismantled by my teachers upon entering drama school? Well, most likely not – but then the question becomes: if not these, then **which** of my fixed set of beliefs must be dismantled? How will my teachers know which are rational, or possibly rational sets of fixed belief and which are sets of fixed beliefs that hinder my development as an actor? If my teachers cannot make this distinction, how will I know that they are dismantling the right set of fixed beliefs? We could take this a step further. Suppose, 99 times out of 100, acting teachers are dealing with 'rational actors'. But what about that 1 per cent who may be a bit irrational about something, and who might find the loss or 'dismantlement' of fixed belief to be profoundly distressing? What if the fixed beliefs might actually be part of what make up a particular student/actor's sense of self or identity?

I once taught a very interesting young man I'll call Terence. Terence had an incredibly powerful imagination and his ability to believe in the given circumstances of any play he worked on actually affected all the other actors around him. Because his belief was so strong, he simply seemed to 'infect' others with that same strength of belief. After one particularly exciting rehearsal, his scene partner, Lisa, said to me 'I really wasn't very inspired today – such a dull rehearsal until my scene with Terence. When he looks at you, you can just see he thinks he IS the king, and he's expecting so much from me, the queen!'

His imagination was quite magical. He also brought his cat to rehearsal every day. It wasn't a live cat. It was a pretty tatty, stuffed ginger cat that came along with him in his bag everyday and sat out on a chair or the floor near where Terence was working. I confess that the cat drove me crazy and I referred to it continually as 'that damned cat' although I seem to recall that Terence had given it a name. I think Terence knew, though, that my anger at the 'damned cat' was something of a joke – said largely to make the other students laugh and take any tension out of what could have been a strange atmosphere. This was, after all, a postgraduate course where one might reasonably expect actors to attend rehearsals without the presence of cuddly toys…

I don't know what importance the cat had for Terence but I sensed that it had some. I also sensed that no young man of Terence's age would risk peer censure over bringing stuffed cats into classes and rehearsals unless there was some strong attachment that overrode his fear of censure. So there we were day after day – me, the company, Terence and the damned cat. I never asked him *not* to bring it, and I never asked him to put it away. He was too good an actor to mess with any of the constituent parts that might have contributed to his unique personality and his obvious skill. Perhaps Terence held a 'fixed belief' that the cat brought him luck? Or that the cat kept him sane? Or that the cat gave him his acting skill? Or was it just a 'lucky' object that he wanted to have around? Irrational thoughts, no doubt – but were Terence's beliefs any more irrational than my own belief that the cat might, in some sense, have been contributing to his acting performances? And that to ask him to remove it might in some way upset the delicate balance of atmosphere and impede his usual imaginative genius?

Moseley's book goes on to describe a kind of 'transactional improvisation' which forms part of his method of training actors and it is interesting to me because I think it illustrates how often we now routinely address the actor's individual psychology when training. The exercises in 'transactional improvisation' are very much like a group therapy – designed to instil trust in a group context, to offer constructive challenge and to encourage the development of new behaviours, etc. While I am sure there is probably much to be gained in these exercises, they do sound surprisingly close to what we might expect a clinical psychology group therapy to achieve. He refers to this exercise both as the 'What-I-Am' game and the 'self-knowledge game' and describes it like this:

> One actor in a group is asked to make a statement about themselves, something which they believe to be true in the form of 'I am a…person'. For example, one actor might say 'I am an insecure person'…The group then 'reprioritises' the individual's statement…so that it becomes a potential threat to group unity and equality. To crush the individual outright would be to expose the group's intolerance, and of course ironically would heighten the individual's reason for being insecure. Instead the group appoints a 'champion' whose job is either to force the individual to withdraw the statement, or to force the individual to offer enough to the group to enable them to accept it…During the process, any one of the champion's response lines may trigger off huge amounts of insecurity in the individual, so that by working off his opponent, the individual may find, and offer, all the insecurity he needs to make the statement [true].[12]

While there may be any number of things that this game might do for an actor, could we ever actually know what they are? Could we ever be certain that this game leads to 'self-knowledge'? It may be that in this case, the teacher has statistical evidence on his side – in 500 out of 500 cases the student observed has gained 'self-knowledge' – but as Nassim Nicholas Taleb points out in his book, *The Black Swan*, statistical evidence is misleading. Until someone discovered a black swan in Australia in the seventeenth century, the whole definition of a swan was bound into its whiteness. Once the black swan was discovered, hundreds of years of statistical certainty were rendered meaningless.[13]

But even putting anxieties about statistical reliability to one side, we are still left with a couple of worries. One is perhaps moral and the second logical. In the first case, it is rare for teachers of acting to have a strong background in clinical or even theoretical psychology and – as Eli Wallach objected many years ago – is group interaction focusing on a single person's admitted weakness really within the purview of the acting teacher? In the second case, isn't there a weakness in the conclusion regarding the actor's purported gain in 'self-knowledge'? Could we trust a student who might 'self-report' as having gained 'self-knowledge'? Studies in the area of self-reporting repeatedly demonstrate its weakness. But even if we adopt the 'heterophenomenological' stance espoused by Daniel Dennett (in which the self-report of a subject is admitted as evidence along with many other kinds of evidence), whatever knowledge that student may or may not have gained would surely have to be centred in the relationship between the self and this particular group. Consequently the question of how we might verify whether that knowledge is transferable to any other group would certainly bedevil any attempts to establish that a student had gained 'self-knowledge'.

Philosophical problems aside, Moseley, to his very great credit, concludes his book with an observation about the limitations of looking at the actor's own inner life: 'The problem with focusing on the emotional and psychological state of the individual, however, is that this can draw attention away from the social gestures and transactions which continually reinforce and influence that individual's behaviour, and which may present a different interpretation of the text.'[14] My point is not to question Moseley in particular. He is surely not the only acting teacher concerned with the actor's psyche. Edward Dwight Easty writes:

> The actor must learn early in his career that his acting talent (and by this I mean his sensitivity, intelligence awareness and even his physical attractiveness) will be closely governed by his personal life. Consequently, his personal problems will affect his talent.[15]

Leaving aside Easty's rather strange description of acting talent, the ways in which contemporary acting approaches and books seem to see the question of the individual actor's psychology as something that is involved in acting (and which therefore may need to be addressed in training), is worrisome.

But this conviction has certainly not always held. If we look, for example, at Michael Chekhov's first chapter in the influential *To the Actor*, which is entitled 'The Actor's Body and Psychology', Chekhov never addresses the first-person psychology of the actor. Instead his chapter is about the relationship of the body to mental states and how the two are connected. He talks of the importance of freeing the body – not simply through what he saw as the traditional curriculum of actor training: gymnastics, fencing, callisthenics, etc., but insisted that the body must be 'fed' with psychological qualities – 'must be filled and permeated with them',[16] which would help to keep the actor's body animated. He sees this 'psychological feeding' as a question of building an arsenal of knowledge about human behaviour through observation, but he doesn't seem to see an actor's difficulties as possibly arising from an 'emotional' block – he sees 'block' as something that happens when the *body* is not free:

> There are certain actors who can feel their roles deeply, can comprehend them pellucidly, but who can neither express nor convey to an audience these riches within themselves. Those wonderful thoughts and emotions are somehow chained inside their undeveloped bodies.[17]

It seems critical to me that Chekhov doesn't assume that actors who can't express emotion are emotionally blocked – he sees the problem as one in which the actor is physically blocked. He also knows that actors must have a 'rich, colourful psychology' but he does not assume that this will be achieved by enhancing self-knowledge, nor by revealing personal memory or experience, nor by having their 'fixed beliefs' eliminated. Instead he advised the actor to get out and observe and think about the behaviour of others. Perhaps the relatively very recent focus on the actor's own psychology has grown out of many diverse contextual influences that Robert Brustein and Richard Hornby, amongst others, have alluded to, but for me the greater question is how we approach and understand the psychology of actors NOW – and whether in the interests of philosophical enquiry it is time to start querying

> **Must we 'expose ourselves' physically or psychologically in order to become better actors?**

the practice of guessing, experimenting, dismantling or in any way tinkering with an actor's own psychology or 'emotional state of being'. It seems to me that there are a number of moral philosophical questions that this practice entails and perhaps it is time for us to engage with these before we engage with the practice of attempting to dismantle the 'fixed beliefs' of actors, or demand that they expose themselves (physically or psychologically) in order to become 'better' actors.

The psychological toy box

There's no doubt that for many of us one of the greatest pleasures of acting and directing lie squarely in the psychological guessing games that inform both performances and overall directorial approaches. The number of 'Lucio-as-drug-dealer/addict', 'Horatio-as-gay-man-in-love-with-Hamlet' or Orsino-as-paedophile' performances I've seen are surely proof that we love to get right into the questions of what motivates behaviour and what kinds of elaborate (if sometimes pretty tenuous) psychological quirks we can impose on our characters. But for all that we play at it, it's always seemed to me that 'psychology' as a subject is more or less expected to be part of the actor's spontaneous intellectual arsenal – since we rarely discuss this in acting texts. It could be said, no doubt, that for actors the whole area of psychology proper gets subsumed into discussions about 'subtext'. In other words, our attempts to ferret out what kinds of psychological motives or states might lay beneath a simple line like Ranevskaya's 'Who's been smoking disgusting cigars?' (Is she avoiding Lopakhin? Is she making a statement about class difference? Is she recalling an ex-lover?) are bound to be psychological inquiries.

As practitioners we spend endless hours discussing what motivates behaviour in the plays that we direct and act in, but we rarely ever take a step backward and ask 'what it is that we can actually KNOW about human psychology and what can we KNOW about the relationship between psychological states, motivation and behaviour?'

From Stanislavski onwards actors have been encouraged to think about subtext, which is in fact an encouragement to embark upon a psychological examination. For most of us, character psychology will take some time for us to work out

> **Where is the 'Psych 101 for Actors' class?**

but the tools with which we shape our conclusions are not in themselves very often the subject of scrutiny. We talk endlessly about subtext and many books on acting consider it – but where is the 'Psych 101 For Actors' class? If psychological examination is such a significant part of the actor's labour, why do we assume that the only thing actors need to carry out such an examination is their own life experience and observation?

For most of us, the process of playing a part moves from analysis to representation in roughly this way:

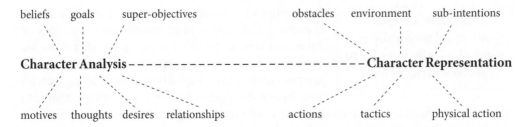

The actual process is not, of course, this linear and for some actors there may be many other things that come into play. I'm leaving out the larger areas of concern in this, which might fall under 'play analysis', 'historical/socio/cultural analysis', etc. Not because we don't need to understand much about Russian history, society and culture to understand fully Turgenev's characters, but because I'm concentrating here on the kinds of analysis we do with regard to psychological behaviour, and I'm going to take it as a given that the actor trying to understand Mikhail Rakitin will have done background research and will understand that Rakitin's historical/social/cultural context informs his behaviour.

But let us look at this rather simplistic framework above – the first question here is how we relate the first part, the Analysis, to the second part, the Representation. This might be simple. In our analysis we may have concluded that Hamlet's suspicion and grief are motivating him to punish his mother. This will affect the relationship between them, as well as the actions and the tactics in the playing. But how are we meant to carry out the psychological analysis that led us to centre on grief, suspicion and mothers in the first place? Why are we so rarely concerned with how to approach psychological analysis in acting books? Why do the profound questions of character analysis remain so often written about only in the realm of academic rather than practical study? In an academic book survey you'll find psychological analyses of Hamlet that run from considerations of his Oedipal frustrations to theories about his aversion to sex to conclusions about his necrophiliac tendencies.

There are of course many times, in rehearsals, when a more formal consideration of psychology sneaks in – as Bella Merlin's account of Nick Hytner's productions of the two parts of *Henry IV* illustrates:

> You could say that the journey in these two plays is the suppression of the real self. If, Matthew, I follow your instinctive connection with the part, it would seem that the self experienced by Hal at this moment could be a perfectly fine self, but it's of no use to him as king. It's easy to get very post-Freudian with Shakespeare as he seems to have 'predicted' so much, but there is this interesting idea here that appetite or libido can be channelled into power. Hal can full-bloodedly express himself in a Falstaffian way as a normal human being – but to be king, he would have to channel that full-blooded self into political power.[18]

Whether or not we can work a little Freudian analysis into rehearsal with quite Mr Hytner's ease, I'm sure it's safe to say that we will generally work our way through some pretty interesting psychological ideas when we're rehearsing. But as we know, in the practical realm of acting, the questions of psychology seem so often these days to be turned back over to the actors' own psychological constitution. Instead of asking first 'how does Angelo's proposition to Isabella affect her psychologically?' actors will often begin by asking 'how would I feel if this happened to me?' In other words (in the manner of Stanislavski's 'magic if') we are quite used to employing the 'simulation' theory of predicting what is in others' heads, outlined above.

The problem for actors who begin with the empathetic 'magic if' exercise is precisely the problem that Stella Adler was addressing in the quotation that we looked at earlier ('The truth of the character is not found in you, but in the circumstances of the royal position of Hamlet, the character you are playing', etc.) While we can see the difficulties in Adler's articulation of this idea – particularly in terms of the metaphorical relationship between actor and character posed here – the force of what she has to say is directed at getting actors to understand that the character circumstances of a Royal Prince of Denmark are going to be different from the character circumstances for most of us. For an 18-year old girl from Bolton to confine her preparation for the role of Isabella to 'I know what I'd do if someone was threatening my brother's life' would be perilous indeed.

This is putting the case rather baldly, of course, and most women playing Isabella recognize that her life as a young novitiate is very different from theirs, but in psychological terms, how do we begin to assess that difference? If, as actors, we want to start with a psychological analysis based only on facts and not on guesses, then we are really only able to look at the character in terms of **behavioural psychology**. In other words we have to make all our decisions about Isabella on the basis of her behaviour and not on the basis of what might be hidden away in her mind. We don't know enough from the text to determine how Isabella's past experiences might affect her current psychological state. And yet, somehow, we have to add up all the clues from text and behaviour to make a credible guess at how things work in her mind (or at least, the part of her mind that she may be aware of).

But always there are some points when we invoke some **introspective psychology** (in which we attempt to guess at her internal mental state rather than to restrict our analysis to her observable behaviour). These points probably occur in the moments when there is not enough information in the play to allow us a 'plausible' explanation for a character action based simply on observable behaviour. We are probably not too worried, for example, about figuring out why Lucio lies. The play gives us ample demonstration of the fact that Lucio's behaviour will always direct itself toward Lucio's advancement with people of power, and toward the advancement of his own physical pleasures. While some actors may enjoy an intellectual dissection of Lucio's inner psychology in what they imagine will deepen their understanding of what *drives*

> **There is certainly some cause to doubt whether the use of introspective psychology can help us at all in our portrayal of a character**

Lucio's *drives* (perhaps imagining any one of a number of dysfunctions in the Mommy-Daddy-Lucio history), there are just as many actors happy to accept the behavioural evidence regarding Lucio's actions as motivated by selfish interests at all times.

I would suggest that there are times when it seems most common to revert to introspective psychological analysis – and the main ones seem to me to be:

1. **Cognitive dissonance**: this is a phrase used to describe a common situation in which one holds conflicting beliefs or behaviours (we'll be looking more closely at this area later). In Isabella's case she says one thing, but then does (or attempts to persuade others to do) another. She initially responds to the news of Angelo's sentence of her brother with 'O just but severe law. I had a brother then.' But of course all of her actions in the play belie her acceptance of the law as 'just'. How does the actor reconcile this?

2. **The 'mysterious'**: might be described as moments that do not initially seem to gibe with all that we know about the character and the circumstances. Or they may be moments that just don't find resonance with us individually. In Isabella's case many puzzle over, for example, her statement in the scene where we first encounter her, in which she bemoans the fact that the convent she inhabits isn't more strict. This seems a bit out of kilter with the ways in which – once called upon – she interacts quite quickly in the outside world, pleading with powerful men, appealing to and then condemning her own brother, cooperating in setting up an elaborate hoax for Angelo and willingly testifying quite publicly against some very powerful men.

3. **Questionable or open decisions**: in Isabella's case, as we know, the very end of the play is left quite open and most actors resort to some kind of introspective psychology to guess what might be going on in Isabella's head as she hears the Duke's proposal of marriage.

While it might certainly be expected that in any rehearsal process the questions of what is in Isabella's head in these three situations will come up, there is certainly some cause to doubt whether the use of introspective psychology can help us at all in our portrayal of Isabella – especially if, in the guise of armchair psychologists we are after finding a 'definite' answer to these questions.

In the case of (1), cognitive dissonance, how can we imagine that introspective psychology will help us? In what ways would it help? If we make the decision that she is really not genuine in her beliefs about the law being just, then we open up an interpretation for which we have very little textual evidence. If we make the decision that she is genuine in her belief, we are still left with the fact that she pleads against the 'just' law and accuses Angelo of pride for administering the punishment. Is it not sufficient to take her at her word – that she is at war with herself? While knowing that she is aware of the 'discomfort' of holding conflicting opinions/behaviour could help us in our portrayal, we don't need to try and reconcile this – to do so risks taking the inherent drama out of this situation.

In the case of (2), the 'mysterious', we might imagine many subconscious reasons why a young woman would desire a more punishing, strict routine in her convent – but of course if these reasons are truly subconscious, then there is nothing that the actor can do with them, so there is no need for us to spend intellectual labour here. If they are not subconscious, but are simply unspoken, then we might perhaps decide that Isabella has a conscious motive in proclaiming this desire – perhaps, for example, she wants to ingratiate herself with the other sisters by looking very devout. In practical language, this theory is a subtextual reading: Isabella *says* she wants a stricter regimen, but what she *means* is that she is very devout. If we make this decision we are privileging our own psychological guessing over Shakespeare's text – but this is common enough practice. For some actors the privileging of subtext over text can result in a great performance. But as we know, there is also a great performance to be had in taking the text as read.

The case of (3) – the unresolved or open question – is not open to subtextual analysis, since Isabella is given no text at the end of the play. This means that we have little choice but to settle down in the armchair and take a guess at what she is thinking. This is all well and good and we must accept that there is no way to demonstrate an innate superiority of one guess over any other. Therefore all the following have an equal place at the interpretative table:

1. I will marry him – I think he is a good man and he loves me.
2. I am going back to convent – I've had enough of this outside world.
3. I will never marry this man – he is a liar and he put us all through a terrible experience.
4. I am going home to my mother – I'm not sure what to do now. Neither marriage nor convent is appealing.
5. I must go back to the convent and pray. God will lead me to the right decision.
6. I will marry him only if he will spare Lucio's life – after all, they both lied in their turn.

When we're told, in our training years, to go away, 'dig deeper', 'ask more profound questions', etc. in our attempts to lend weight and dimension to the roles we take on, what can we be reasonably expected to produce in terms of psychological substance?

One night many years ago when I was still in grad school, my friend Theresa and I went to see a 'full uncut' version of Hamlet in a small theatre somewhere in LA. It was one of those decisions I really can't explain. The cast were – as might be expected – all veterans of daytime soap operas and small film parts, and had little idea about playing Shakespeare. They were unfortunate in their director, who seemed to suffer a similar inability to gauge the difference between a television performance and performing Shakespeare live. The consequent small dimension of the playing made for a tedious evening. It was a tiny audience – only about ten of us I seem to recall – and at the first interval everyone left – with the exception of my friend and me. At the second interval we decided that the other eight had been wise and headed for our car which was parked behind the little theatre. As Theresa got her keys out to unlock the doors we were suddenly aware that a number of the cast had followed us out to the parking lot. It was an uncomfortable moment as they asked why we were leaving. Tactfully we explained that we had early classes in Irvine the next day and hadn't realized how late the production would run. Being actors with sensitive egos you could see that they were grateful for this explanation and the actor playing Hamlet asked us if we had enjoyed it. My friend Theresa skilfully countered his question with one of her own: had HE enjoyed the performance and did he think that Hamlet was mad? The actor, who was the best-known soap star in the company replied that it wasn't his job to think about what went on in Hamlet's head – his job was to behave like the Prince of Denmark. At the time I rather smugly assumed that he was the product of LA-soap-opera-airheadedness. These days I'm not so sure. In fact, I think he was onto something…

If we take the case of Isabella in point, how are we to navigate this final decision, given the huge gaps in knowledge that we have about her? For instance, it may be that her mother died when she was very young and that her father sent her away to a convent. Or it may be that her father died when both she and her brother were very young and they have lived most of their lives as orphans. Although she only ever mentions her (dead) father in the text, it may very well be that Isabella's mother is alive and has remarried a wealthy Viennese merchant who, along with his new wife, is perplexed at the choice of the young girl in becoming a nun. As we might imagine, all three of these scenarios could result in very different kinds of psychological effects – and might certainly affect our list of guesses above.

So many psychologies

These days there are a lot of different psychologies. And in the wake of the 'cognitive revolution' behaviourism and Freudian approaches have suffered a distinct fall from favour in terms of understanding the mind. The question of how we know what is in someone else's head has been at the forefront of some of the cognitive debates. At the extreme end of those who are looking at these questions anew is the conclusion that psychology as it is currently understood is doomed to become a victim of scientific advance. In much philosophy and cognitive studies literature these days, psychology is already referred to as a 'folk theory'. 'Folk psychology' is the particular target of a philosophical school called 'eliminative materialism', which considers all psychology – as it deals with things like 'mental

There are no such things as beliefs or hopes or desires. This is just a cosy 'folk' story…

states' (such as beliefs or desires) – to be 'folk psychology'. This may sound initially like a relative of behavioural psychology, but it is a wholly different project:

> Modern versions of eliminative materialism claim that our common-sense understanding of psychological states and processes is deeply mistaken and that some or all of our ordinary notions of mental states will have no home, at any level of analysis, in a sophisticated and accurate account of the mind. In other words, it is the view that certain common-sense mental states, such as beliefs and desires, do not exist. To establish this claim, eliminativists typically endorse two central and controversial claims…The first scenario proposes that certain mental concepts will turn out to be empty, with mental state terms referring to nothing that actually exists. Historical analogs for this way of understanding eliminativism are cases where we (now) say it turned out there are no such things, such as demons and crystal spheres. The second scenario suggests that the conceptual framework provided by neurosciences (or some other physical account) can or should come to replace the common-sense framework we now use…Given these two different conceptions, early eliminativists would sometimes offer two different characterizations of their view: (a) *There are no mental states, just brain states* and, (b) *There really are mental states, but they are just brain states (and we will come to view them that way).*[19]

Admittedly, a bit heavy going in this description – but the point is easy enough to grasp: there are no such things as beliefs or hopes or desires. We will come to realize this in time and the idea that there ARE beliefs and hopes and desires will come to be seen by us eventually for just what it is: a cosy folk story.

Of course, these ideas seem *seriously at odds* with our common sense way of thinking about the mind and the way that people function. But most of those who write from the eliminative materialist perspective do NOT deny the complexity of 'folk psychology'. Nor do they deny its function – as an everyday theory, most of the 'EM' crowd admit, 'folk psychology' works. But they do deny that it is an idea that will last much longer in its current state against the advance of scientific research. Like old theories about witches, or the sun moving around the earth, most consider that the whole category of 'folk psychology' will be superseded by advances in knowledge about how the brain works. And the result of this will be our realization that 'mental states' or 'propositional attitudes' (such as beliefs, desires, hopes and other mental states that might motivate behaviour) do not actually exist.

Now this is a radical idea. For those of us who have spent much time in the rehearsal studio wondering if Hamlet truly believes in God, or if Hotspur hopes to hear that his father is proud of him, or if Juliet's desire for Romeo is really a form of teenage rebellion, the idea that desires, hopes or beliefs simply do not exist is almost unthinkable. How else can we explain human behaviour? What else are we motivated by if not our beliefs, hopes and desires? That is a good question – and one not immediately answered by those who are predicting the imminent demise of 'folk psychology'. Because in truth, their theories are not actually proposing that we don't experience beliefs, hopes and desires, but only that these mental states or brain states do not work in the way that we have commonly come to think of them as working.

But if eliminative materialists – or those who claim that folk psychology will one day be supplanted by another, better science of human behaviour and motivation – have no hard alternatives to offer at present (beyond pointing to things like 'neural substrates' or 'dual processes' or 'brain plasticity'), they do at least have the virtue of raising a lot of sticky points about the overall weaknesses in 'folk psychology'. And what might be of interest to practising actors/directors are the ways in which those weaknesses might illuminate our own work. If we take Isabella in case, we know that much of the analysis we did earlier was based on our 'folk-psychological' theories about how her own internal mental states could be driving her behaviour – but we also know that this analysis in itself did not overcome what we might describe as 'cognitive dissonance' or, more simply, did not really help us to understand the apparent contradictions between her behaviour and her stated beliefs.

If the theory of folk psychology assumes a model of mind in which there is normally a link between beliefs or desires and action or behaviour, then we know that in the case of Isabella we have some difficulties (if only in terms of how often her actions contradict her stated beliefs and desires). This particular view of how our minds work (the view that there IS a link between 'beliefs' and action or behaviour) is precisely what eliminativists might point to in order to demonstrate the limits of 'folk psychology' as a tool for understanding or predicting behaviour. Steven Stich, for example, suggests that we may have an entirely different structure of mind, and asks us to consider the possibility of a brain structure that 'keeps two sets of books'. One of these sets, he suggests, might interact with brain systems responsible only for belief-like states (Isabella believes in the word of God as revealed in the Bible), and one of those systems might interact only with the brain systems responsible for non-verbal behaviour, or action (Isabella still involves herself in an elaborate deception of Angelo). While it might rightly be observed that often these two systems are compatible, in many cases concerning Isabella they are not:

> If we really do have separate verbal and nonverbal cognitive storage systems, then the functional economy of the mind postulated by folk theory [in other words, the idea that we have one cognitive system for both verbal and behavioural systems] is quite radically mistaken. And under those circumstances I am strongly inclined to think that the right thing to say is that *there are no such things as beliefs*.[20]

Stich seems to be referring here to recent theories of the mind as a 'dual processing' system – although dual processing isn't usually posed in the way that Stich asserts. More commonly the two cognitive processes are separated by consciousness. One system, sometimes referred to as System 1 or Type 1 processing is largely unconscious (what Lakoff and Johnson have called the cognitive unconscious), works quickly, is independent of general intelligence and is contextualized, in that it is always responding to our immediate environment. This is the evolutionarily 'old' system of cognition. Type 2 or System 2 cognition is conscious, uniquely human, slower and more reflective and works from rule-based reasoning. Of course the concept of dual systems of thinking is not new – indeed, Freud posited three systems. But the ways in which these processes are currently described is new. Theorists recognize that the 'systems' can be in conflict with each other – and some see this as a problem to be overcome. Others feel that the need for a rational integration of these cognitive systems is not necessarily desirable, and see the tension in these conflicts as a constituent part of human cognition.

Clare Saunders and David Over consider the difficulties in areas like Type 1 desires for fat and sugar in our diets (a kind of genetic hangover from the days when food was scarce and calorie density important) and Type 2 desire for a celery stick (the rational recognition that these days, for some, food is not scarce and the avoidance of fat and sugar in our diets will lead to better health):

> More generally, there will always be conflicts between longer term goals and the desire for immediate gratification…Nevertheless dual-process theorists – insofar as they have addressed this problem at all – have tended to argue (or simply assume) that we should at least seek to minimize such conflicts. Indeed, it is often taken to be obvious that 'psychological consistency is itself valuable'…Our primary concern, for present purposes, is the implication that the pursuit of 'rational' integration is sometimes not just unfeasible, but also undesirable – that it is not always rational for us to try to get into a high level frame of mind where we no longer experience the conflict between (for example) justice and sympathy.[21]

Saunders and Over write about desires and beliefs, but they do so in terms of the different ways which these mental states are processed. Type 1 desires are unconscious desires – but they originate from genetic drives rather than from, say, childhood trauma or Freudian categories of the subconscious. Type 2 desires result from a more instrumental rationality. I'm interested in their point about the ways in which we tend to assume that psychological consistency is valuable or even achievable.

As actors and directors we tend to expend much of our intellectual labour in pursuit of some psychological consistency of character because we want to be able to identify what drives behaviour. We may come to conclusions such as: 'Constantine believes that his play is good' or 'it is Coriolanus' desire to avoid the public mob'. We don't necessarily expect that there is a science that can prove our statements about the internal workings of Constantine's or Coriolanus' minds; indeed we expect a little slippage between our reading of a character's mental state (which we take to have a causal effect on their behaviour) and someone else's reading (I might think Antigone's overriding belief in her own importance drives her behaviour, you may think her superstitious belief about burying the dead drives her behaviour – or we might split the difference). But is there any other way – apart from this psychological guessing game about a character's inner beliefs and desires – in which we can think about Antigone's behaviour?

For me, one of the most fascinating things about delving into this area has been reading some of the studies that have been carried out when looking into mysteries of what motivates human behaviour, beliefs and decisions. And perhaps the two most recurring themes amongst these studies are (1) the relative lack of accuracy in the area of 'introspection' – or in other words, how we explain to someone what we were thinking when we did X; and (2) how even what we might consider our bedrock beliefs can be influenced significantly by unconscious factors, particularly in the area of dissonance. In many cases where experimental situations have been set up and subjects were then asked to explain their behaviour in the set up, it has been proved that subjects are as likely to guess (or to supply 'plausible theories') about the thinking processes behind their behaviour as they are likely to be able to 'self-report' with accuracy.[22] Studies have also shown a remarkably fluid relationship with our own 'beliefs'. For example, a study carried out in which groups of people were offered various amounts of money for writing an essay completely opposed to their own beliefs determined that most people will hold on to their beliefs (despite what they may write) if the money offered is high enough. But if the money offered (50 cents in this case) is too low, then the study participant actually reports that they aren't quite so opposed to the ideas as they thought. Psychologists describe this kind of behaviour as our way of lessening dissonance. In other words, we can write an essay on the virtues of slavery if someone offers us $100. We KNOW that we're only writing it for the money. But if we write it for only 50 cents, we can't actually justify it to ourselves in any other way than to say that we can see some virtue in slavery.

One set of researchers set up an experiment in which subjects were asked to eat a grasshopper:

In one condition, the experimenter who presented this somewhat bizarre request was friendly and affable. In another condition, he was cold, unfriendly and generally unlikeable. As might be predicted from dissonance theory, the subjects who agreed to eat the grasshoppers for the aloof and unfriendly experimenter rated themselves as being more in favour of eating grasshoppers than did the subjects who agreed to eat the grasshoppers for the friendly experimenter. Apparently, trying to please a friendly and likeable person served as a justification for engaging in grasshopper eating, whereas changing private attitudes toward eating grasshoppers was necessary for reducing dissonance when the experimenter was unfriendly.[23]

Clearly our minds can only tolerate a certain amount of dissonance and lack of justification for things. In the absence of reconciliation or justification we will simply adjust our inner attitude – which is a polite way of saying that we will lie about things. Not consciously – of course – but when we need this little mental fluidity, we seem happy to accommodate. These studies suggest that we don't ourselves understand why we do things and that even if we could imagine that we are psychologically consistent, we are probably *only* consistent after we've 'adjusted' ourselves mentally and tried to convince ourselves that we enjoyed eating that grasshopper...

A recent study published by researchers at the Cambridge Centre for Brain Repair suggests another way in which 'folk psychology' is threatened by advances in cognitive research. The study looked at the behaviour of traders on the stock market floors in the City of London and demonstrated a clear link between brain chemistry and behaviour. The clear message of their report was the importance of brain chemistry in rapid decision-making:

> The research team followed 17 traders in the City of London for nearly two weeks, taking samples of their saliva before and after each day's trading. Testosterone levels were found to be significantly raised in those who had enjoyed a particularly good day's business. The scientists also discovered that levels of the stress hormone cortisol rose in direct relation to market volatility and that an increase in cortisol leads to risk aversion and can exaggerate downturns in the markets.
>
> The report's lead author, Dr John Coates, said: 'Too much testosterone can turn risk-taking into a form of addiction, while extreme cortisol during a crash can make traders shun risk altogether. In the present credit crisis traders may feel the effects of chronic cortisol exposure and end up in a mental state known as "learned helplessness". If this happens, central banks may lower interest rates only to find traders still refuse to buy risky assets. At times like these economics has to consider the physiology of investors, not just their rationality'.[24]

There are a number of interesting questions raised by this – probably the first is how we conceive of the cause and effect going on here. Was the chemistry causing the behaviour or was the behaviour causing the chemistry? But while there might be any number of things we could imagine were going on psychologically with these traders ('If I fail, my dad will be right about me'; 'When I make this quick million, she'll have to take me back'; 'One more big win and I'll start feeling good about myself again', etc.), that individual psychological information does not appear to be germane to the *behaviour* of the trader.

While these examples might help us to understand why some contemporary philosophers increasingly see 'folk psychology' as a passing paradigm for explaining human behaviour, it doesn't do much for us in a practical way. We can't begin to guess the chemical composition of Isabella's brain – and even if we could it wouldn't help us much in our desire to create a credible portrayal of her. But these studies are surely one or two nails in the 'folk psychology' coffin. If Young Actor X can't or doesn't know why he doesn't want to 'open up' in the scene of the play where his mother died – how on earth is Guru A to know? I am suggesting here that if our own motivation for our behaviour is

> **Would it aid our understanding of our fellow human beings to know that purchasing a tub of Ben & Jerry's Chunky Monkey ice cream has everything to do with brain chemistry and context?**

so mysterious to us and if we are so willing to adjust our internal landscape in order to accommodate dissonance, then it must be equally mysterious to those around us. And yet this 'folk psychological' guessing remains the only game in town when it comes to most rehearsal rooms. If we abandon 'folk psychology' what do we have left?

I can't find much apart from the predictions – some coming from our eliminative materialist friends – that in a fine, glorious future, cognitive science will have so completely understood the workings of the brain that we will come to see that 'intentional states' like belief and desire are simply illusions – and that, in fact, our behaviour is determined by neurological patterns and workings that we have hitherto not understood. Suppose we are convinced by this proposition? Suppose one fine day we rise up in a new world, where all human behaviour can be explained by brain chemistry, neural substrates, context and dual processes? Would it help actors in any practical way? Would it aid our understanding of our fellow human beings to know that purchasing a tub of Ben & Jerry's Chunky Monkey has nothing to do with our *desire* for expensive designer ice cream and our *belief* that Chunky Monkey is particularly yummy, but has instead everything to do with chemistry, context and S1 cognition?

Is there any possibility that we could, as actors or directors, throw aside the whole category of psychology as a strategy for understanding human behaviour? Might the idea of discovering motivations that are NOT psychologically based be helpful? Or enlightening?

Where do we start?

As we've considered, most actors and directors don't tend to use any specific school of psychology when they're working. We tend, instead, to alternate between simulation and fact/reason-based theories of mind. We also seem to assume two things: (1) that our character's experience has shaped their personalities; that human beings LEARN and adjust behaviour in accordance with their experience and (2) that human beings are very likely to make future decisions based on our past and that our future behaviour is very likely to be consistent with our past behaviour.

This assumption of consistency, as we've seen, is not entirely logical, nor do we know if it is even valuable in considering human behaviour. And we know from our own lives that even if someone is consistent 99 days out of 100 there is every chance that on the hundredth day they may exhibit very 'uncharacteristic' behaviour (we're back to the black swan!). It is equally absurd to assume that we necessarily learn from experience – most of us can list a number of people about whom we might say 's/he never learns'. The human propensity to persevere in the face of failure is particularly endearing – and is as Dr Johnson observed, 'the triumph of hope over experience'. This means that we must tend to see dramatic characters as perhaps more fundamentally 'logical', consistent and predictable than the real people we know – whose behaviour we often can't predict or are surprised by. But there are very few actors or directors I've known who had the courage to say that a character is behaving in a particular way for reasons we can't fathom, nor to accept easily Saunder and Over's conclusion that 'rational integration' of conflict is not always necessary or even appropriate.

When I was head of acting at Central we had a guest director who we often called on to direct first-year plays. This was because his specialty was a painstaking thoroughness in terms of getting every young actor to explain every second of what his or her character was thinking and how that thinking motivated every action and how every action was directed toward a series of sub-objectives and how those sub-objectives added up to an overall character 'arc' or journey. Admirable stuff, we thought, and certainly every young actor he worked with exuded a sense of what we referred to positively as 'groundedness'. It seemed the right kind of approach for beginning actors and his method was nothing if not meticulous, emphasizing the importance of discipline and process for the students.

I remember watching one of his productions of an Ibsen play, sitting next to my good friend, the veteran director George Roman. At the end of the play George (clearly not elated by the production) asked me why on earth I insisted on bringing this director back over and over again and I replied that his care and attention to detail 'grounded' the young actors. With his usual charming smile George informed me that he didn't come to the theatre to see actors grounded. He came to see them fly.

We wouldn't probably know where to begin our representation of Isabella if we didn't have SOME theory of psychology that hinges on her demonstrating a consistency of character. But this brings us to a very interesting philosophical question – can anyone's behaviour be predicted when they find themselves in dramatic circumstances? Do most people simply take one of two roads in dramatic circumstances: think and consider before acting [Hamlet] or strike now and question later [Hotspur]? This probably depends on what we consider dramatic circumstances – but would we be safe in saying that circumstances are dramatic when we are forced to make decisions when the correct choice is not obvious or even immediately 'explainable' – in other words, drama emerges when we face the 'unobvious decision'? A.D. Nuttall describes what is revealed when characters make the 'unobvious' choice:

Is it not the mark of a good dramatist to offer characters that are both complex and intelligible? Not necessarily. There is a place in the surviving collection of crabbed lecture notes known as the *Poetics* of Aristotle where the philosopher remarks that moral character is shown when a person makes an 'unobvious decision'…[I]f one thinks about drama one can see what Aristotle meant…If I am about to cross a road but decide not to, because I see a bus coming, I have made an obvious decision and an observer will have learned absolutely nothing about my moral character. If a man smelling faintly of whisky knocks at my door and asks politely for the price of a cup of tea, it is not obvious what I should do. If I kick the man down the steps, an observer will have learned a lot about me, at once.[25]

This quotation is from a passage where Nuttall is looking at the difficulty in determining motivation behind Iago's dishonesty, but in the end he seems content to enjoy the contrast of the *unexplained* behaviour in Iago's case and the *understandable* behaviour of Othello. He recognizes that to ascribe 'hatred' as Iago's motivation is simply the same thing as summarizing his behaviour – in Nuttall's opinion 'it accounts for nothing'.

But are there times when we can content ourselves, like Professor Nuttall, with not digging away at the psychology/motivation/deep recesses of the human mind and simply let ourselves concentrate on behaviour – or even enjoy the ways in which our characters demonstrate conflicting behaviours?

Psychology and survival

The great blossoming and then subsequent fall from grace of the 'behaviourist' theories of psychology more of less occurred as people became increasingly disillusioned with what seemed to be an insistence that human behaviour can be explained without reference to non-behavioural (i.e. mental!) aspects or activities. Clearly, we are not happy to confine our analysis of human activity simply to the sphere of our behaviour. The emerging area of evolutionary psychology makes people similarly nervous (as all apparently 'reductive' approaches do) but evolutionary psychology seems to strike a balance between the individual psychological flexibility of people and the ways in which we, as an evolutionary species, have evolved certain kinds of behaviours and preferences that have served our continued and prospering survival. In his book *The Moral Animal* Robert Wright describes the ways in which evolutionary psychologists look not so much for *specifics* as for *tendencies* in human behaviour and the process is not unlike the way he describes the work of evolutionary biologists, who focus on a given trait and then attempt to explain how it might serve as a solution for a given challenge to survival.

> **What on earth can Darwin teach an actor?**

We could look at evolutionary psychology in this way and say that what these psychologists are doing is looking at a psychological trait and trying to figure out what survival challenge it is a solution to. In other words, it is a way of applying Darwin's theories of evolution to an understanding of human behaviour. But what on earth can Darwin teach an actor?

The whole Darwinian endeavour seems to raise hackles a bit – not least because we are naturally resistant to ideas that might suggest somehow that all of the gorgeous complexity of the human psyche could be reducible to rather uncomplicated ideas like 'all human beings are simply programmed to ensure their own survival'. But the field of evolutionary psychology has arisen precisely because of the intellectual acknowledgement that we have evolved in the ways that we have in order to preserve and enhance our species, but that we are also beings with such flexible and adaptive minds that we demonstrate an extraordinary range of behaviours that extend far beyond this simple and fundamental truth of our 'selfish' genes.

Let us imagine for a moment that we all became 'crude' and reductive evolutionary psychologists as actors and began every analysis of our characters by acknowledging that we are all the bearers of 'selfish' genes and that we will all be naturally driven toward behaviour that will guarantee both the survival and proliferation of our genes. Of course, for someone like Richard Dawkins, author of the classic *The Selfish Gene*, we might put it more accurately by saying that our genes are the bearers of our illusion of 'selfhood' – but for the moment, let us allow our selfhood-centric view to hold here. Even if we begin with this fundamental truth – that most human behaviour is directed toward survival and propagation – we are still left with some tough questions. Of course Hamlet wants to survive, and yes, perhaps he is unconsciously disturbed by the ways in which his uncle's marriage to his mother may be disrupting the natural genetic succession in the royal line of Denmark, but what has that to do with his extraordinary meditations on human existence? And why bring this area into a consideration of acting? Surely acting is concerned precisely with that second point above – the ways in which the complexity of human behaviour extends far beyond our genetic drives?

Well, one reason for doing so is that it might offer an actor as much (in terms of a solid staring point) as any other kind of psychological analysis. In order to demonstrate this point, let's go back for a moment and consider the psychological complexities of Isabella.

For many people, the lively nature of Isabella's interventions in the shenanigans surrounding the Duke's absence in Vienna make her choice to enter a convent in the first place rather puzzling in itself. For someone like Harold Bloom – who calls Isabella 'pragmatically mindless', 'apocalyptically chaste' and 'sublimely neurotic'[26] – presumably nothing Isabella does would be too puzzling, but for those of us who need to work at portraying Isabella, we may find her decision to be a nun at odds with her behaviour out in the real world. So where might we start? If we decide to look to a kind of Freudian model of psychological motivation for her religion, we would have to construct some elaborate theories about the thwarting of Isabella's sexual drive (perhaps imagining some trauma that might have happened in her childhood that caused her to abandon the usual role of wife and mother and to connect so powerfully with a religious experience that she would turn away from seeking gratification of her own sexual drive) and the ways in which her sexual desires might now be 'repressed' or renunciated through religious ecstasy or obedience of some kind. This is interesting and could provide hours of fun for an actor in terms of imagining her innermost mind. The problem is that when we're analysing like this, we're actually analysing through a theory that would insist that something like repressing the sexual drive is an unconscious thing anyway – so it becomes difficult for an actor to know how to employ the knowledge they might feel they've gained.

Let us turn for a moment from introspective to evolutionary psychology, where we might find something that is less 'buried' in terms of the mind and also more immediately applicable for the actor. Dawkins' classic, *The Selfish Gene*, might in many ways be said to have thrown open all the questions of what human beings are and what 'individuals' could be said to be, and to have inspired much of the growth of interest in the area of evolutionary psychology.

His version of human 'beingness' differs significantly from the kind of 'psychologically real' human 'beingness' that most actors and directors work from:

> The individual organism…is not fundamental to life, but something that emerges when genes, which at the beginning of evolution were separate, warring entities, gang together in co-operative groups as 'selfish co-operators'. The individual organism is *not exactly an illusion*. It is too concrete for that. But it is *a secondary, derived phenomenon*, cobbled together as a consequence of the actions of fundamentally separate, even warring, agents…Perhaps the subjective 'I', the person that I feel myself to be, is *the same kind of semi-illusion*. The mind is a collection of fundamentally independent, even warring, agents…Whether or not these agents are to be identified with memes…the subjective feeling of 'somebody in there' may be a *cobbled, emergent, semi-illusion* analogous to the individual body emerging in evolution from the uneasy co-operation of genes.[27]

Like eliminative materialists, Dawkins is asking us to consider that the idea of an individual with specific psychological mental states is something of an illusion. We are not what we think we are. Indeed, the individual is a bit like a 'host' for the billions of warring genes that have temporarily ganged together to advance themselves. The mental states that may accompany the mission of advancing genes are actually brain states. They are various configurations of neural operations. This is an oversimplification of the issues, but it will do for our purposes. Dawkins also proposes another kind of virulently self-replicating unit – units of human culture, which we might see as interacting with genes. This 'second replicator unit' is another way of saying that all this selfish, self-replicating genetic activity is modified and influenced by the cultural, historical, social context in which are genes are fighting to exist. He calls these units of human culture 'memes':

> We need a name for the new replicator, a noun that conveys the idea of a unit of cultural transmission, or a unit of imitation. 'Mimeme' comes from a suitable Greek root, but I want a monosyllable that sounds a bit like 'gene'. I hope my classicist friends will forgive me if I abbreviate mimeme to meme…Examples of memes are tunes, ideas, catchphrases, clothes fashions, ways of making pots or building arches. Just as genes propagate themselves in the gene pool by leaping from body to body via sperms or eggs, so memes propagate themselves in the meme pool by leaping from brain to brain via a process which, in the broad sense, can be called imitation.[28]

For Dawkins, both genes and memes are self-replicators (meaning they make copies of themselves), and genes are *selfish* self-replicators. Dawkins' view of the selfish gene is relatively simple to comprehend in terms of Darwinian survival theories – indeed, in Dawkins' view, 'we are survival machines'. We are designed to survive, adapt and thrive and natural selection favours whatever changes enhance our capacity to survive and thrive. For this reason, 'good' genes – in the eyes of nature – are those that have 'the ability to build efficient survival machines – bodies'.[29] The aim of these good genes is to increase and insure their own survival:

A survival machine is a vehicle containing not just one gene but many thousands. The manufacture of a body is a cooperative venture of such intricacy that it is almost impossible to disentangle the contribution of one gene from that of another...This means that any one individual body is just a temporary vehicle for a short-lived combination of genes. The combination of genes that is any one individual may be short-lived, but the genes themselves are potentially very long-lived. Their paths constantly cross and recross down the generations. One gene may be regarded as a unit that survives through a large number of successive individual bodies.[30]

Dawkin's argument puts me in mind of a cat that I once knew. It showed up unannounced one day at my father's office where I was working, took a liking to my dad and me, and just stayed on. It was the hungriest cat we'd ever known and we jokingly called it 'tapeworm' as we were convinced that it was not a cat at all, but a tapeworm that had rented a cat costume.

It seems to me that Dawkin's view of us is similar – we are not so much individual persons as collections of genes that have 'rented' a 'person' costume in order to secure their survival. It may be a relatively ruthless picture he has painted – millions of warring genes battling for selection, but in terms of evolutionary science it's difficult to argue with the logic of his view, and his book has survived 30 years of fierce debate, more or less victorious.

At first glance his theory seems unsettlingly reductive. What can we say about the idea that all of human history and endeavour boils down to a simple Darwinian skirmish amongst the unseen – surely this is biological reductionism at its most extreme? But before we start to worry about this reductionism, let us go back to consider Dawkins' cultural 'replicator' – the meme.

Although Dawkins' description of the meme and its self-replication might put us in mind of theories about ideologies, or how particular ideas take hold and influence us, he is really talking about a simpler kind of metaphor for the ways in which replicating cultural ideas *may* come to affect replicating genetic trends. In the case of Isabella, we might need a consideration of the 'God meme'.

For Dawkins (and others) religion is a challenge to explain in evolutionary terms. What in the world can belief in a supernatural being do to enhance the survival possibilities of our genes? He has a theory, but his theory only has force if we look at WHY human beings fall in love so passionately, and so 'irrationally'. From a Darwinian point of view, falling in love is a way of ensuring loyalty to one 'co-parent' for as least as long as it takes to rear a child. Darwinists DO take the romance out of things. Instead of love being a romantic, ethereal stirring of our soul it turns out we just need to ensure the propagation of our species,

> **"You fall in love and chemicals start pole-dancing around the neurons of your brain…"**

and we do that best if we remain loyal as partners until the issue of union is old enough to go off and fall in love him/herself. Because men are biologically programmed to 'spread their possibilities around', if they did not have the capacity to fall in love, remaining loyal long enough to rear their offspring would be out of the question. Because women may make poor genetic choices sometimes, it is still important for them to stick with that choice come what may – at least until their children are grown. Having parents who are in love helps to ensure a child's best chances. Being in love has been shown to be accompanied by very specific brain states – brought about by very specific brain chemicls:

> Dopamine. God's little neurotransmitter. Better known by its street name, romantic love. Also, norepinephrine. Street name, infatuation. These chemicals are natural stimulants. You fall in love, a growing amount of research shows, and these chemicals and their cousins start pole-dancing around the neurons of your brain, hopping around the limbic system, setting off craving, obsessive thoughts, focused attention, the desire to commit possibly immoral acts with your beloved while at a stoplight in the 2100 block of K Street during lunch hour, and so on.[31]

Given the theories about why evolution has provided the rush of brain chemicals that result in love or infatuation, Dawkins asks:

> Could irrational religion be a by-product of the irrationality mechanisms that were originally built into the brain by selection for falling in love? Certainly religious faith has something of the same character as falling love (and both have many of the attributes of being high on an addictive drug).[32]

In other words, rather than directing the rush of brain-chemical infatuation toward our target 'dream man', we misfire and hit God. The idea of God and the survival of the religious 'meme' is possibly related to genes, as explained by Susan J. Blackmore:

> In many cultures priests or rulers are given divine status. We know that women prefer to mate with high status men, and that these men leave more offspring by having more wives or by fathering children by women who are not their wives. Even in societies in which the priesthood is celibate and could not (or at least should not) pass on their genes, other people could acquire power by association. If this religious behaviour helped people to acquire more mates, then any gene that inclined them to be more religious in the first place would also flourish. In this way *genes* for religious behaviour would increase because of religious *memes.*[33]

I think Blackmore's theory is a challenge to accept. And Isabella as a 'poor shot' who misfires and 'hits God' is a stretch, I'll grant you. But perhaps this idea is no more challenging for us to *use* in our portrayal of Isabella than a Freudian theory of unconscious 'displacement'. At the very least, Dawkins' theory means that our emphasis remains on behaviour (and on the ways in which love makes us behave) and not on churning through deep, half-hidden emotion. Suddenly, not only her entry into the convent but also her desire for a stricter regime (in which lengthier enforced silences and prayer might allow her more time with her religious love/ecstasy) makes sense.

If we look at her 'war 'twixt will and will not' we might also see something in the ways in which the usual casting of love of her brother vs the desire to obey the laws of God and man becomes more acute: it is now not the struggle between love and obedience, but the struggle between two kinds of equally strong love.

Viewed in this way what seems clear from her behaviour in the play is that Isabella is a very passionate young woman. She is passionate in her religious love and passionate in her love of life. If we see her religion as a kind of intense love, the play becomes centred NOT on an internal struggle between duty and familial love so much as on two very active passions. This strikes me as a very immediate reading and therefore possibly very useful in acting terms. Not the only reading, of course, but one that might answer the challenge I began this section with: what on earth can Darwin teach actors?

But I can't help wondering whether, in evolutionary psychological terms, there isn't a much simpler explanation for religion. Stephen Pinker notes that according to a survey by ethnographers, 'religion is a human universal'.[34] He goes on to consider that there are a couple of plausible evolutionary explanations for this, one of which is that religion brings a community together. But surely the argument makes more sense if we reframe it a bit to say that religion *defines* a community – and conversely defines who is NOT in that community. As we know, our survival depends on our ability to detect threats. This is pretty easy in the case of sabre-tooth tigers or grizzly bears. But of course it's much more difficult when it comes to detecting the threat that comes from another human. We can't always determine by face or clothes or manner if we're likely to be threatened or not. The way in which a specific religious belief works means that these beliefs can be used as a highly portable 'values-tester', in the absence of ID cards or anything else. Particularly since, with most religions, 'a story goes with it', as Damon Runyon would say. I could be tested pretty quickly by a Christian fundamentalist because my knowledge of the bible is pretty sketchy. I'm familiar with the main narrative arc, but I'm fuzzy on the detail. Similarly, I could be pretty quickly caught out if I claimed to be a Muslim. I just don't know the stories well enough. Which means that no matter how broadly I smile, or whether I bring a casserole or not, the members of the Seventh Day Adventist tribe will know pretty quickly that I am NOT ONE OF THEM.

In Isabella's case, this possible survival mechanism is right at the heart of her every action. She continually tests everyone around her to determine whether their beliefs are a match for hers. Presumably, if they are a match, the level of threat to her or to her brother is lessened. The whole of her first scene with Angelo can be seen as an elaborate test of the match of

Angelo's professed Christianity with her own, pure faith. The real drama begins when she then has to test whether Claudio's Christianity is a match with hers – and initially it appears that it is not. This creates a terrible dilemma for Isabella – yet it never shakes her sense of her own faith or her own rightness. Perhaps this is because for her 'rightness' is not the issue so much as finding and securing her 'tribe' of like-minded people is. In this sense, Isabella's religion is an instrument of her survival. And in the end, even trying to determine what Isabella makes of the Duke's proposal could be a question of whether she can – in analysing his actions over the whole course of the story – see in him a true member of her religious 'tribe'. Or perhaps she is about to take a journey beyond the 'safe' world of the convent tribe and try her luck with a new community with more secular ways.

It may be a long time – if ever – before the day comes when actors will routinely talk about their characters in terms of evolutionary psychology, but perhaps Stanislavski was something of a closet evolutionary psychologist. We must admit that most acting theory from Stanislavski onward promotes a kind of 'selfish' analysis that Dawkins would be proud of – even if that 'selfishness' is not posed as genetic selfishness. We begin most character analyses by asking 'what do I want?' and 'how am I going to get what I want?' and 'what's in my way?' From this starting point it isn't particularly hard to see that before we ask 'what do I want?', we could ask 'what is most important for my survival at this moment?' The answers won't always be immediately connected with genetic survival. For Constantine becoming a successful writer is important for his (healthy) continued survival at the opening of *The Seagull*, and we see the disastrous consequences of his failure. For Ophelia, marrying Hamlet is important for her (and her genes'!) healthy survival and we also see the disastrous consequences of her failure.

Darwinian approaches are regularly taken to task for reducing everything to simple survival and propagation. While it may not be the place we want to finish after many weeks of rehearsal, it may be just as valid a starting point as any other psychology when we're faced with the mysteries and varieties of human behaviour. Maybe the point is much simpler than it looks and perhaps the 'loss of psychology' isn't as radical as it first sounds.

Robert Wright looks at a number of possibly puzzling behavioural issues in evolutionary terms and demonstrates a strong link to the promotion of genetic survival – many of which seem to me to avoid the charge of simple 'reduction' that is so often aimed at evolutionary psychology. Here he considers what possible advantage bad moods or low self-esteem may serve in terms of our survival interests:

> …you could say that low self-esteem evolved as a way to reconcile people to subordinate status when reconciliation is in their genetic interest…It may be in their genetic interest not only to accept low status, but, in at least some circumstances, to convey their acceptance of it – to behave submissively so that they aren't erroneously perceived as a threat and treated as such…Feeling bad about yourself is good for things other than sending people self-serving signals…[A]s the evolutionary psychiatrist Randolph Nesse has stressed, mood can efficiently focus energy. People of all statuses may get lethargic and

glum when social, sexual, or professional prospects look dim, and then grow optimistic and energetic when opportunities arise. It's as if they had been resting up for a big match. And if no opportunities arise, and lethargy passes into mild depression, this mood may goad them into a fruitful shift of course – changing careers, jettisoning ungrateful friends, abandoning the pursuit of an elusive mate.[35]

These are interesting possibilities but, like so much of introspective psychology, they are of limited practical use to the actor faced with the possibility of portraying characters in bad moods or with low self-esteem.

Rational actors

One of the difficulties in looking at the area of how we model or 'metarepresent' the state of someone else's mind goes back to Dennett's idea that we are always assuming rationality. This is a precarious position in the case of Hamlet and many other dramatic characters, but leaving these more 'literary' or interpretative questions aside, the whole question of what constitutes 'rational' for human beings is a bit fraught. There are probably many experiential things we could identify that attest to the difficulty of this, but perhaps one might be a 'weak' version of Rational Actor theory. The idea of the rational actor is one used extensively in areas like economic and political judgements. The overall idea is that we could analyse a given situation and identify the potential gains and losses, the potential risks and rewards. Essentially, the Rational Actor theory is a mathematical model in which we can express gain/loss or risk/reward mathematically and on the basis of the numbers determine that an ideal person (the rational actor) would make a decision based on the logic of mathematical demonstration. This, of course, neatly sidesteps the problems of psychology.

But in simply proposing a rational actor, we've already identified the problem. The proposition is based on an ideal, and we know that human decisions vary widely in terms of the way that they make choices. If a simple comparison of statistics and figures had the power to sway human decision no one would smoke and no one would order sticky toffee pudding. These decisions, as we considered earlier, give rise to the 'how can we explain C' philosophical problem.

So we know that a more or less mathematical model like Rational Actor theory is of limited use in the case of human decision, but of course we don't rule rationality out when we're attempting to determine what is in someone else's mind. As an actor, we would find it very difficult to do much of anything if our general outlook on how other people's minds work did not in large measure assume a kind of fundamental rationality – even if that rationality is only expressed in terms of basic survival. As we've considered, even in those cases where we can't begin to theorize an answer to the question 'why would this character do that' we know that we can possibly look to evolutionary drives as a 'secret' motivator (my character is smoking because smoking is part of sexual display behaviour) – always acknowledging that this kind of question is only going to concern the actor and not the character. In other words, Don Draper isn't worrying about why he's smoking – but the actor playing Don Draper may be worried about why he's smoking. In these cases, we need be careful about not transferring our worry. But this aside, why DO we worry, as actors, about motivation? Is it because we can't imagine formulating action unless we can determine what lies behind the action? If so, then we are essentially certain that action is more interesting/engaging/compelling when the actor knows WHY s/he did what s/he did. But is this true?

I remember working many years ago with a wonderful actor named William Needles. I was in grad school, and the university policy was to bring in professional actors from time to time – especially to play parts that were beyond our callow student understanding. Bill was a veteran member of the ensemble of the Ontario Stratford Shakespeare Festival and working with someone of his skill both in comedy and classical text was an extraordinary opportunity for all of us. He was playing Monsieur Jourdain in *Le Bourgeois Gentilhomme* and I was playing his wife. Bill had a wonderful way of whispering asides during rehearsal, and they were invariably of the rather satiric, campy variety. His quick wit came to be a cherished part of being in rehearsal with such a seasoned performer. I can recall early on being in a rehearsal with an undergraduate actor who asked of director, Robert Cohen, at one point 'What's my motivation here?' Bill and I were tucked away over on stage right and he leaned down to whisper 'Your paycheck, love.'

It's an old theatrical joke, but played with Bill's usual insouciance, I was suddenly reduced to giggles, which left the poor young actor thinking that I had been laughing at his question. The truth is, I suppose I often DO laugh at that question, but only because it has become a pretty pompous-sounding stereotype. There was a kind of gentle anti-intellectualism about Bill's work, it seemed to me, because he had that kind of comic ability that is so hard to understand intellectually. He was also very much an 'old school' actor as he explained to us once. When asked what he meant he said that he always started with instinct and that he could just 'feel' when something was working. And of course, I never once heard him ask 'What's my motivation?'

Is it ever fair in acting to say that you DON'T know what motivated your character to do X just at point Y? Can we ever find the courage to defy the actor stereotype and stop worrying about motivation?

I think we have come to the conclusion that deep analysis of given circumstances, determining every motivation (i.e. going through all the intellectual Stanislavski exercises) promotes efficiency. As we know, the more that we can convert to automaticity in mental terms, the more energy we have to do what we think matters in performance – focused action. We need to nail things down as much as we can in rehearsal so that our work has a lucidity and consistency to it that contributes to clear storytelling in performance. But we can do all this *and* still decide, at points, that we DON'T know what's motivating a given character choice. We can decide that an action makes NO sense to us, yet still act it with conviction. If we make this decision we are living with ambiguity – in just the same way that we live with ambiguity about human motivation/action every day of our lives. We can do this, of course we can. But we don't. We might come up with many reasons why we don't, but perhaps the most interesting is that the drive to make sense of things is *not* a voluntary one. It is in the make-up of our brains to make sense of things. We are natural 'sense-makers' and we naturally tell stories, or 'narrativise' things so that they make sense in some way:

> When a hospital patient with severe anterograde amnesia is asked 'What did you do yesterday?' he does not have any memories from the previous day to call to mind. In many cases, the patient will construct a narrative from scraps of older memory and weave them together to make a coherent and detailed story. 'I stopped in to visit my old pal Ned at his store and then we went out for lunch at the deli...' This process, which is called confabulation, is not merely a face-saving attempt. In almost all cases, amnesiacs believe their own confabulations and will act upon them as if they were true. Confabulation in anterograde amnesia is not a process under voluntary control. Rather it's what the brain does when confronted with a problem it cannot begin to solve: it makes a story from whatever bits of experience it can dredge up, in much the same way that narrative dreams are created from scraps of memory.[36]

As actors our drive to find motivations is no doubt the same drive to confabulate. It may well be that the most interesting choice we could make when playing Hamlet is to choose irrationality, to choose to say that we DON'T know what drives an action, but to play it anyway.

Summary

Perhaps it is time for us to think more about what it is we do when we employ our theory of mind in the attempt to understand and portray literary characters. We might start simply by broadening the way that we look at the psychology of characters – at what makes them tick, what might explain their behaviours, etc. – and contemplate approaching these questions in a kind of two-fold way. One might be mapping them against the bigger, broader canvas that evolutionary psychology paints. This canvas is a larger kind of representation of what might be driving a number of complex human behaviours (as demonstrated above) but it won't be enough on its own. One might be to consider the 'S1' and 'S2' types of cognitive processes of a character, and to consider the fact that not all actions are going to be reasoned actions, and not all goals are going to be reasoned goals. As Herbert Simon points out:

Reason is wholly instrumental. It cannot tell us where to go; at best it can tell us how to get there. It is a gun for hire that can be employed in the service of any goals we have, good or bad.[37]

Some of the goals or actions of our characters are going to be the result of S1 'cognitive unconscious' process. As we know from our own experience, there are times when we bring in the 'hired gun' of reason to help us understand these things and there are times when we don't want to go to that trouble and expense.

What makes the actor's art great is not simply understanding (possibly larger, possibly more 'universal' than we might have thought) motivation, but in representing the behaviours that result from these motivations in ways that are at once engaging, sometimes surprising, but which always serve to make the story of a play clear. For some of us, the only way to create that kind of representation may be through the more traditional psychological or simulation models. It seems to me that we have come to assume that psychological consistency is innately valuable, but whether that consistency is really the most interesting way into portrayal is worth questioning.

It might be flying in the face of the way in which our 'confabulating' brains want to operate, but maybe it's time for us to have the courage sometimes to explore beyond the rational and the consistent and just sometimes – when it feels right – play an action we don't understand. No doubt this will worry some because it sounds like an anti-intellectual proposal and most of us who have taught actors have known all too many unarticulated, irrational choices in untrained or young actors. I'm sympathetic with this worry, and believe me I know the danger of presenting this idea to a young actor. But I've watched the opposite happen, often as actors gain more experience and come to rely on some kind of process or method that they begin to operate in all situations with all characters. It can seem sometimes as if we go from neophytes with no system to journeymen with too much. No observation like this is universally true, and not all experienced actors need to be reminded that systems (acting or otherwise) can sometimes inhibit unexpected brilliance. A decision to explore beyond the rational, the consistent and 'the motive' might make for some very interesting, unexpected acting, but we would have to work very hard against our own 'confabulating' and 'dissonance-adjusting' instincts to do this.

Notes

1. *Philosophy in the Flesh: The Embodied Mind and its Challenge to Western Thought* (New York: Basic Books, 1999), p. 1.
2. David Krasner, 'Strasberg, Adler, and Meisner' in Alison Hodge (ed.), *Twentieth Century Actor Training* (London: Routledge, 2000), p. 134. (Internal quotations taken from David Garfield's *A Player's Passion*.)
3. Jonathan Pitches, *Science and the Stanislavsky Tradition of Acting* (London: Routledge, 2006), p. 115.

4. *Ibid.*, p. 116.
5. *Ibid.*, p. 115.
6. Stephen Stich & Shaun Nichols, 'Folk Psychology: Simulation or Tacit Theory?', *Mind & Language*, 7(1), 1992, p. 35.
7. Daniel C. Dennett, *Brainstorms: Philosophical Essays on Mind and Psychology* (London: Penguin, 1981), p. 10.
8. Quoted in Alison Hodge (ed.), *Twentieth Century Actor Training* (London: Routledge, 2000), p. 134.
9. Sanford Meisner, *On Acting* (New York: Vintage, 1987), p. 87.
10. Jerzy Growtowski, *Towards a Poor Theatre*, ed. Eugenio Barba (London: Eyre Methuen, 1976), p. 96
11. Nick Moseley, *Acting and Reacting* (London: Routledge, 2005), p. 33.
12. *Ibid.*, p. 38 and p. 42.
13. Nassim Nicholas Taleb, *The Black Swan: The Impact of the Highly Improbable* (London: Allen Lane, 2007).
14. Moseley, *Acting and Reacting*, pp.196–197.
15. Edward Dwight Easty, *On Method Acting* (New York: Ivy Books, 1989), p. 82.
16. Michael Chekhov, *To the Actor* (New York: Harper & Row, 1953), p. 2.
17. *Ibid.*, pp. 1–2.
18. Nicholas Hytner, quoted in Bella Merlin, *With the Rogue's Company* (London: Oberon Books, 2005), pp. 27–28.
19. http://plato.stanford.edu/entries/materialism-eliminative/.
20. Stephen Stich, *From Folk Psychology to Cognitive Science* (Cambridge, MA: MIT Press, 1983), p. 231.
21. Clare Saunders and David E. Over, 'In Two Minds about Rationality?' in Evans & Frankish (eds), *In Two Minds: Dual Processes and Beyond*, (Oxford: OUP, 2009), pp. 326–327.
22. The most often-quoted report in this area is Richard E. Nisbett and Timothy DeCamp Wilson's *Telling More Than We Can Know: Verbal Reports on Mental Processes*, which can be accessed at: http://www.lps.uci.edu/~johnsonk/philpsych/readings/nisbett.pdf.
23. http://www.scribd.com/doc/499078/The-Theory-of-Cognitive-Dissonance, p. 5.
24. 'How Testosterone Can Make a City Trader Earn a Slicker Million', 16 April 2008 (report on research can be found at: http://www.admin.cam.ac.uk/news/dp/2008041501).
25. A.D. Nuttall, *Shakespeare the Thinker* (New Haven and London: Yale University Press, 2007), p. 283.
26. Harold Bloom, *Shakespeare: The Invention of the Human* (London: Fourth Estate, 1999), pp. 358–380.
27. This is Mary Midgley quoting Dawkins in an article on the Royal Institute of Philosophy website: www.royalinstitutephilosophy.org/think/article.php?num=6.
28. Richard Dawkins, *The Selfish Gene*, 30th Anniversary Edition (OUP: 2006), p. 192.
29. *Ibid.*, p. 86.
30. *Ibid.*, pp. 24–25.
31. Neely Tucker, 'An Affair of the Head', *Washington Post*, 13 February 2007.
32. Richard Dawkins, *The God Delusion* (London: Bantam Press, 2006), p. 185.
33. Susan J. Blackmore, *The Meme Machine* (Oxford: OUP, 2000), p. 197.
34. Steven Pinker, 'The Evolutionary Psychology of Religion' at http://pinker.wjh.harvard.edu/articles/media/2004_10_29religion.htm.
35. Wright, *The Moral Animal*, pp. 270–1.
36. David J. Linden, *The Accidental Mind* (Cambridge, MA: Harvard University Press, 2007), p. 226.
37. Herbert Simon, *Reason in Human Affairs* (Stanford: Stanford University Press, 1983), pp. 7–8.

Chapter 5

Where Am I?

I remember once being in a restaurant in Southern California, sitting next to a family with a toddler, who was seated in a high-chair. The baby was at that in-between age – perhaps a bit too big for the high-chair, but certainly too young and too unruly to be allowed free seating at the table. My companions and I attempted to ignore the family as it struggled to please/placate/feed the child but our attention was immediately drawn when the baby smashed into the high-chair tray with a fistful of silverware and shouted 'Where am I?' It was a funny moment for so many reasons – not least of which was the fact that the baby was not in a position to control where he was, nor to get up and leave should it turn out that the baby felt this particular restaurant was not up to the standard he wished to maintain. The incongruity of his demand coupled with the sound of sudden human self-awareness made me laugh and still makes me laugh when I recall it.

But 'where am I?' (and that same sense of sudden self-awareness) might well be the question on your mind right now. In a sense, after looking at some of the contradictions and variables in the last few chapters, I begin to wonder myself where we are…So let's try to reach some helpful conclusions, based on things we've already looked at, and by tossing a few more intriguing ideas into the mix.

Actors are not green

If we go back to looking at the scholarly history of acting theory in Joseph Roach's book, *The Player's Passion*, published in 2001, we can follow a thread through his chronology that suggests the whole history of acting theory has been a classic kind of 'dialectical' development – which begins with two opposing ideas finding a kind of synthesis and then moving forward to a new set of oppositions. Although in the case of acting theory it seems that the advance is slightly more of a circular than a linear one. We seem to go around and around over two critical questions.

- **Internal or external?** Do we start from the mind and 'filter out toward' the body? Or do we begin with the 'psychological gesture' or a physical 'hook' of some kind and then 'work inward' toward the mind? Do we begin with what we imagine is in our character's (our own) head? Or do we respond to things occurring around us? Are we 'character' actors or are we 'playing out of ourselves'? What is psychophysical acting – does the very existence

of interest in psychophysical technique suggest that somehow there may be such things as *exclusively* physical acting or *exclusively* psychological acting?
- **Real or simulated?** Are we REALLY feeling the emotion we portray? Or are we simply intellectualizing the idea of emotion and 'portraying' unfelt emotion with skill?

But might it be that we're at a point where these oppositions are no longer tenable? We've looked at the fact that in terms of cognitive science research, it would appear that actors do (or can) use their OWN emotions and feelings, but because they are doing so while simultaneously working through the language/reasoning part of the frontal cortex, those 'real-actorly' emotions are rarely experienced in exactly the way that our own spontaneous 'real-life' emotions are. This is because working through that cortical area of the brain creates a very different kind of feeling from that resulting straight from the fast-response amygdala reactions to anger, fear, etc. So it is very likely that a good actor is working through a combination of portraying and feeling – both 'portraying' emotion (which is more immediately physically based) and 'feeling' feelings (which are a more naturally reflective phenomena). But it is almost certainly true that neither 'actorly feelings' nor 'actorly emotion' have the force that real-life feelings and emotions do because when we are acting we are involving a set of neural patterns that are engaged differently than they are in our everyday cognitive/emotion experience. These patterns involve the language/reasoning part of the cortex that responds to direction (like 'move upstage' or 'don't drop the end of your line') and that also 'knows' that we're acting in the same way that we 'know' when we're going to try and tickle ourselves. Also, we're involving areas of the medial prefrontal cortex that 'knows' we're being watched.

We've considered how we can affect our own bodies through well-imagined emotional memory. Conversely, we can work from externals since we know that we can affect our own emotions simply by making faces. And we also know that an actor can base an action on a kind of internal psychological 'guessing' and empathy, and we know that an actor can throw out psychology altogether and base an action on something simply external, such as 'what action might guarantee my character's survival?' Indeed, there are so many interesting variables at work here – is it time to jettison altogether the 'oppositional' questions above about how actors work?

However we answer that question, or wherever it is that we find ourselves either geographically, or in our careers or our education, there is one pretty obvious constant in our coordinates: we're in the twenty-first century, still writing and reading books debating acting theory written in the eighteenth, nineteenth and twentieth century, and glancing nervously around, lest we are infected by the ideas of a seventeenth-century philosopher. This is not necessarily a bad thing – philosophers still read Aristotle and Spinoza. Good/challenging ideas are good/challenging ideas no matter when they were first recorded. But unlike philosophy, we don't seem to move on and evolve much in the world of acting theory, particularly when it comes to following up research in areas like cognitive science and psychology or philosophy. I think this may be because, in philosophical terms, we haven't often enough considered what is *essential* to the whole practice of acting.

In a wonderfully readable book on philosophy and jokes, Thomas Cathcart and Daniel Klein consider the philosophical issue of essentialism:

> Aristotle drew a distinction between essential and accidental properties. The way he put it is that essential properties are those without which a thing wouldn't be what it is, and accidental properties are those that determine *how* a thing is, but not *what* it is.[1]

And I can't resist including the joke they use to illustrate the problem:

Abe: I got a riddle for you, Sol. What's green, hangs on the wall, and whistles?
Sol: I give up.
Abe: A herring.
Sol: But a herring isn't green.
Abe: So you can paint it green.
Sol: But a herring doesn't hang on the wall.
Abe: Put a nail through it, it hangs on the wall.
Sol: But a herring doesn't whistle!
Abe: So? It doesn't whistle.[2]

The point, I hope, is that perhaps much of what we busily debate, write about, lecture on and experiment with in rehearsals is often confusing because we aren't always sure exactly what it is we're talking about – what IS acting? Surely the whole area could be simplified somewhat if we could determine – in Aristotles's terms – what acting is. In a sense, when acting books advise us to do one thing or another, they are always postulating a theory on what acting is, but they rarely do this in a rigorous way. Instead we are left to infer for ourselves what a particular theorist takes to be the essential quality that constitutes acting, because most of their work concentrates on the accidental qualities. But is it possible for us to define an essential property of acting? We could, of course, begin with our own riddle (with apologies to Cathcart and Klein):

Abe: What is emotionally 'connected' and emotionally 'expressive', physically free, psychologically 'real' and green?
Sol: I give up.
Abe: An actor.
Sol: But an actor isn't always emotionally 'connected', emotionally 'expressive' or psychologically 'real'.
Abe: So do some sense memory exercises, use the 'magic if' and keep repeating phrases at each other.
Sol: But an actor isn't always physically free.
Abe: Do some training in a powerful, possibly Eastern physical practice.
Sol: But actors aren't green.
Abe: So sue me.

It's a challenge to determine what the essential properties of acting might be, although we can spend much time considering – as we did in our riddle above – the accidental properties. And in doing so we direct our attention away from the fundamental question. I think many might say that the essential property of acting is action. Meisner would have said 'to be doing something'. In fact, he was probably closer than most other theorists to considering whether there is an essential quality to acting. As we know, he certainly didn't see emotional display as an essential quality. And he probably didn't see character as an essential property – but he is not alone in these things. We can all think of many actors for whom these are not essential properties of their work as actors. If we were to agree that the essential property of acting is action – isn't it a bit strange that we've spent so many years in debate over what might be called the *accidental* properties of acting? Much of the difficulty in our debates is that most acting texts confuse the essential properties of acting (the WHAT) with the accidental properties of acting (the HOW).

We know that we're not likely to determine this essential property simply by choosing amongst the internal/external, real/fake oppositions. As we considered earlier in this section, Joseph Roach poses the main oppositions surrounding the history of acting in terms of 'mechanistic' or 'vitalistic' approaches – which he considers to be the fundamental difference between a kind of systematic or 'craft'-based approach, and might include 'portraying' rather than 'feeling' emotion (this is a mechanist approach) and a spontaneous expression in the art of acting (which is a vitalist one). But even these long-standing and much debated oppositions are concerned with the accidental properties of acting. And they are troublesome oppositions in this sense, because while we might *say* we value spontaneous expression in the art of acting, when it comes to playing King Lear, we wouldn't say of a more studied or laboured expression that the actor wasn't *acting*. We would probably just say that the performance wasn't a very good one. Besides, although this talk of spontaneous expression is widespread in acting books, we know that we're always considering that spontaneity in the very specific context of theatre – which includes endless repetition and multiple performances. In this context, the amount of spontaneous (i.e. that which arises from impulse) expression we can accommodate while acting is limited. We wouldn't really want to see an actor spontaneously give way to his or her emotions, as it would be dangerous, might alarm the other actors or look like a psychotic episode.

Let's leave the oppositions aside and simply concentrate on identifying the *essential* ingredient of acting – in this way, perhaps we'll come to an agreement about how we might go on from there to improve our performance in all the *accidental* properties. While we may be sympathetic with the idea of action being the essential quality of acting we know that it doesn't serve. 'Action' is too general as a description to be of use to us and is no more helpful in our attempt at getting to the essential quality of acting than is 'breathing'. Of course an actor needs to breathe and an actor needs to engage in action, but these things apply broadly to most areas of our life and do not constitute the essence of acting.

So you want to be a selective quasi-amnesiac?

Okay, I'll admit this doesn't have the ring of something like 'So you want to be an actor?', but as a way of describing the very specific quality that is fundamental to acting – and which must exist in order for all else (imagination, character, intention, action) to operate – I believe that selective quasi-amnesia is useful. If I wanted to provide a fuller statement of the essential quality of acting it would be that acting is selective quasi-amnesia in the service of theatrical performance. So what is selective quasi-amnesia? First of all it is Colin McGinn's description, which he uses to describe the experience of immersing ourselves in something that we know to be fictional. In order to allow ourselves the experience of being fully immersed in a fictional world, we employ a kind of selective 'forgetting'. As McGinn points out, we 'cannot be immersed in a fiction and consciously thinking "this is only fiction". Your attention cannot be both on the fictional work *qua* fictional artefact *and* on the fictional world depicted.'[3] Instead, at moments of immersion in a story we select to forget that 'this is only fiction'. The 'quasi-' modifier in McGinn's description refers to the fact that when we are immersing ourselves in a fictional world (or for our purposes – when we are acting), we *pretend* to forget. Let's rehearse this idea a bit.

When we set about trying to understand a character we are always employing a theory of mind (ToM), as we considered earlier. Exactly how we model that ToM is still a very hotly debated issued, but actors need only consider the fact that we DO have one. We do this in our folk-psychological ways for the most part. And however we conceive of a ToM, we must have a way of deciding not so much what Hamlet will do next – that's pretty neatly laid out for us – but what Hamlet will *think* next. This is, of course, just part of the actor's labour in response to the ambiguity of texts. For example, we know that after 'The Murder of Gonzago', Hamlet is called to speak with his mother. But we don't know what he thinks about this particularly. On the way he stumbles upon Claudius praying. And we DO know what he thinks about this, because he outlines it for us very clearly in the 'Now might I do it pat' monologue. But even when we know what Hamlet is thinking because he *tells* us what he's thinking, we are in the territory of higher order thinking and this is because we have knowledge that Hamlet doesn't have – both our own and that provided by Shakespeare. And once we've heard Claudius' confession of 'words without thoughts' we might very well conclude:

'I believe that Hamlet mistakenly believes that Claudius is sincerely penitent.'

This is what we might consider a 'second order intentional' thought. In other words, we have to perform a two-fold operation before we can come to this 'second order' conclusion: (1) we have to have a representation in our own minds of what is in Hamlet's mind and (2) we also have to form our own belief about Hamlet's belief. Daniel Dennett puts this pretty clearly (or at least as clearly as this sort of thing can be put!):

A first-order intentional system has beliefs and desires about many things, but not about beliefs and desires. A second-order intentional system has beliefs and desires about beliefs and desires, its own or those of others. A third-order intentional system would be capable of such feats as wanting you to believe that it wanted something, while a fourth-order intentional system might believe you wanted it to believe that you believed something, and so forth. The big step [is] the step from first-order to second-order.[4]

Now of course, we have some textual evidence that Claudius' prayer was (in his own estimation) ineffective, but we have no evidence about whether in his private moments Claudius is sincerely penitent or not. Still, if we come to the above conclusion (I believe that Hamlet mistakenly believes that Claudius is sincerely penitent), we must have decided that Claudius is NOT penitent, so we believe that Hamlet's belief is mistaken. It is this mistaken belief that prevents him from using his sword at that moment. So when we're on stage as Hamlet, we put up our sword and perhaps we've decided (as Hamlet) that we do this slowly; reluctantly. Of course, in the moment of putting up our sword, we have left all our higher order thinking in the rehearsal room. We need to forget that we have even exercised our second order intentional thinking ability, because on stage we need to immerse ourselves in the story and pretend to BE HAMLET (who is, at this moment, busily engaged in his own second order intentional thinking: he is busy thinking about his own beliefs about Claudius' belief). While acting, we strive to forget our own higher order thinking or metarepresentation, because we want to focus simply on what it feels like to be Hamlet, and to be in *his* situation with *his* higher order thoughts, which lead to action – or in this case, inaction. We know this world is imaginary, but we select to approach it as quasi-amnesiacs who have temporarily 'forgotten' about our own world – although of course, we can never really do that.

But our fictional cognitive process (what it feels like to be Hamlet), as we know, can only be the product of our OWN cognitive process, which by a metaphorical process we are transferring into Hamlet's domain – we are thinking 'as if' we are Hamlet. That we affect this metaphorical transfer when acting is clear. But once again, we must now, in essence, make it our business to forget that we are in the midst of metaphorically transferring our own knowledge and subjective lived experience into the domain of Hamlet's knowledge and 'subjective lived' experience (insofar as we can imagine this). In this sense, actors are also (forgive me!) meta-pretending. We know the truth (we are *pretending* to be Hamlet), but we pretend that we do not. We pretend to forget so that we can pretend convincingly. We must be meta-pretending, selective quasi-amnesiacs onstage.

This means, of course, that actors are always pretending on two fronts. They are pretending to forget and they are pretending to be Hamlet. I would say that this dual forgetting is the essential quality of acting. In McGinn's terms, dual forgetting is what allows us fictional immersion – a state which he describes as

A *sui generis* state of mind…It is that state of mind in which fictions, acknowledged to be such, take on some of the functional features of known facts, in which imaginative products function *as* genuine experiences…Perhaps a metaphor will say it best: fictional immersion occurs when the work *disguises* itself as reality, while never concealing the fact that it is a disguise.[5]

I outline all of this because along with everything else we have looked at in terms of the actor's cognitive process, this additional 'forgetting' (which is necessary once we get on stage) makes it very clear just how wonderfully complex the actor's cognitive processes are, and also leads me – surprisingly, perhaps – back to Duse. Despite all the 'metas' and the forgettings and the pretendings and everything else we've considered, can we ever assert that our acting has the power to instigate an autonomic response? First of all – we know that WE CAN'T voluntarily affect anything that is controlled autonomically. So I would venture to say that in Duse's case, she wasn't acting. Now there's a contentious thought. A blush that has been admired for decades was not produced by acting, but by being, genuinely, embarrassed for some reason. We admire this. But would we admire it if the autonomic behaviour had been stimulated by an amygdala response of fear, leading to rage (think back to my friend James who attacked during the *'Tis Pity She's a Whore* scene). We admire Duse's blush because it is harmless. But we would condemn James's actions because they had potential to harm others. Still, what is really the difference between these two things?

I would suggest that the moment the actor forgets that they are pretending, or forgets that they are transferring meaning from one domain to another in a metaphorical process, and that they are engaging their imaginations in a wholly imaginary context, they really are entering a different territory. This is the territory of the self. And theorists (perhaps like Strasberg) might think that this is what we want on stage, but this territory is fraught with danger, since we can only admire its workings if the emotion involved is benign.

The complexity of the whole operation has, many times, defeated our ability to be comfortable in all this rational analysis of meta-processes. Drama is *play*. Pretending and imagining are *playful* activities. Acting is pretending and imagining in the service of great story-telling. Doesn't all the analysis get in the way of our approaching the practice freely?

Well, yes. It probably does – if our thoughts *remain* there. In fact, there is much strong scientific research that backs up the view that too much analysis while performing is worse than too little. And too much analysis at the wrong point is absolutely counter-productive. Many researchers have studied the effects of thinking about activity that has passed into automaticity, and their findings corroborate the long-held suspicion that the reason actors 'choke' is because, mid-performance, they suddenly start thinking about activity that has long since been mastered.[6] Indeed, actors can often find themselves tripping up over their own thinking because part of what we tend to do in the late stages of rehearsal (or even in performance) is to try new ideas in the hope of keeping our approach fresh and our work appearing spontaneous. But when introducing new ideas on top of thought, movement, action and memory that we've rehearsed in a (relatively) given way many times, then we're interfering with the brain's natural propensity to transfer the familiar from high-resource thinking intensity to low-resource automaticity. And that interference can lead to trouble for the actor, as noted by Jonah Lehrer:

> The part of the brain that monitors behaviour – a network centred in the prefrontal cortex – starts to interfere with decisions that are normally made without thinking. It begins second-guessing skills that have been honed through…diligent practice…When you overthink at the wrong moment, you cut yourself off from the wisdom of your emotions…[7]

It seems to me that this whole area constitutes another kind of fundamental actor's paradox: the neophyte actor often wants to rush into performance because they fear that too much rehearsal/thinking will dull the immediacy of their emotional connection, hence they face the danger of juggling too much high-resource thought intensity to cope with effectively in performance. The experienced actor knows the importance of extended rehearsal time in order to allow a sufficient level of conscious activity to pass into automaticity, but once that is in place faces the danger of undermining themselves by applying fresh, high-resource thought to low-resource or automatic thought/behaviour that has been laid down through weeks of diligent rehearsal.

The only answer, of course, is to trust that the rehearsal process has been solid and thorough and then to remain 'in the moment', open to nuance; responsive to small things that change and may suddenly inspire fresh emotion/cognition in a completely spontaneous, NON-ANALYTICAL way. This gets neatly around the danger Lehrer cites when involving the prefrontal cortex, and allows, in his words, access to the 'wisdom of emotion'.

But of course, not thinking about all that thinking we've been doing over four or five weeks of rehearsal requires some dedicated focus, because it's very hard for the Western mind to comprehend that sometimes NOT THINKING is the key to a great performance. And no doubt this explains our history of turning to the mysterious East in times of trouble…

The Orient(al) Express(iveness)

The complexities of the process described above are probably fairly described as mind-boggling. This is no doubt because I'm engaging my cortical, S2 cognitive processes in the attempt to engage your cortical, S2 cognitive processes with a detailed outline of the complicated interplay of the ways in which we pretend on stage. I have to hope at this point that we can be comfortable with the fact that we are pretending to be Hamlet (although as we've seen, for many theorists the idea of pretending on stage is anathema). The stubborn fact is that when we're on stage we're pretending. It is an extraordinary and often detailed and highly engaged type of pretending but in the most fundamental ontological terms when we're acting we're pretending. Some actors do this better than others. For some actors, the ability to imagine, empathize and pretend to forget that they're pretending is a truly marvellous thing to behold. But it's complicated. And for that reason I can't help wondering if the long history we have now of turning to Eastern performance practices isn't an attempt to bypass all this complex thinking and dream about something more holistic, mystical and liberating. Because just about every major theatre practitioner from Stanislavski to Brecht, Meyerhold to Artaud, Grotowski and Brook have been enthralled by Eastern performance practice and were no doubt inspired to do so by concluding that Western intellectualism was ruining something unnamed but essential to the art of theatre, and spoiling any pleasure in the art of acting:

> Western directors and teachers have looked to the East since the time of Stanislavski and Meyerhold for new acting and directing techniques. Brecht was astounded by Chinese theatre, Artaud was inspired by Balinese dancers and Grotowski learned from the Peking Opera.[8]

And of course, we know that Stanislavski was fascinated by Yoga. Phillip Zarrilli's recent *Psychophysical Acting* is the most recent turn to the East and is a nice example of the ways in which Western theatre practitioners can find something valuable in the more holistic ideas of non-Western performance. Like so many, Zarrilli begins with worrying a bit about Descartes:

> When psychology emerged as a separate discipline from philosophy in the nineteenth century, the sciences of mind and the self were often considered separate from the science(s) of the physical body. This split reflected the long-term Western binary dividing mind from body that so problematically crystallized in the mind-body dualism of the seventeenth-century French philosopher René Descartes (1596–1650).[9]

As we've seen in our considerations, Zarrilli is certainly not the first acting theorist to aim his bow at poor René. Richard Hornby weighs in with (what recent cognitive science would recognize to be) a naive point of view about the way in creative activity works and manages to take a shot at Descartes in passing:

> Artistic creation flows in one direction only, from within to without. Externals like costuming, props, blocking, and even the playwright's words are unimportant artistically – they are of course unavoidable, but they have no more artistic significance than a printing press has to a poem or a movie projector to a film. The actor has indeed become a ghost in a machine.
>
> In place of Cartesian dualism, we need an integrated model of acting that sees it as a skilled, felt activity.[10]

But surely it is time to move on from this worry – if only because no serious Western thinker would defend Cartesian dualism these days – at least not in the form that Descartes proposed.

But more importantly, we need to ask ourselves first whether it's really true that acting theory has in any way been bedevilled by a perverse adherence to a seventeenth-century philosophy. The fact is that from Stanislavski onward we've been considering something called psychophysical action. From the earliest half of the twentieth century, Stanislavski was talking about psychophysical actions, and Meyerhold was training actors through his biomechanical methods in the 1920s. Michael Chekhov was teaching and writing about psychological gesture in the 1930s and 1940s. Numerous theatre practitioners throughout the 1960s and 1970s were centring much of their focus on the body as the site of performance and significance, and practitioners like Barba and Suzuki continue to do so today. Surely this suggests that actors are MORE liberated from the mind/body problem than your average Joe/Josephine. But for reasons that are hard to work out, there is still a kind of widespread worry that the actor's nemesis is that master of provisional epistemological solipsism: Descartes. Zarrilli's worry is significant enough that he refers throughout his book to the 'bodymind' – as if, somehow, if we aren't careful we will unwittingly find ourselves prey to talking about bodies and minds separately.

But I can't help wondering if the Cartesian dualism that provokes such worry isn't actually located *in the ontological assumptions of the worrying theorist*. Perhaps I can make this clearer by looking at something that Zarrilli writes about the things he means to explore in his book, which include:

- The 'white space' in the etching we call acting;
- The silences that have the potential to render form when we perform;
- One process for inhabiting the silences of this inner space 'not visible or conscious to the mind, but there' (Griffin:1992: 172)
- How in that space the actor's being-in-the-moment resonates with the traces, associations, and/or images called memory, feeling, emotion.[11]

There are a number of ways in which we can interpret Zarrilli's ambiguous text but let us take 'white space' to be not the absence of meaning but the unintelligible shape-maker that determines intelligibility; the thing that gives significance form or lends contour to content. Perhaps we can imagine that Zarrilli is attempting to describe aspects of performance that don't have a describable content. This puts us in mind, no doubt, of the mysterious descriptions of Stanislavski and Chekhov's work that we examined earlier.

This 'white space' is not simply a question of something like 'stage silence' – although it could be related to that. In the process of performance the text demands that a kind of describable analytic process be brought to bear: we examine text in terms of structure, logic, semantics, syntax, we express text in ways that demonstrate our particular take on the relation of structure and meaning in a text overall. We engage in a recognizable cognitive process which emerges from and gives shape to language and communication. But white space or silence lends us some relief from all this cognitive activity. It opens up the possibility, perhaps, for something more *profound* than analytical cognition. But how should we formulate a theory of organization for these working aspects of our performance activity? Lost in our Cartesian dualism, perhaps, like poor administrators, we misfile this positive content (text/analytical labour) under 'brain activity'. We further miscategorize the brain as 'the body's boss, the pilot of the ship'.[12] Now as we look around 'the office' we have little choice but to consider, metaphorically, that perhaps this silent white space (the non-thinking/the non-analytical) should be filed or categorized elsewhere. But of course, the only drawer left is the body. The body – making no unreasonable demands for analysis or systematizing, or conceptualizing – seems like the natural home for the kind of zen white space in performance. Perhaps the underlying idea then is that by paying attention to the body – the stubborn, irreducible, silent body – we can transcend the chattering analytical brain from which we seek some respite.

The question remains, however, whether we've filed things in the right place and, of course, we know that we have not. In fact we know that there is no decision, analysis, action, empathy or even abstract thinking like moral judgement that does not involve an intricate interplay with emotion. And we know that emotion is always an intricate interplay of mind and body – a product of the 'bodymind' in Zarrilli's language. And we know that even the ways in which we metaphorically conceptualize our abstract thoughts are modelled on physical states (affection = warmth, difficulties = burdens, time = motion, mental states = locations, etc.). Our reason accedes to the world through the body and our models of reasoning reflect and involve the body.[13]

This means that even when we're falling prey to the idea of the brain as the 'captain of the ship', we aren't really dualistic brain/body beings. The mind, we know, is inherently embodied.

Yet that 'white space' remains. It is a sense of something 'extracognitive' or ineffable that slips away from our grasp and plagues the attempts of the acting theorist to capture and describe the practice of performing. And so perhaps we turn to the pure physicality of the body, of being, and breath and motion that is kick-started into performance mode through custom-designed performance exercises. The sorts of things that Zarrilli describes in his book certainly seem like the stuff that might fire up the extracognitive as it is manifested in genius or creativity or inspiration. He outlines the kind of accomplished practice that can result from the right kind of training, which I present here in partial form:

- Awakening energy: through attentive breathing, the practitioner gradually awakens, discovers and then is able to circulate the energy (*ki/qi/prana-vayu*) that lies within...
- Attunement: through psychophysical exercise the practitioner attunes the body and mind into a gestalt or a whole...
- Heightening awareness: during the process of attunement one's perceptual/sensory awareness is opened both inward and simultaneously outward...
- Doing and being done: at optimal virtuosic levels of performance, one does the action/task while simultaneously being done by the action/task...[14]

This specific training, according to Zarrilli, 'prepares both body and mind for integration'. But of course it is at precisely this point that we detect the 'closet Cartesianism' – for Zarrilli is suggesting that our natural state is dualistic – and that this dualistic state is only to be overcome by training. Along with many others, Hornby included, Zarrilli is worried about Cartesianism because acting theory is still working through some very old conceptions about how our 'beingness' is constituted. We don't require training exercises in order to connect our minds and bodies more securely. Our minds and bodies are already connected in secure, multiple and complex ways.

I think we might be forgiven if, at this point, we want to throw in the towel and simply conclude that we'll never escape the long shadow of dualism. But it may be that what we've been considering all along in the world of acting theory is simply the WRONG dualism. Perhaps we need to look at another dualism in order to understand the reason why, throughout nearly 100 years of discourse and debate, acting theorists turn their thoughts to the East.

In testing East/West cultural preferences for employing either formal or intuitive reasoning when faced with problem-solving tasks, researchers found that there is decidedly a difference in the preference for one form of reasoning over the other:

> An analytic mode of thought has been held to be more prevalent in Western cultural groups. This mode is characterized by decoupling of the object from its context, assigning the object to categories based on necessary and sufficient features, and a preference for using rules, including the rules of formal logic, to explain and predict the object's behaviour. In contrast a holistic mode of thought has been held to be more prevalent in East Asian cultural groups. This mode is characterized by attention to the context or field as a whole, a concern with relationships among objects, and between the field and the object, and a preference for intuitive approaches, as well as 'dialectical' reasoning, which seeks the 'middle-way' between conflicting propositions.[15]

No doubt the descriptions of these two kinds of thought bring to mind some of the descriptions that we associate with hemispheric specialism in the brain, where the left side is concerned with systematizing and solving particulars through algorithmic logic and the right side is concerned with contextualizing, empathizing and seeing the whole picture. It has been further noted that the cultural differences mentioned above are related to the idea of dual processes of thinking or distinctly different processes of thinking. And one of the more interesting conclusions was that:

> East Asians also prefer dialectical resolutions to apparent contradictions, so that the contradiction is tolerated or a compromise solution is sought. Americans respond to contradiction by 'polarizing' their opinions – deciding that one proposition is true and the other false.

This passage seemed particularly interesting to me in view of the persistent polarizations that seem to plague our attempts to get to the bottom of things in Western acting practices. These kinds of distinctions between the East/West in cognitive approaches have been called by Jonathan St B.T. Evans a difference in cognitive *styles* – not a difference in cognitive processes.[16] In other words, these styles – analytical and holistic – are *not* in themselves reflective of a difference in cognitive *architecture*. Instead, they are part of the commonly held System 2 or Type 2 cognition. In a further consideration of this, Keith Stanovich sees these differentiated styles as algorithmic and reflective modes of cognition that both arise from Type 2 cognition.[17]

As helpful as our friends in cognitive psychology are, we might be best advised at this point to leave the hard science of all this out and simply acknowledge that the conscious mind does seem to have two cognitive styles – and I think the one that might be of interest to us at this point is the more holistic, reflective and intuitive style. Guy Claxton calls this the 'tortoise brain' and he sees significant value in the slow, non-rule-based, ruminative way of problem-solving that could almost be described as the 'white space' of thinking:

> Recent scientific evidence shows convincingly that the more patient, less deliberate modes of mind are particularly suited to making sense of situations that are intricate, shadowy or ill defined. Deliberate thinking, d-mode, works well when the problem it is facing is easily conceptualised...But when we are not sure what needs to be taken into account, or even which questions to pose – or when the issue is too subtle to be captured by the familiar categories of conscious thought – we need recourse to the tortoise mind...
>
> It is only recently, however, that...the newly formed disciplined of 'cognitive science'... [has revealed] that the unconscious realms of the human mind will successfully accomplish a number of unusual, interesting and important tasks if they are given time. They will learn patterns of a degree of subtlety which normal consciousness cannot even see...[18]

Claxton, unlike Evans or Stanovich, directly proposes that the reflective mind is influenced by the unconscious mind, and he goes on to note that Western societies have lost the value in contemplation and that 'only active thinking is regarded as productive'.

If we go back for a moment to consider that we have hard research evidence pointing to the Eastern preference for this kind of reflective, 'tortoise brain' approach to things – might it be *the Eastern cognitive style* that acting theorists have been pining after all these years, rather than the Eastern BODY? Might it be that in exercises that place heightened concentration on non-verbal (non-reasoning) things like breath and body we slow ourselves down to the extent that this 'tortoise brain' (which is indigenous to the 'white space' of cognition) is coaxed out into the open? Might the connection between 'reflective' S2 cognition and the unconscious (as it is posed by Claxton, above) be one way of understanding what constitutes the underlying system of the extracognitive? These are compelling questions, I think, and they make sense in terms of the ways in which we have so often taken the Eastern BODY to be a kind of antidote to the Western MIND.

Some cognitive researchers have looked closely at the effect on the brain of two different approaches to training focus or concentration: one is attention training and the other is attention *state* training. These distinctions follow along the lines of mindfulness meditation (where the meditator has an open and 'empty' mind) vs concentration meditation (where the meditator concentrates on a given object). We can see something like this kind of distinction in the way that a practitioner like Meisner approached training the actor's concentration on repetition and observation of an acting partner vs the way that Zarrilli focuses training on body-based processes like breathing, flow of energy and physical alertness. Meisner is training the actor's attention, whereas Zarrilli is training the actor's *state* of attention. In an article on attention training, Yi-Yuan Tang and Michael Posner look at studies done in attention state training, which they call integrated body mind training (IBMT) and describe an experience that sounds very close to what Zarrilli and others, like Daniel Meyer-Dinkgräfe,[19] see as an optimal actor-training:

> IBMT does not stress efforts to control thoughts, but instead induces a state of restful alertness, enabling a high degree of awareness of body, mind and external instructions. It seeks a balanced state of relaxation while focusing attention. Control of thought is achieved gradually through posture and relaxation. The coach works to achieve a balanced and harmonious state rather than by having the trainee attempt an internal struggle to control thoughts in accordance with instruction.[20]

One might expect that this kind of attention state training would have any number of positive effects on alertness and overall sense of heightened balance, but the particular study that Tang and Posner consider has an even better outcome from the actor's point of view: 'The combined use of body and mind training is also supported by studies of embodied cognition, in which changes in the body, particularly in facial expression, influence emotional processing and facilitate retrieval of autobiographical memories.'

If we go back to Colin McGinn we find a further issue to consider in the value of the reflective 'slow' mind for the actor. The research on preferences for intuitive or formal reasoning demonstrated that in reflective mode, we are more 'contradiction-tolerant'. In other words in this cognitive mode we can entertain contradiction without feeling the pressure to reconcile or polarize. In his analysis of the dream state of consciousness, and ways in which we 'believe' what is happening in our dreams, McGinn see a powerful relationship between the ability to tolerate contradiction and 'fictional immersion':

> Dream belief stems from fictional immersion plus extreme suggestibility. What we must do now is examine this theory in the light of the data I have itemized: is it consistent with the agreed data of dream belief?
>
> I think it is easily seen that it is. Tolerance of inconsistency is essentially the same phenomenon that we find in ordinary cases of fictional immersion: I know very well that the actor on the stage is not about to stab the other actor, but I 'believe' that he is. I

become absorbed in a novel in which a certain world leader has been assassinated, but I know very well that he has not. I am hypnotized into believing that I am a barking dog, but part of me knows that this is rubbish. The dreamer's tolerance of inconsistency is therefore not some kind of preternatural irrationality or disregard for logic; it is simply the correlative of fictional immersion. Without fiction immersion the contradictions would be intolerable, but with it we get belief insulation.[21]

Trust McGinn to have the eloquence for capturing the essential state of the actor: belief insulation. As actors, we marry that state of selective quasi-amnesia with fictional immersion onstage in order to achieve this kind of 'belief insulation'. We're concerned here with the essential qualities of acting, however, and not with the accidental qualities. This means that even when we are in that state where our quasi-amnesia and pretend beliefs are insulated from the real world, we might still turn in an absolutely dreadful performance. *But we would still be acting.*

And so it may be that the continual turn to the East for inspiration makes much sense for the actor – but probably NOT for the reasons that most theorists seem to think that it does. Of course, most training systems based in Eastern technique (like Zarrilli's) promote things that will go a long way toward enhancing an actor's arsenal: heightened physical fitness, enhanced concentration and sensory responsiveness, and of course these things are a tremendous added benefit. There may also be more to consider about the way in which Eastern training practices often induce or sail very near a meditative state – and this state in itself is close to the hypnotic state. This may mean that actors trained in these ways will – like hypnotic subjects – demonstrate enhanced suggestibility and tolerance of contradiction, both of which would heighten the sense of belief.

Conclusion

Training in the arts tends to be a pretty tribal affair. Those in the Meisner tribe often see their technique as the 'only' valuable technique for training an actor. Those who teach Hagen or Suzuki are often similarly convinced that their systems are innately superior to all others and can sometimes be pretty inflexible about approach. While I hope that everything we've looked at in this book leads us to realize that there is probably not a single superior way to approach the complex practice of acting, it's likely that such tribalism will continue to flourish. I've learned that acting isn't the only performing art that can be pretty tribal about technique. The dance and vocal worlds have their tribes and each are always as happy to encounter fellow tribesmen as they are suspicious of members belonging to other or newer tribes.

The Philosophical Actor looks on this with some understanding (an understanding no doubt bolstered by a modicum of knowledge about evolutionary psychology!). What we've concerned ourselves with in these pages has not been about any one particular approach to acting, but rather with looking at a broad-based analysis of the tools and the language we use when we're working or training. It seems evident that there are a number of ways into the mystery of acting, and we know that there are some people who seem to be 'naturals' and some of us who have to work harder at the whole enterprise. Advances in cognitive science may ultimately uncover what, exactly, it is that makes a great actor – and early indications may be that along with many other traditional things we might identify (such as good 'raw materials' in terms of voice and physicality, an openness to play and imaginative plasticity) there may be some tangible 'neuro-markers': (1) extensive or hyper-efficient brain connectivity – which would enhance an overall connectedness with the distributed complexity of perception and response; and (2) hyper-efficiency in mirror neuron systems – which would enhance embodied empathetic responses and increase the sense of self-belief.

It seems likely to me that the tools we use for rehearsing are not necessarily the tools we use for performing, and that the ways in which we achieve our own 'fictional immersion' may emerge as much from the ways in which we harness our attentional state as it does from connecting with our imaginations. We certainly know that the actual process of performing for an audience is likely to involve areas of the brain that rehearsal (particularly once we've grown used to the director and other actors watching us) will not.

It is important that we strive to entertain some contradiction when we're thinking about something quite as complex as acting. Which means that while there are some dualisms that persist in our practice, they are not the old dualisms (mind/body; personality/character; internal/external) but perhaps dualisms like S1 and S2 cognitive processes (hare/tortoise brain); attention training and attentional state training; 'meta-pretending' and non-acting; emotion and feeling; self-generated and context-generated emotion and character; directed and autonomic responses; Subject and Self; and compound relationships like primary/background/social emotions and display 'rules'; or metaphorical/metonymical relationships between actor and character.

As a complex operation, acting needs complex thinking that gives way to uninhibited imagination and free physicality in order to do it well. The more we attempt to get a grip on that multifaceted activity through simple breakdowns or definitions (action/transitive verb = acting, 'acting is being' or 'good acting is truthful acting'), the more we undo our ability to really comprehend that complexity. I think the whole purpose of philosophy is to force a little reflection into practice by encouraging us to do a rigorous examination our working assumptions. Writing this book has given me many moments of reflection in terms of how theory fits into and sometimes explains the practical work of actors. I hope this book provides a set of powerful intellectual weapons that you can pack when you get back into the rehearsal studio. An 'armed and dangerous' actor is bound to bring the unexpected into play – and I don't know any actor or director who doesn't value that in rehearsal and performance.

Notes

1. Thomas Cathcart & Daniel Klein, *Plato and a Platypus Walk into a Bar: Understanding Philosophy through Jokes* (New York: Abram Image, 2006), pp. 10–11.
2. *Ibid.*, p. 12.
3. Colin McGinn, *Mindsight: Image, Dream, Meaning* (Cambridge, MA: Harvard University Press, 2004), p. 111.
4. Daniel Dennett, *Kinds of Minds* (New York: Basic Books, 1996), p. 121.
5. McGinn, *Mindsight*, p. 184.
6. See particularly study done by Sandra Bielock, cited by Jonah Lehrer, *How We Decide* (New York: Houghton Mifflin Harcourt, 2009), pp. 137–138.
7. *Ibid.*, pp. 138, 142.
8. Richard Brestoff, *Great Acting Teachers and their Methods* (San Val Publishing, 1995), p. 163.
9. Phillip R. Zarrilli, *Psychophysical Acting: An Intercultural Approach after Stanislavski* (London: Routledge, 2009), p. 13
10. Richard Hornby, *The End of Acting: A Radical View* (New York: Applause Books, 1992), p. 115.
11. Zarrilli, *Psychophysical Acting*, p. 2.
12. Daniel Dennett, *Kinds of Minds: Toward an Understanding of Consciousness* (New York: Basic Books, 1996), p. 77.
13. 'From a biological perspective, it is eminently plausible that reason has grown out of the sensory and motor systems and that it still uses those systems or structures developed from them. This explains why we have the kinds of concepts we have and why our concepts have the properties they have. It explains why our special-relations concepts should be topological and orientational. And it explains why our system for structuring and reasoning about events of all kinds should have the structure of a motor-control system.' George Lakoff and Mark Johnson, *Philosophy in the Flesh: The Embodied Mind and its Challenge to Western Thought* (New York: Basic Books, 1999), p. 43.
14. Zarrilli, *Psychophysical Acting*, p. 83.
15. B. J. Kim, R. Nisbet, A. Norenzayan & E. Smith, *Cultural Preferences for Formal vs. Intuitive Reasoning* (http://www-personal.umich.edu/~nisbett/formalreas.pdf), p. 4.
16. See 'How Many Dual Process Theories do We Need? One, Two or Many?' in J. Evans & K. Frankish, *In Two Minds: Dual Processes and Beyond* (Oxford: OUP, 2009), pp. 33–54.
17. See 'Distinguishing the Reflective, Algorithmic and Autonomous Minds: Is it Time for a Tri-Process Theory?' in Evans and Frankish, *In Two Minds*, pp. 55–88.
18. Guy Claxton, *Hare Brain, Tortoise Mind* (New Jersey: ECCO Press, 1997), p. 3.
19. See 'Consciousness Studies and Utopian Performatives' in Daniel Watt & Daniel Meyer-Dinkgräfe (eds), *Theatres of Thought* (Newcastle: Cambridge Scholars Publishing, 2007).
20. Yi-Yuan Tang & Michael I. Posner, 'Attention Training and Attention State Training', *Trends in Cognitive Science*, 13(5), 2009.
21. McGinn, *Mindsight*, pp. 108–109.

Bibliography

Adler, Stella (1988) *The Technique of Acting* (New York: Bantam)

Assagioli, Roberto (1990) *Psychosynthesis: A Manual of Principles and Techniques* (Northampton: Crucible)

Auslander, Philip (1997) *From Acting to Performance: Essays in modernism and postmodernism* (London: Routledge)

Baggini, Julian (2006) *The Pig That Wants to Be Eaten* (New York: Plume)

Barash, David P. & Barash, Nanelle R. (2003) Madame Bovary's Ovaries: a Darwinian Look at Literature (New York: Delacorte)

Baron-Cohen, Simon "Theory of Mind in Normal Development and Autism", *Prisme*, 2001, 34

Bateson, Gregory (2000) *Steps to an Ecology of Mind* (University of Chicago Press)

Benedetti, Jean (1998) *Stanislavski & the Actor* (London: Methuen)

Bild, Kathryn Marie (2002) *Acting From a Spiritual Perspective* (Hanover: Smith & Kraus)

Blackmore, Susan J. (2000) The Meme Machine (Oxford: Oxford University Press)

Bloom, Harold (1999) *Shakespeare: The Invention of the Human* (London: Fourth Estate)

Boleslavsky, Richard (1965) *Acting: The First Six Lessons* (New York: Theatre Arts Books)

Boston, Richard (1974) *"Theories of Laugher" in An Anatomy of Laughter* (London: Collins)

Boyd, Robert and Richerson, Peter J. (2005) *Not By Genes Alone: How Culture Transformed Human Evolution* (Chicago University Press)

Bredin, Hugh (1984) "Metonymy", *Poetics Today*, Vol 5, No. 1

Brestoff, Richard (1995) *Great Acting Teachers and Their Methods* (San Val Publishing)

Brizendine, Louann (2007) *The Female Brain* (London: Bantam Press)

Brown, Ann L. (1977) Knowing When, Where and How to Remember: a Problem of Metacognition (http://www.eric.ed.gov/ERICDocs/data/ericdocs2sql/content_storage_01/0000019b/80/32/8c/0d.pdf)

Buckner, Randy L. & Carroll, Daniel C., "Self Projection and the Brain", *Trends in Cognitive Science*, Vol 11, No 2, 2006

Carnicke, Sharon M. (1998) *Stanislavsky in Focus* (Amsterdam: Harwood Publishers)

Carter, Rita (1998) *Mapping the Mind* (London: Phoenix)

—— (2008) *Multiplicity: The New Science of Personality* (London: Little Brown)

—— (2002) *Consciousness* (London: Widenfeld & Nicolson)

Cashmore, Ellis (2002) *Sports Psychology: the Key Concepts* (Leeds: Human Kinetics)

Cathcart, Thomas & Klein, Daniel (2006) *Plato and a Platypus Walk Into A Bar: Understanding Philosophy through Jokes* (New York: Abrams Image)

Claxton, Guy (1997) *Hare Brain, Tortoise Mind* (New Jersey: ECCO Press)

Changeux, Jean-Pierre & Ricoeur, Paul (2000) *What Makes Us Think?* (Princeton University Press)

Chekhov, Michael (1991) *On the Technique of Acting* (New York: Quill)

—— (1953) *To the Actor* (New York: Harper & Row)

Cole, Toby, ed. (1983) *Acting: A Handbook of the Stanislavski Method* (New York: Three Rivers Press)

Churchland, Patricia (1986) *Neurophilosophy* (Cambridge: MIT Press)

Csikszentmihalyi, Mihaly (1996) *Creativity: Flow and Psychology of Discovery and Invention* (New York: HarperPerennial)

Damasio, Antonio R. (1994) *Descartes' Error* (Oxford: OUP)

—— (2000) *The Feeling of What Happens*

—— (2004) *Looking For Spinoza* (London: Vintage Books)

Darwin, Charles (1979) *The Expression of Emotion in Man and Animals* (London: J. Friedman Publishers Ltd)

Dawkins, Richard (2006) *The Selfish Gene: 30th Anniversary Ed* (Oxford U Press)

—— (2006) *The God Delusion* (London: Bantam Press)

Dennett, Daniel C (1978) *Brainstorms: Philosophical Essays on Mind and Psychology* (London: Penguin Books)

—— (1991) *Consciousness Explained* (London: Penguin Press)

—— (2005) *Sweet Dreams* (Cambridge: MIT Press)

—— (1996) *Kinds of Minds* (New York: Basic Books)

Eagleton, Terry (1983) *Literary Theory: An Introduction* (Oxford: Blackwell)

Easty, Edward Dwight (1989) *On Method Acting* (New York: Ivy Books)

Edelman, Gerald M. (2004) *Wider Than the Sky* (London: Penguin)

Ekman, Paul, Ed. (2005) *What the Face Reveals*, 2nd Ed (Oxford: OUP)

—— (2003) *Emotions Revealed* (London: Widenfeld & Nicolson)

Esper, William & Damon Dimarco (2008) *The Actor's Art and Craft* (New York: Anchor Books)

Evans, J. & Frankish, K. (2009) *In Two Minds: Dual Processes and Beyond* (Oxford: OUP)

Fink, Joel Gary (1980) *Depersonalization and Personalization as Factors in a Taxonomy of Acting* (Ann Arbor: University Microfilms International)

Flor, Richard & Dooley, Kevin (1998) "The Dyamics of Learning to Automaticity", *Noetic Journal* 1(2)

Freedberg, David, & Gallese, Vittorio (2007) "*Motion, Emotion and Empathy in Esthetic Experience*" *Trends in Cognitive Science,* Vol. 11 No 5

Gertler, Brie & Shapiro, Lawrence (2007) *Arguing About the Mind* (New York: Routledge)

Gladwell, Malcolm (2008) *Outliers* (New York: Little, Brown and Company)

Greenfield, Susan (2002) *The Private Life of the Brain* (London: Penguin)

Greenwood, John D. (1991) *The Future of Folk Psychology: Intentionality and Cognitive Science* (Cambridge: CUP)

Growtowski, Jerzy (1976) *Towards a Poor Theatre*, ed. Eugenio Barba (London: Eyre Methuen)

Hagen (1973) *Respect for Acting* (New York: Wiley)

Hanin, Yuri L., ed. (1999) *Emotions in Sport* (Champaign: Human Kinetics)

Harrison, Charles & Wood, Paul (eds) (1992) *Art in Theory, 1900–1992* (Oxford: Blackwell)

Hildegard, Ernest R. (1986) *Divided Consciousness* (Chichester: John Wiley & Sons)

Hodge, Alison, Ed. (2000) *Twentieth Century Actor Training* (London: Routledge)

Hornby, Richard (1992) *The End of Acting: A Radical View* (New York: Applause Books)

Huther, Gerald (2006) *The Compassionate Brain* (New York: Trumpeter)

Kandel, Eric R. (2006) *In Search of Memory: the Emergence of a New Science of Mind* (London W.W. Norton & Co.)

Kim, B. J., Nisbet, R., Norenzayan, A., & Smith, E., *Cultural Preferences for Formal vs. Intuitive Reasoning* (http://www-personal.umich.edu/~nisbett/formalreas.pdf)

Kosuth, Joseph (1992) "Art After Philosophy", *Art in Theory, 1900-1990* (Oxford: Blackwell)

Lakoff, G. and Johnson, M. (1999) *Philosophy in the Flesh: The Embodied Mind and its Challenge to Western Thought* (New York: Basic Books)
—— (1980) *Metaphors We Live By* (University of Chicago Press)
Law, Stephen (2003) *The Philosophy Gym: 25 Short Adventures in Thinking* (London: Review)
LeDoux (1998) *The Emotional Brain* (New York: Touchstone)
—— (2002) *The Synaptic Self* (New York: Penguin)
Lehrer, Jonah (2009) *How We Decide* (New York: Houghton Mifflin Harcourt)
Levitin, Daniel (2006) *This is Your Brain on Music* (London: Atlantic Books)
Lewis, Robert (1980) *Advice to the Players* (New York: Theatre Communications Group)
Linden, David J. (2007) *The Accidental Mind* (Cambridge: Harvard University Press)
Marian, David (2005) "The Correspondence Theory of Truth", *The Stanford Encyclopedia of Philosophy*
Mamet, David (1997) *True and False: Heresy and Common Sense for the Actor* (London: Faber Books)
McGinn, Colin (2002) *The Making of a Philosopher* (New York: HarperPerennial)
—— (2004) *Mindsight: Image, Dream, Meaning* (Cambridge: Harvard University Press)
MacNab, Geoffrey (2007) "*The Wild One Tamed*" *The Independent*: London, June 15
Meijers, Anthonie (2001) *Explaining Beliefs* (Stanford: CSLI)
Meisner, Sanford (1987) *On Acting* (New York: Vintage)
Mellalieu, Stephen D. & Hanton, Sheldon, eds. (2009) *Advances in Applied Sport Psychology* (New York: Routledge)
Merlin, Bella (2001) *Beyond Stanislavski: The Psycho-Physical Approach to Actor Training* (London: Nick Hern Books)
—— (2005) *With the Rogues Company* (London: Oberon Books)
Meyer-Dinkgräfe, Daniel, ed (2006) *Consciousness, Theatre, Literature and the Arts* (Newcastle: Cambridge Scholars Press)
Modell, Arnold H. (2003) *Imagination and the Meaningful Brain* (Cambridge, MA: MIT Press)
Moran, Aidan (2009) "Attention in Sport" in *Advances in Applied Sport Psychology* (Oxford: Routledge)
Moseley, Nick (2005) *Acting and Reacting* (London: Nick Hern Books)
Moser, Paul K., and Trout, J.D. (1995) *Contemporary Materialism: A Reader* (London: Routledge)
Nideffer, R.M. (1992) *Psyched to Win* (Leeds: Human Kinetics)
Nisbett, Richard E. & Wilson, Timothy D, "*Telling More Than We Can Know*", *Psychological Review*, Vol. 84, No. 3, May 1977
Nuttall, A.D. (2007) *Shakespeare the Thinker* (New Haven and London: Yale University Press)
Orlick, Terry (2000) *In Pursuit of Excellence* (Leeds: Human Kinetics)
Ornstein, Robert (1986) *Multimind* (London: Macmillan)
Peterson, Eric (1981) *A Semiotic Phenomenology of Performing* (Ann Arbor: University Microfilms International)
Pinker, Stephen (2003) *How the Mind Works*
—— (2003) *The Blank Slate*
—— (2007) *The Stuff of Thought* (New York: Viking)
Pitches, Jonathan (2006*) Science and the Stanislavski Tradition of Acting* (London: Routledge)
Plutchik, Robert, (2002) *Emotions and Life :Perspectives from Psychology, Biology and Evolution* (American Psychological Association)
Prowse, Robert R. (2000) *Laugher: A Scientific Investigation* (London: Faber and Faber)
Ramachandran, V.S. (2005) *Phantoms in the Brain* (London: Harper Perennial)
—— (2003) *The Emerging Mind* (London: Profile Books)

—— (2004) *A Brief Tour of Human Consciousness* (New York: Pi Press)

Ratey, John (2001) *A User's Guide to the Brain* (NY: Little Brown and Co.)

Restak, Richard (2006) *The Naked Brain: How the Emerging Neurosociety is Changing the Way we Live, Work, and Love* (New York: Harmony Books)

Rix, Roxane "*Alba Emoting: A Revolution in Emotion for the Actor*" found at: http://albaemoting.org/_wsn/page2.html

Roach, Joseph R. (1993) *The Player's Passion: Studies in the Science of Acting* (Ann Arbor: University of Michigan Press)

Rose, Steven (1993) *The Making of Memory* (London: Bantam)

Rowan, John (1997) *Subpersonalities: The People Inside Us* (London: Routledge)

Shavinina, Larisa V. & Ferrari, Michel (2004) *Beyond Knowledge: Extracognitive Aspects of Developing High Ability* (New Jersey: Lawrence Erlbaum Assoc.)

Shawn, Wallace (2008) *Wish I Could Be There* (New York: Penguin Group)

Shermer, Michael (1999) *How We Believe: The Search for God in an Age of Science* (New York: W.H. Freeman and Co.)

Siddons, Henry (reissued 1968) *Practical Illustrations of Rhetorical Gestures*, 2nd Ed. (New York: Benjamin Blom)

Simon, Herbert (1983) *Reason in Human Affairs* (Stanford: Stanford University Press)

Smith, E. and Kosslyn, S (2007) *Cognitive Psychology* (New Jersey: Prentice Hall)

Solomon, Robert C. (2007) *True to Our Feelings* (Oxford: OUP)

Sparshott, Francis (1982) *The Theory of the Arts*, (New Jersey: Princeton University Press)

Sperber, Dan ed. (2000) *Metarepresentations: a multidisciplinary perspective* (Oxford: OUP)

Stanislavski, Constantin (1990) *An Actor's Handbook*, ed. & tr. Elizabeth R. Hapgood (London: Methuen)

—— (1991) *My Life in Art*, tr. J.J. Robbins (London: Methuen)

—— (1989) *An Actor Prepares*, tr Elizabeth R. Hapgood (New York: Theatre Arts Books)

Stanovich, Keith (2009) "Distinguishing the Reflective, Algorithmic and Autonomous Minds: Is it Time for a Tri-Process Theory?" in *In Two Minds* (Oxford: OUP)

Stewart, Ian and Cohen, Jack (1997) *Figments of Reality* (Cambridge, CUP)

Stich, Stephen (1983) *From Folk Psychology to Cognitive Science: The Case Against Belief* (London: MIT Press)

Stich, Stephen & Nichols, Shaun (1992)"*Folk Psychology: Simulation or Tacit Theory?*", *Mind & Language*, v. 7, no. 1

Stucky, Nathan & Wimmer, Cynthia (2002) *Teaching Performance Studies* (Carbondale: Southern Illinois University Press)

Taleb, Nassim Nicholas (2007) *The Black Swan: The Impact of the Highly Improbable* (London: Allen Lane)

Tang, Yi-Yuan & Posner, Michael I. (2009) "Attention Training and Attention State Training", *Trends In Cognitive Science*, Vol 13 Issue 5 May

Tassi, Aldo (2000) "Performance as Metamorphosis", *Consciousness, Literature and the Arts* (Vol 1 No. 2, July)

Watt, Daniel & Meyer-Dinkgräfe, Daniel eds (2007) *Theatres of Thought: Theatre, Performance and Philosophy* (Newcastle: Cambridge Scholars Publishing)

Wright, Richard (1994) *The Moral Animal: Evolutionary Psychology and Everyday Life* (New York: Pantheon Books)

Yakim,Moni (2000) *Creating a Character* (New York: Applause Books)

Yi-Yuan Tang & Michael I. Posner, (2009) "Attention Training and Attention State Training", *Trends In Cognitive Science*, Vol 13 Issue 5 May

Zarrilli, Phillip R. (2009) *Psychophysical Acting: An Intercultural Approach After Stanislavski* (London: Routledge)

—— ed. (1995) *Acting (Re)Considered: A Theoretical and Practical Guide*, 2nd Edition (London: Routledge)

—— (2002) "*Action, Structure, Task, and Emotion*" in *Teaching Performance Studies* (Carbondale: Southern Illinois University Press)

Zimbardo, Philip (2007) *The Lucifer Effect* (London: Rider Books)

Index